MW00399572

ENDOR[S]

SETTING THE STAGE FOR ETERNITY

"Here's a book that will clarify a lot of confusion. A must read!"

—Dr. Gene A. Getz, Ph.D.

President, Center for Church Renewal
Author of *The Measure of a Man* and others.

"In this comprehensive work on believers' rewards, Dr. Betz lays bare the sobering truth that in this life we are to weave the threads of time into the loom of eternity. Or to change the figure, when we get to heaven, all our cups will be full—but we will have different size cups! Where, when, and by whom this will be determined is the subject of this book."

—Dr. Norman L. Geisler, Ph.D.

President and Dean, Southern Evangelical Seminary
Author of *I Don't Have Enough Faith to Be an Atheist* and 60 others.

"Here is a book that represents a lifetime of study on an altogether neglected subject: the judgment seat of Christ and the Christian's rewards. Simply written, well illustrated, and definite in its conclusions, any person will enjoy reading this book and will probably be convicted at the same time."

—Dr. Stanley D. Toussaint, Th.D.

Senior Professor Emeritus of Bible Exposition
Dallas Theological Seminary
Author of *Behold the King*

"Harlan Betz reminds me that I am in a race. Not the super-competitive rat race of American acquisition and performance, but a race to invest my time and talents in opportunities for meaning and glory before the clock runs out. And he makes me want to win! With deeply biblical straight-talk, Betz 'Sets the Stage for Eternity' explaining the crowns and commendations, the overcoming and understanding of how it can be such a joy to become the person God longs for us to be. He helps us imagine the eternal rewards and deficits that flow from today's choices in a way that torches our desire for Christ's glory, not our own."

—Lael Arrington

Author of *Godsight: Renewing the Eyes of Our Hearts*

Broadcast co-host: *The Things That Matter Most*

"Harlan Betz has spent many years studying the divine revelation of the judgment seat of Christ in Scripture. This book is the fruit of that study and is one of the most thorough and biblical expositions of that subject available."

—Dr. Thomas L. Constable, Th.D.

Professor of Bible Exposition, Dallas Theological Seminary

Author of *The Bible Commentary* at soniclight.com

"This volume is an extremely valuable contribution to the often neglected, but important, biblical doctrine of rewards."

—Zane Hodges

President, Kerugma, Inc.

Author of *The Hungry Inherit* and others.

"*Setting the Stage for Eternity* is 'must reading' for everyone who longs to reach their God-designed potential. Harlan Betz provides biblical insight into what the coming kingdom of Christ will be like, how to get there, and how to glorify God in this life and throughout eternity. This book includes Basic Truths for those who long to know Christ and Ranger Training for those who long to reign with Christ. Anyone who reads this book will be inspired and challenged. *Setting the Stage for Eternity* is a life-changing book! I whole-heartedly endorse this book."

—Dr. Earl Radmacher

President Emeritus and

Distinguished Professor of Systematic Theology Emeritus

Western Seminary

Author of *The Disciplemaker*

"Harlan's thorough and biblical study will benefit many believers. He challenges your thinking and motivates your preparation so that when you stand before the Lord, He can say, 'Well done thou good and faithful servant.'"

—R. Larry Moyer

President and CEO

EvanTell

Author of *31 Days with the Master Fisherman* and others.

"(*Setting the Stage for Eternity*) is challenging and inspirational. I appreciate (Betz's) simple and clear presentation of the gospel. Regretfully, the gospel has become confused in many of our churches today. Knowing and believing the gospel is just the beginning of a delightful journey to all who give their lives to serve our wonderful Lord! (*Setting the Stage for Eternity*) outlines this journey very well!"

—**Art Rorheim**,
Co-founder and President Emeritus
AWANA Clubs International

"Here is a book that every Christian should read thoughtfully. It lends itself to discussion and self-reflection and giving to others. In terms of vital information, it may be one of the most significant books a twenty-first century Christian reads."

—**Dr. Howard Hendricks**
Distinguished Professor and Chairman
Center for Christian Leadership
Author of *Living by the Book*, *Teaching to Change Lives,* and others.

FalconPublishingLTD

Setting the Stage for Eternity

A study of the judgment seat of Christ
and its impact on a believer
in this life
and
in the life to come.

Dr. Harlan D. Betz

Foreword by Dr. Howard D. Hendricks

FalconPublishingLTD

Setting the Stage for Eternity

Verses marked "Greek" are the author's translations and paraphrases from the Greek New Testament according to the Majority Text.

Cover layout design by Lorna Branon
Cover background artwork by Dee Day.
Interior sketches by Daniel Ellis.
Edited by David L. Fey

PRINTING HISTORY

FIRST PRINTING 2006

ISBN-13: 978-0-9746959-3-8
ISBN-10: 0-9746959-3-9

FALCON PUBLISHING LTD.
P.O. Box 6099
Kingwood, TX 77345
713-417-7600

www.falconpublishing.com

Library of Congress Control Number 2004117553

10 9 8 7 6 5 4 3 2 1

DEDICATION

This book is gratefully dedicated to Jesus Christ.

He is my Savior, my Lord, and my Shepherd.

He is my Master, my Model, and my Mentor.

He is my Joy, my Strength, and my Song.

He is my Love, my Inspiration, and my Friend.

He is in me. He is with me. He is for me.

He is my Hope of Glory.

CONTENTS

Appendices:

FOREWORD

Dr. Howard G. Hendricks

"What is this world coming to?"! More than ever before that cry erupts from uneasy earthlings as we stare at the headlines or hear the breaking news on television. Fear and uncertainty always arise from a lack of knowledge; most of us don't know what to expect next. The unknown hovers over us like a dark cloud with daily lightning strikes of bad news.

For centuries mankind has studied the stars and unearthed ancient predictions of the future. Very few of those forecasts have been accurate. Yet there remains the gnawing insistence that there is a future, and the unraveling of the mystery must lie outside of human intelligence. But who is smart enough, who is tuned in most clearly to the real truth we long to know?

The Bible reminds us that God the Creator has revealed Himself to humans, first by His magnificent natural world, then by His prophets through whom He spoke from time to time and finally through the coming of His Son, Jesus Christ, born in human flesh. He is the living Word who breathed human breath in history, who died a bona fide death and rose from the dead, as witnessed by hundreds. Now ascended into heaven, He is preparing an eternal home for His own people. If these facts are examined logically, then the only rational conclusion is that the Bible has the answer to the bewildering future.

The Holy Spirit makes known to believers what actually has been, what is and what will be in the future. The Apostle Paul, inspired by the Spirit, wrote, "I would not have you to be ignorant . . . ." God is more interested than we are that we be apprised of His plan for what lies ahead.

A general consensus among Bible scholars is that we are drawing near to a climax, a culmination of life as we have known it for more than two millennia. It is of utmost importance that we understand what God has in His plan for everybody. But many of us cling to the falsehood that this is privileged information, classified for scholars and certain mystical minds. Since Satan is the sworn enemy of our holy God, it only makes sense that he would want us to believe that the doctrine of future things is reserved for a select few and is irrelevant for people in our contemporary, sophisticated world.

It is true that God's plan for the ages is an enormous and complicated design. The vast scheme of life is far beyond our limited scope, but God has pulled back the curtain in the scriptures to reveal what will take place. Equally noteworthy is the biblical counsel about how we are to prepare for what is ahead. The implications have eternal impact.

From his long and dedicated pastoral role, Harlan Betz senses the eagerness of Christians to know the truth about the future of our world and how we should arrange our lives accordingly. His diligent study and gifted ability to express profound truth in simple language combine to produce a clear explanation of God's plan, complete with helpful clarifying charts.

Numerous reminders are scattered throughout the New Testament that all of us will be called to give an account to God for the deeds done while we were "in the body." I have a strong conviction that one question we will all have to answer is "Did you read My Word?" We cannot afford to stand before our heavenly Father with an alibi that we didn't know what would happen. Here is a book that every Christian should read thoughtfully. It lends itself to discussion and reflection—and giving to others. In terms of vital information, it may be one of the most significant books a twenty-first century Christian reads.

Howard G. Hendricks
Distinguished Professor
Chairman, Center for Christian Leadership
Dallas Theological Seminary

ACKNOWLEDGMENTS

I am very grateful to the following people for their inspiration and encouragement:

Pastor Norm Adamson, whose walk and words encouraged me to consider the ministry;

Professor Zane Hodges, whose teaching enabled me to interpret the New Testament;

Dr. Howard Hendricks, whose discipleship showed me the importance of motivation;

Dr. Stanley Toussaint, whose life gave me a pattern for the ministry;

Dr. John F. Walvoord, who met with me personally on several occasions and encouraged me to write this book;

Dr. Gene Jeffries, whose encouragement enabled me to complete this project.

I also want to acknowledge the following people for their assistance in helping me to arrange my thoughts and words into publishable form:

Katrina Shinn, thank you for your very gracious assistance in typing the manuscript and in laying out the charts found in the appendices.

Susie Sellner, thank you for your gracious help in proof-reading the manuscript.

David Fey, thank you for your technical assistance in editing the many drafts and formatting the text of this book.

Gwen Fey, thank you for your encouragement and your leadership in getting this book published.

Finally, I want to express my love and appreciation to the following people:

My son Joshua and his wife Jill, and my daughter Sarah and her husband Mark, who by walking in the truth and giving spiritual direction to their children, have brought great joy to my life;

My wife Sharon, whose love and prayers are my constant companion. Sharon, you have always been in my corner, and I thank God for giving you to me.

There are many others who have been there for me and have encouraged me along the way. I cannot list all your names, but I want you to know that I praise God for you. I want to express my love and appreciation to all of you who have prayed with me and for me and have encouraged me to boldly follow Christ.

Harlan D. Betz

INTRODUCTION

Most people get so caught up in the affairs of this life that they fail to prepare for the next. The person who prepares for this life but not for the next is wise for a moment but a fool for eternity. Now, no one really wants to fail. No one really wants to be a fool for eternity, but very few seem to know how to prepare for eternity. Benjamin Franklin was right on target when he said, "By failing to prepare, you are preparing to fail!"

While I was a student at Dallas Theological Seminary, I was discipled by Dr. Howard Hendricks, mentored by Dr. Stanley Toussaint, and taught by Dr. John F. Walvoord and Professor Zane Hodges (as well as many others). In the spring of 1974, at the close of those four years at Dallas Seminary, I wrote my thesis on *The Nature of Rewards at the Judgment Seat of Christ!* This study has had an incredible impact upon my life. I came to understand that what I am doing and becoming right now is setting the stage for the rest of eternity!

This year is the 32nd anniversary of my graduation from Dallas Theological Seminary. During those thirty-two years, I have been serving as a pastor. Over and over, I have seen lives changed by the truths gleaned from this Bible study. Most believers have little or no understanding about the judgment seat of Christ and the nature of rewards that will be awarded to victorious believers. When believers come to understand the purpose of the judgment seat of Christ and the nature of the rewards God desires to give, their lives are radically changed! It is my desire to share these truths with you.

From 1996 to 1998, I did further study on the judgment seat of Christ and its impact on a believer. Under the direction of Dr. Gene Jeffries at Cambridge Graduate School, I contacted Dr. Harold Hoehner, Dr. Robert Lightner, Dr. Charles Ryrie, Dr. J. Dwight Pentecost, Dr. Donald Campbell, and Dr. Stanley D. Toussaint. Each of them gave me some input for this study. During that time, I met personally with Dr. John F. Walvoord. He and I discussed the judgment seat of Christ and the nature of rewards at length. Following that time of input, as a part of my doctoral studies, I wrote a doctoral dissertation. It was a study of the judgment seat of Christ and its impact on a believer in this life and in the life to come.

I want to share the results of these studies with you. I join with the Apostle Paul in praying this prayer for you:

> Therefore I also, after I heard of your faith in the Lord Jesus and your love for all the saints, do not cease to give thanks for you, making mention of you in my prayers: that the God of our Lord Jesus Christ, the Father of Glory, may give you the spirit of wisdom and revelation in the knowledge of Him, the eyes of your understanding being enlightened; that you may know what is the hope of His calling, what are the riches of the glory of His inheritance in the saints, and what is the exceeding greatness of His power toward us who believe. (Eph. 1:15-19)

The request Paul brings before our heavenly Father is twofold. First he is praying for wisdom. This is a prayer for insight and deeper understanding and skill in living. Second he is praying for revelation. This is a prayer for instruction and greater understanding and growth in knowledge.

The results Paul desires for these believers is spelled out in this prayer. He longs for them to know:

> the hope of God's calling—that they might be conformed to Christ,
> the riches of God's inheritance—that they might be a glorious inheritance,
> the greatness of God's power—that they might be divinely empowered!

Why is it that so many believers have failed to gain this wisdom? Why is it that so many Christians have not received this instruction? I believe the basic problem is threefold:

> They are living only for now (Mt. 6:31-33)!
> They are loving only this world (1 Jn. 2:15-17)!
> They have lost sight of eternity (1 Cor. 2:9-13)!

The unaided human mind cannot understand eternity. The Bible says we can look, we can listen, and we can learn, but our eyes have not seen, our ears have not heard, and our minds have not imagined the things that God has prepared for those who love Him! Most people have no understanding of:

> the marvelous blessings they could enjoy,
> the spiritual riches they could inherit,
> the glorious opportunities they could experience, or
> the incredible glory they could bring to the Lord!

Fortunately, God has revealed them to us in His Word! The only way we can discover these truths is to dig into His Word! These truths cannot be found anywhere else!

Ray Steadman tells the story of a television producer for the British Broadcasting Corporation who was preparing a documentary about Christianity in England. In the course of his research he sent a memo to a clergyman who served as an advisor to the BBC on church affairs. The memo read, "How might I ascertain the official church view of heaven and hell?" The clergyman replied with a memo consisting of only one word: "Die!" Fortunately, we do not have to die to discover God's truth about heaven and hell! What does the Bible teach us?

Heaven is a paid-for place! One of the most central and most simple truths in the Bible is found in John 3:16: *"For God so loved the world that He gave His only begotten Son, that whosoever believes in Him should not perish but have everlasting life!"* The Bible makes it clear that God so loved each one of us that He sent His Son Jesus Christ to die in our place and pay for our sins, so that if we would simply believe in Him, we would not perish but would have eternal life! It is critical that we understand that getting to heaven is based on faith in Jesus Christ. Getting to heaven is incredibly costly because it cost the life of the Lord Jesus Christ who died on the cross to pay for our sins; but it is free to us because Jesus has already paid the price. All we have to do is believe in Him and accept this free gift of forgiveness and eternal life in Jesus Christ! Heaven is a paid-for place.

Heaven is a permanent place. Just as the womb is not a permanent residence but simply a few months preparation for life on earth, even so life on earth is not a permanent residence, but is simply a brief time of preparation for all eternity! As the Bible says, *"It is appointed for men to die once, and after that judgment"* (Heb. 9:27, Greek). Following physical death, man will experience eternal joy in heaven or eternal judgment in hell. Going to heaven is based solely on faith in Jesus Christ. Those who go there will never be cast out. Those who have eternal life have it as a permanent possession. Heaven is a permanent place.

Heaven is a preferred place. Death is inevitable, but physical death is not the end of our existence! For those who are believers in Jesus Christ, death is not a termination; it is a graduation and the commencement of our life in heaven! It is our great loss that we fail to live in the light of eternity. Our eyes become so focused on things down here that we forget the things up there. We live as though this life is all there is, when in fact, this life is but a brief moment, a vapor, in contrast to all eternity. Our life here is simply setting the stage for all eternity. And the eternity God has planned for us is far better than life here on earth.

George Bernard Shaw once complained, "Heaven as conventionally conceived, is a place so inane, so dull, so useless, and so miserable that nobody has ever ventured to describe a whole day in heaven, though plenty of people have described a day at the seashore."

I have to agree with George, but remember, he was describing heaven as conventionally conceived. When most people think of heaven, they think of people clothed in white, with angel wings, playing harps, and singing until they are hoarse. For most people that is indeed a rather dull and boring prospect for eternity. The good news is that heaven is not what it is conventionally conceived as being. The Bible says,

"Eye has not seen and ear has not heard, nor has the human mind ever conceived of the things that God has prepared for those who love Him" (1 Cor. 2:9, Greek). Heaven is not just another place, it is another plane! It will be a whole different dimension of life! It is beyond our comprehension. It is beyond our imagination. It is beyond our wildest dreams.

I understand that life here on earth can be exhilarating, exciting, romantic, and adventurous; but life here also has its trials and troubles. Life here has its hurts and heartaches. Life here has its diseases and deaths. God has something better for us. It is referred to as heaven.

If we could get a sneak preview of heaven,
if we could see the amazing beauty of heaven,
if we could hear the majestic music of heaven,
if we could experience the joy of reunion with loved ones gone on before us,
if we could catch a glimpse of the loving Lamb of God,
if we could realize the glorious joys that could be ours in heaven,

we would be so overcome with eager anticipation of entering that heavenly home that we would have trouble waiting to go there. Heaven is a preferred place.

Heaven is a perfect place. The gates will always be open, the glory will always be evident, and the goodness will never be defiled. There will be no more defiled hearts, no more degraded passions, and no more depraved minds. There will be no more deceit, no more desecration, and no more darkness. There will be no more idolatry, no more immorality, and no more illegality. There will be no more stubbornness, no more sinfulness, and no more selfishness. There will be no more sin, no more sorrow, and no more sickness. There will be no more lying, no more lewdness, and no more loneliness. There will be no more drunkenness, no more dissensions, and no more death! There will be no more worry, no more weakness, and no more war.

Heaven will be a place of freedom and fullness, peace and prosperity, health and happiness. Heaven will be a place of security and significance and service. The wonders, the joys, and the phenomenal delights of heaven are far better than anything we could ever experience here on earth. Heaven is a blessed hope. It encourages us to keep on. It enables us to endure hardships. It inspires us to honor God. It motivates us to reach out. Heaven is a perfect place.

Heaven is a precious place! While descriptions of heaven are not numerous, there is one feature that is prominent above all others. This feature must not be missed. The center of attraction in heaven is our Lord Jesus Christ.

To the discouraged apostles, Jesus said, *"I go to prepare a place for you . . . that where I am, there you may be also"* (Jn. 14:2-3).

To the grieving Thessalonians, Paul tells of the rapture and the resurrection and reunion with loved ones in heaven, and he notes that they will *"always be with the Lord"* (1 Thess. 4:17)!

To the repentant thief, our Lord Jesus Christ said, *"Today you will be with Me in Paradise"* (Lk. 23:43)!

The Apostle Paul said he wanted to depart from this life *"and be with Christ, which is far better"* (Phil. 1:23).

Someone has said, "The light of heaven will be the face of Jesus. The music of heaven will be the name of Jesus. The theme of heaven will be the work of Jesus. The joy of heaven will be the presence of Jesus. The employment of heaven will be the service of Jesus."

Jesus went to the cross so we could go to heaven. Jesus died so we could live! Jesus paid the enormous debt of our sins by dying in our place and taking our punishment, but make no mistake about it, this payment must be accepted. Jesus died so that we could be given eternal life as a free gift, but we must personally accept that gift. You must place your faith in Jesus Christ, trusting in His death and resurrection as the full and final payment for all your sins. God offers you eternal life as a free gift. Have you received that free gift by trusting in Jesus Christ as your own personal Savior? If not, you can do so right now, right where you are.

Jesus has gone to heaven to prepare a place for those who have placed their faith in Him. The Bible tells us that if we believe in Jesus, though we may die physically, we will never die spiritually. Those who have placed their faith in Christ are guaranteed entrance into heaven . . . not because of *who* they are, but because of *whose* they are. By God's grace and through their faith, they belong to God, purchased and paid for by the blood of Christ. They have the blessed assurance that Jesus is their Savior, and they have the blessed hope of going to heaven! Heaven is a precious place.

Now that is a fantastic blessing. It is great to have the settled assurance that your sins are forgiven, and that you are bound for heaven! But unfortunately, far too many believers are settling for just getting there. The often missed truth is that Christ not only invites us to come to Him, He also challenges us to follow after Him. God wants us to lay up treasures in heaven! God wants us to be an honor to Him and bring glory to His Son! God wants believers to experience far more than merely reaching heaven; He wants us to experience riches in heaven!

Books on prophecy have flooded the marketplace, and yet many believers are still left with some important questions:

- What is heaven like?
- What do I have to do in order to get to heaven?
- What is the judgment seat of Christ?
- Why will God judge believers?
- How will God determine if what we have done is rewardable?
- Could the judgment seat of Christ be a time of sorrow and shame?
- What is the nature of the rewards given at the judgment seat of Christ?
- Are those rewards a justifiable motivation for godly living?
- Does the way I live my life here on earth have an impact on my life in eternity?
- Should my potential for rewards in eternity have an impact on my life now?

This study is designed to bring answers to those questions, motivation to our lives, and glory to our God! This study is designed to guide you into the Word of God and to help you understand the judgment seat of Christ and its impact on a believer in this life and in the life to come. This study is designed to be instructive and corrective. It is not designed to be exhaustive. This study is designed to be easily understood and personally applied.

I want to encourage you to dig into your Bible and search the Scriptures with me. Open your heart and allow the Holy Spirit to reveal new truths to you. The Scriptures were not revealed simply to challenge us; they were revealed to change us. The Bible is not designed simply to inform us; it is designed to transform us.

Pray that you will not simply be challenged, but that you will be changed! Pray that you will not simply be informed, but that you will be transformed!

It is my prayer that this study will provide:

1. A loving call to those who do not yet know Christ as their own personal Savior.
2. A clear message to those who are confused about the gospel.
3. A new direction for those who have lost a sense of purpose and meaning in life.
4. A stirring challenge to those who have become complacent.
5. An encouraging word to those who have fallen away or are tempted to give up.
6. An inspiration for those who want to bring honor and glory to our Lord!
7. A powerful motivation for becoming like Christ.

It is my hope that Jesus Christ will not only be exalted through this book, but that He will also be magnified in the lives of those who read it.

Harlan D. Betz

> Brethren, I do not count myself to have apprehended; but one thing I do, forgetting those things which are behind and reaching forward to those things which are ahead, I press toward the goal for the prize of the upward call of God in Christ Jesus. (Phil. 3:13-14)

Study Guide – Introduction - Heaven

"The person who prepares for this life but not for the next is wise for a moment, but a fool for eternity!"

—Harlan D. Betz: *Setting the Stage for Eternity*

1. What is hell like?
   It is a place of everlasting ________________. Mt. 25:41
   It was prepared for ____________ and ____________. Mt. 25:41
   It is a place of everlasting ______________________. Mt. 25:46

2. Consider these quotes:
   "There is a dreadful hell, and everlasting pains; where sinners must with devils dwell in darkness, fire, and chains."
   —Isaac Watts: *Heaven and Hell.*
   "Tis not where we lie, but whence we fell;
   The loss of heaven's the greatest pain of hell."
   —Pedro Calderon de la Barca: *Adventures of Five Hours,* Act V

3. What is heaven like?
   Jesus called it His Father's ________________. John 14:2
   Jesus said it was a place of many ________________. John 14:2
   Jesus told his followers, "I go to prepare a place for ________________." John 14:2
   Jesus said heaven is "where ____________________!" John 14:3
   "If God hath made this world so fair where sin and death abound, how beautiful beyond compare will paradise be found."
   —James Montgomery

4. What else do we know about heaven from Revelation 21 and 22?
   List several things that won't be there.
   List several things that will be there.
   What is it that you most look forward to doing in heaven?

5. Reflect on these truths:
   "Has this world been so kind to you that you should leave with regret? There are better things ahead than any we leave behind!"
   —C. S. Lewis: *Living Quotations*
   "The joys of heaven are not the joys of passive contemplation, of dreamy remembrance, of perfect repose; but they are described thus, 'They rest not day or night,' 'His servants shall serve Him.'"
   —Alexander MacLaren

6. What must I do in order to get to heaven?
   There are things I must realize:
   I am a ____________________. Rom. 3:23
   I deserve ____________________.Rom 6:23
   There is something I must recognize:
   Jesus Christ ____________ for me! Rom 5:8
   I can be saved by ____________ in Jesus Christ! John 3:16

7. Meditate on these statements:
   Salvation is by grace alone through faith alone in Christ alone! Eph. 2:8-9
   "For cap and bells our lives we pay,
   Bubbles we buy with a whole soul's tasking;
   Tis heaven alone is given away,
   Tis only God may be had for the asking."
   —James Russell Lowell: *The Visions of Sir Launfal,* Prelude
   "Heaven's gates are not as highly arched as princes' palaces; they that enter there must go on their knees."
   — John Webster: *The Duchess of Malfi*

CHAPTER 1

THE REALITY OF THE JUDGMENT SEAT

In an art gallery there is a beautiful piece of statuary representing "The Blind Watcher." A young lady had been engaged to a lover who had gone to sea. Each evening she went to the harbor and looked for signs of his promised return. Her father opposed both her attitude and her actions, and one day in anger he struck her across the face. This blow destroyed her vision, but it did not destroy her love.

When she could no longer see, she came and listened, in hopes that she might catch some sound of her lover's coming. At last, after a long and unavoidable delay, he did come. Her waiting was one of absolute trust and persistent expectation. It was the affectionate expression of a constant love. It was rewarded by the incredible warmth of her lover's embrace, the inconceivable commitment of her lover's life, and the indescribable joy of her lover's fellowship.

In like manner, many believers are gladly anticipating the promised return of Christ. Will they go unrewarded for such steadfast love? The Apostle Paul answers this question when he writes:

> Finally, there is laid up for me the crown of righteousness, which the Lord, the righteous Judge, will give to me on that Day, and not to me only, but also to all who have loved His appearing. (2 Tim. 4:8)

Those who are living in the light of His return will be rewarded by the warmth of Christ's embrace, the thrill of Christ's praise, and the blessing of Christ's joy! Unfortunately, there are some believers who are not living in the light of Christ's return. They will be called into account for their manner of living, and they will be justly dealt with for their selfish attitude and their foolish actions. The Bible tells us that we will all give an account to the Lord Jesus Christ at the judgment seat of Christ!

Carl F. H. Henry, noted scholar and church leader, said, "Never in all history have men spoken so much of end-time, yet been so shrouded in ignorance of God's impending doomsday." He is exactly right. There has been a lot of information written on prophecy, but there is only a little information written on the judgment seat of Christ.

It is critical that we come to understand the judgment seat of Christ and its impact on a believer in this life and throughout eternity. It is vitally important for us to know the hope of God's calling, the riches of God's inheritance, and the greatness of God's power. Understanding the purpose of the judgment seat of Christ can be life-changing.

Before a person can realistically consider the purpose of the judgment seat of Christ, he must be convinced of its reality. It is critical that you understand that we must all give an account for what we have done in this life. Far too many believers think they will not have to give an account for their attitudes and actions. Far too many believers think they can do whatever they want and say whatever they want because all their sins are covered by the blood of Jesus. They do not think God will hold them accountable for any good thing they failed to do or for any bad thing they found themselves doing.

Are Christians going to be held accountable for their thoughts and words and deeds? The Word of God leaves no room for debate with respect to the reality of the judgment seat of Christ. The Bible declares that *"We must all appear before the judgment seat of Christ, that each one may receive the things done in the body, according to what he has done, whether good or bad"* (2 Cor. 5:9-10). This judgment was so real to the Apostle Paul that it actually drove him to live a life that would be pleasing to the Lord. Talk about reality! This judgment seat, which Paul referred to as the **bema**, is certainly worth investigating.

THE MEANING OF THE BEMA

The Greek word **bema** is translated "judgment seat." Dr. Alford Plummer, in his commentary on 2 Corinthians, explains that the **bema** is the tribunal, whether in a civil court or in a military camp.[1] In either case the tribunal was a platform on which the seat of the presiding officer was placed. Moulton and Milligan note that **bema** is commonly used in the official sense of "tribunal" and "judgment seat" in the papyri as it is in the New Testament.[2] Usually the **bema** was the place where civil officials heard legal cases and rendered judgment.[3]

There is one other use of the term **bema**, which must be brought into our thinking. This term was also used to denote the platform on which the judges sat at the Olympic Games. It was to this judgment seat that each contestant had to answer. It was at the **bema** that the victorious contestants were rewarded.[4] This is a picture with which we are very familiar. We have all watched the Olympic Games. We have seen the judges sitting at a **bema** during the ice-skating, swimming, and gymnastic competitions.

Just as the **bema** was real to the athlete, it was real to the Apostle Paul. However, Paul viewed the **bema** he was going to face with a much greater sense of awe and respect, because he was going to face a much greater judge. "Who is the judge at the **bema**?"

THE JUDGE AT THE BEMA

There are actually twelve occurrences of the term **bema** in the New Testament. Two of these occurrences are very distinctly set apart:

1. Only the Romans 14:10 and 2 Corinthians 5:10 passages are not references to past historical events;

2. Only the Romans 14:10 and 2 Corinthians 5:10 passages are found in the epistles;

3. Only the Romans 14:10 and 2 Corinthians 5:10 passages have God serving as the judge at the **bema**.

Consequently, Romans 14:10 and 2 Corinthians 5:10 are the only passages that deal specifically with the judgment seat of Christ. These two passages are the ones that speak to the issue we are investigating.

Who is the judge at the **bema**? The Apostle Paul wrote it this way to the Roman Christians, *"We shall all stand before the judgment seat of Christ"* (Rom. 14:10). Paul explained it this way to the Corinthian Christians, *"For we must all appear before the judgment seat of Christ"* (2 Cor. 5:10). Jesus Christ himself declares, *"The Father judges no one, but has committed all judgment to the Son"* (Jn. 5:22).[5] God the Son is the judge at the judgment seat of Christ. This truth is confirmed in Paul's words to Timothy as he speaks about *"the Lord, the righteous judge"* (2 Tim. 4:8).

George Sweeting, former President of Moody Bible Institute, writes:

> God gives Jesus authority to judge all men because of who He is. Jesus is uniquely qualified to judge because He is God and has existed from eternity (Jn. 1:1). As God, He knows everything, can be everywhere at once, and has unlimited power and authority. He knows everything we think and He

> sees everything we do. Thus He can judge perfectly, with wisdom and full understanding and without error or partiality. Christ is also uniquely qualified to judge because of what He has done. By dying for our sins on the cross, He demonstrated perfect love for all men. Thus, when He judges, His perfect righteousness is balanced by His perfect love.[6]

Jesus will be a righteous judge. His judgment will be fair and balanced, just and impartial, true and unbiased. Jesus will be a wise judge. He will not be deceived or duped. We have all heard the saying, "You can fool some of the people all of the time, and you can fool all of the people some of the time, but you cannot fool all of the people all of the time." Well, there is another line we should have burned into our thinking, "You can never fool God!" He knows the secret thoughts of our minds and the true motives of our hearts. Jesus Christ will serve as the judge at the judgment seat of Christ!

Having determined the identity of the judge, the next obvious question is . . . Who will be judged at the judgment seat of Christ?

THE SUBJECTS AT THE BEMA

The Bible says, *"It is necessary that we all appear before the judgment seat of Christ"* (2 Cor. 5:10, Greek.). In order to determine who will be judged at the **bema**, one must determine who Paul was referring to in this passage when he used the term "we."

Let's look at the context. In reading through the fifth chapter of 2 Corinthians, one is confronted with a number of descriptions about this group of people with whom Paul is identifying himself (by means of the first person plural pronoun). He uses several phrases that clearly distinguish this group:

1. We have a house not made with hands, eternal in the heavens (v. 1);
2. We have been given the Holy Spirit by God as a down payment (v. 5);
3. We walk by faith, not by sight (v. 7);
4. We will be at home with the Lord when our bodies die (v. 8).

These four descriptive phrases can only be applied to New Testament church-age Christians. Therefore, it is only Christians who will be judged at the judgment seat of Christ. Contrary to popular opinion, the Bible does not teach that there will be one great all-inclusive judgment. There will be no unbelievers at the judgment seat of Christ. Most unbelievers will be judged at the great white throne judgment spoken of in Revelation 20:11-15. The judgment seat of Christ is designed uniquely and exclusively for those church-age believers who trust in Jesus Christ as their own personal Savior.[7]

There is a threefold judgment for Christians . . .

The first phase of judgment is past. It took place when Christ died on the cross and rose from the dead. It was a judgment of sin by Christ as a substitute for all and on behalf of all for whom He died (1 Pet. 2:24; 2 Cor. 5:21). The sinner was declared righteous before God by faith in Christ in that judgment (Rom. 3:25; 5:9; Heb. 9:26-29). That judgment enabled justification and deals with our relationship with Christ.

The second phase of judgment is present. It consists of judgment of the believer's character and conduct by himself (1 Cor. 11:31-32; 1 Jn. 1:9), by the church (Mt. 18:17; 2 Thess. 2:14), and by God (1 Cor. 11:3-32; Heb. 12:3-15). This judgment enhances sanctification and deals with our fellowship with God.

The third phase of judgment for the believer is future. It will take place at the judgment seat of Christ (Rom. 14:10; 2 Cor. 5:10). This judgment will examine believers in regard to their faithfulness to God. This judgment will examine our faithfulness and deals with our rewards from God.

The believer was judged in the past as a sinner. He is being judged in the present as a son. He will be judged in the future as a steward.

We have determined that every believer will stand before Jesus Christ at the judgment seat of Christ. The next question we must ask is this, "When will this judgment take place?"

THE TIME OF THE BEMA

The Bible indicates that the judgment seat of Christ will take place immediately following the rapture of the church. Near the end of Paul's earthly career, Paul wrote these words to Timothy:

> Finally, there is laid up for me the crown of righteousness, which the Lord, the righteous Judge, will give to me on that Day, and not only to me, but also to all who have loved His appearing. (2 Tim. 4:8)

It is clear from this passage that Paul did not expect to receive his reward immediately after death. It was his belief that he and all other Christians who love the Lord's appearing would receive their reward *"on that day."*

What day is that? It is the day of *"His appearing!"* The Apostle Paul, in his epistles, often refers to *"the day of Christ"* as the time of reward and rejoicing for the church.[8]

In writing to the Corinthians, Paul speaks of the judgment seat and identifies it with the day of the Lord's coming.

> Therefore do not judge anything before the time, until the Lord comes, who will both shed light on the hidden things of darkness and reveal the motives of the hearts. Then each one's praise will come to him from God. (1 Cor. 4:5, Greek)

Jesus associates the reward of believers with the resurrection when He says, *"You will be rewarded at the resurrection of the righteous"* (Lk. 14:14, Greek). According to 1 Thessalonians 4:13-18, those who are believers in Jesus Christ will be resurrected at the rapture. This associates the judgment seat of Christ with the time of the rapture.

Peter also connects the rapture and reward when he writes to the shepherds of a local church and says to them, *"When the Chief Shepherd appears, you will be rewarded the unfading crown of glory"* (1 Pet. 5:4, Greek.).

The beloved Apostle John lends his support to this identification by noting that the church has already been given her reward when the Second Coming of Christ to the earth takes place:

> Let us be glad and rejoice and give Him glory, for the marriage of the Lamb has come, and His bride has made herself ready. And to her it was granted to be arrayed in fine linen, clean and bright, for the fine linen is the righteous acts of the saints. (Rev. 19:7-8)

Jesus Christ declares: *"Behold, I am coming quickly, and My reward is with Me, to award every man according to his work"* (Rev. 22:12, Greek.).

I heard about a young man who had just finished his seminary training and was excited about preaching without notes. He was asked to preach at a country church that was interested in possibly calling him to serve as their pastor. This was his opportunity to preach without notes. He got up on the platform and announced that his text was Revelation 22:12. He quoted the words of Christ, *"Behold, I am coming quickly!"*—and at that moment his mind went completely blank. He could not remember a thing he was going to say. Fortunately, he remembered the advice of his preaching professor. The professor had told the students that if their mind ever went blank when they were preaching they should simply take a step back from the pulpit, then take a bold step towards the pulpit repeating the phrase they had just shared with just a little more enthusiasm. The preaching professor assured them that reclaiming the pulpit and repeating the words would help them remember what they were planning to say. So this young man took a step back, gathered himself, stepped forward, and boldly pounded the pulpit saying, *"Behold, I am coming quickly!"* Unfortunately his mind was still blank. So he stepped back from the pulpit again, and this time, with even more energy and enthusiasm, he stepped forward, pounded the pulpit, and said, *"Behold, I am coming quickly."* Unfortunately, the pulpit was not stable and the young man launched himself right over the pulpit and into the lap of a lady in the front row. Immediately he got up off of her lap, straightened out his coat and tie, and began to profusely apologize. The lady looked up at him with a smile and said, "Oh, that's all right, young man. You warned me three times!"

She was listening! Dear believers, do you have ears to hear? The Bible warns us over and over that there is going to be a day of reckoning. Jesus, Peter, Paul, and John all speak of a day of judgment. They all seem to be saying that the judgment seat of Christ will take place between the rapture of the church to heaven and the return of Christ to the earth.

SUMMARY

We have been considering the reality of accountability. The Bible says, *"Do not be deceived, God is not mocked; for whatever a man sows, that he will also reap"* (Gal. 6:7). There will be a payday some day. There will be a day of reckoning. We will be held accountable for every thought, every word, every attitude, and every action.

The Bible says we must all appear before Christ! Every believer in Jesus Christ will one day stand before Jesus Christ at the judgment seat of Christ. A Bible believing Christian cannot deny the reality of this coming judgment. Someone said to the great scholar, Daniel Webster, "You have a colossal mind. What is the greatest thought you have ever had?" Webster's response was gripping. He said, "I've thought about many things, but the most awesome, the most terrifying, the most shattering thought I've ever had, is my personal accountability to God one day!"[9]

At times it may seem that there is no judgment for sin, but that judgment will come. The Bible warns us with these words: *"Be sure your sins will find you out"* (Num. 32:23). Achan thought he could hide his stolen goods. He couldn't. He was stoned to death. David thought he could hide his adultery. He couldn't. His life was miserable until he dealt with his sin. Gehazi thought he could hide his greed. He couldn't. He contracted leprosy. Ananias and Sapphira thought they could hide their deceit. They couldn't. They were slain by the Spirit. Disobedience will not go unjudged.

On the other hand, there is this remarkable encouragement . . . even a very little thing, such as giving someone a cup of cold water in Jesus' name, will not go unrewarded (Mt. 10:42). At times it may seem that there is no reward for faithfulness, but faithfulness will not go unrewarded! *"God is not unjust."* He will not *"forget your work and labor of love which you have shown toward His name"* (Heb.6:10). *"The judgments of the Lord are true and righteous altogether"* (Psa. 19:9).

The Bible challenges us to live in the light of eternity. Paul's challenges in 1 Thessalonians 5 could be summarized in three phrases:

1. Be watching seriously for Christ to return. Are you watching faithfully, waiting patiently, and longing eagerly for Christ's return?

2. Be living righteously until Christ returns. Are you walking by faith, encouraged by hope, and manifesting love?

3. Be building spiritually into the lives of others. Are you encouraging others, comforting others, and building up others?

Are you living in the light of eternity? Are you ready to face Christ at the judgment seat? Are you ready to meet your maker? At a news conference in Washington, 1954, Winston Churchill said, "I am prepared to meet my Maker. Whether my Maker is prepared for the great ordeal of meeting me is another matter."[10] Believe me; our divine Lord will be prepared!

Will you be prepared? Christ wants His bride to be without spot or wrinkle. Will you, like the blind watcher, be living in the light of your Lover's return? Those who live in the light of Christ's return will be rewarded by the warmth of Christ's embrace, the thrill of Christ's praise, and the blessing of Christ's joy!

Study Guide – Chapter 1 - The Reality of Accountability!

"Those who are living in the light of Christ's return will be rewarded by . . . the warmth of Christ's embrace,
the thrill of Christ's praise, and
the blessing of Christ's joy!"
—Harlan D. Betz: *Setting the Stage for Eternity*

1. **Read 2 Corinthians 5:1-11.**

2. Who is the judge at the judgment seat of Christ?
How would you describe this judge?

3. Who will be judged at the judgment seat of Christ?
How do you feel about being judged at the **bema**?

4. When will the judgment seat of Christ take place?
It could be soon. Are you ready?

5. Take some time to reflect on the long-suffering patience of our God.

Our God is a God of power and a God of patience. Some folks may mistakenly think that since they have seen no clear evidence of God's judgment in their life, God doesn't care and He will not ever judge them. The Bible teaches otherwise!

"Though the mills of God grind slowly, yet they grind exceedingly small;
Though with patience He stands waiting, with exactness He grinds all."

—Friedrich von Logau

6. **Read 1 Thessalonians 5:1-11.**

7. Are you sensitive to the signs of the times?
What are some of the signs of the times that you have observed in recent days?

8. Are you watching faithfully and waiting eagerly for Christ's return?
How is your life impacted on a daily basis by the knowledge that Christ could return at any time?

9. Is it evident that you are walking by faith?
In what ways does hope bring encouragement to your life?
How can we manifest love toward others?

10. What are some ways God has designed you to be an encourager to others?
Can you think of a couple of people who might need that encouragement today?

11. Take some time to look at your own life in the light of this following quotation:
"If you read history you will find that the Christians who did most for the present world were precisely those who thought most of the next. It is since Christians have largely ceased to think of the other world that they have become so ineffective in this."
—C.S. Lewis: *Mere Christianity*

[1] Alfred Plummer, *The Second Epistle to the Corinthians* (Edinburgh: T. & T. Clark, 1915), p. 156.
2 James Moulton and George Milligan, *The Vocabulary of the Greek Testament* (Grand Rapids, Michigan: Wm. B. Eerdmans Publishing Company, 1930), p. 109.
3 Jesus before the **bema** of Pilate, John 19:13; Paul before the **bema** of Festus, Acts 25:6.
4 Clarence E. Mason, Jr., "*A Study of Pauline Motives as Revealed in 2 Corinthians 4:16-6:4a," Bibliotheca Sacra*, CXI (July, 1954), pp. 219-220.
5 Bruce Metzger notes that this judgment is referred to as the "**bema** of Christ" in 2 Corinthians 5:10. He also notes that Romans 14:10 refers to this judgment as the "**bema** of Christ" in the Textus Receptus (T.R.) while the editors of the critical text (U.B.S.) favor the reading "**bema** of God." *A Textual Commentary on the Greek New Testament* (London: United Bible Societies, 1971), p. 531. Either way there is no real conflict, for in the critical view one has "God being said to do Himself what He does through His Son," according to Alfred Plummer, *The Second Epistle to the Corinthians*, p. 156.
6 George Sweeting, *Who Said That?* (Chicago: Moody Press, 1995), p. 283.
7 I have constructed "A Survey of the Judgments" in Appendix 5.
8 George E. Guille, *The Judgment Seat of Christ* (Chicago: The Bible Institute Colportage Association, 1916), pp. 15-23. Paul talks about "holding fast the word of life, so that in the day of Christ I may have cause to glory because I did not run in vain nor toil in vain" (Philippians 2:16). Guille identifies the "Day of Christ" with the rapture and the time immediately following the rapture (1 Cor. 1:8; 3:13; 5:5; 2 Cor. 1:14; Phil. 2:16; 1 Thess. 4:16-18; 2 Tim. 4:8; 1 Pet. 5:2-4). He identifies the "Day of the Lord" with the Second Coming of Christ in glory as King of kings and the millennial reign (2 Samuel 7:8-16; Psalm 89:3-4; Luke 1:31-33; 2 Thessalonians 2:2). He identifies the "Day of God" with the ushering in of the eternal State, the new Heaven, and the new Earth (2 Peter 3:12; 1 Cor. 15:24-28). See appendix chart number 2.
9 Leonard Ravenhill, *The Last Days Newsletter*, "The Judgment Seat of Christ" (Garden Valley, Texas: Last Days Evangelical Association, March-May, 1983), p. 7.
10 Winston Churchill, at a news conference in Washington, 1954, in New York Times, January 25, 1965 (Supplement), p.7.

CHAPTER 2

THE PURPOSE OF THE JUDGMENT SEAT

Too many people are far too short-sighted. They are living only for now. They are failing to prepare for eternity! They are a lot like Hagar. In a cartoon, Hagar is asked if he believes there is life after death. He says, "I am not even sure I believe there is fun after forty!" How about it? Do you know there can be fun after forty? Do you know there could be phenomenal delights beyond this life? Have you looked beyond your years? Have you looked into eternity?

Thomas Carlyle once wrote, "He who has no vision of eternity has no hold on time." He is exactly right!

We have discovered the incomparability of heaven, and that getting to heaven is a free gift granted to all who believe in Jesus Christ. We have also discovered the reality of accountability, and that every believer in Christ will stand before Christ at the judgment seat to give an account for all he has thought and said and done and become.

Perhaps a battle is taking place in your mind. Two thoughts are fighting for acknowledgement. Your Bible says every Christian will be judged at the **bema**. Your emotions say, "Surely God won't judge believers, will He?" You know that the facts of the Bible must take precedence over the feelings of your heart. According to the Bible, the judgment seat of Christ is a reality. It is coming. It is inescapable. It is for every believer. The battle ends, and the reality of the judgment seat of Christ is acknowledged.

Now you ask, "Why is God going to judge believers at the **bema**?" That is an excellent question, and I'm glad you asked it. A study of the Bible reveals two basic reasons for the judgment seat of Christ.

First, there is the present motivation of the believer.

Second, there is the future manifestation of the believer.

THE PRESENT MOTIVATION OF THE BELIEVER

One of the driving aspirations of the Apostle Paul was to live a life that was well pleasing to His Lord. Paul not only had this as his ambition but also saw it as the proper ambition for all Christians. This is revealed in 2 Corinthians 5:9 where Paul writes: *"Therefore, we make it our aim, whether present or absent, to be well pleasing to Him."* We must certainly agree that this is a noble and a worthy aspiration. But we must also admit that many Christians fail to live up to this aspiration.

At the end of his life, Paul was able to declare, *"I have fought the good fight, I have finished the race, I have kept the faith."* How was it that Paul was able to fulfill his aspiration to please the Lord? What was it that motivated Paul to live a life that would be satisfying to the Lord? He is not silent on this point! Let Paul answer in his own words:

> Therefore, we make it our aim, whether present or absent, to be well pleasing to Him. For we must all appear before the judgment seat of Christ, that each one may receive the things done in the body, according to what he has done, whether good or bad. (2 Cor. 5:9-10)

The reason Paul gives for this desire to be pleasing to Christ is the fact that one day he will appear before the judgment seat of Christ, there to be recompensed for the things he did during his life here on earth. The judgment seat of Christ was a very powerful motivating factor in the life of the Apostle Paul.

Paul was motivated by his desire to be pleasing to his Lord. Paul was motivated by an awareness of his accountability to God. Paul was motivated by his desire to be rewarded by Christ! Paul saw this as a justifiable motivation for Christ-like living!

Paul never tried to motivate a believer by having him question his eternal life. He knew that eternal life was given freely, unconditionally, and eternally to everyone who believes in Christ. Paul did try to motivate believers by having them question their eternal lot! He challenged Christians to be aware of the fact that the person they are becoming now and the way they are living now is setting the stage for eternity! He challenged them to consider the fact that they would have to give account of their attitudes and actions, their character and conduct, and their thoughts and motives, at the judgment seat of Christ. He challenged them to consider whether their life was pleasing to the Lord and worthy of reward. He reminded them of the two basic options:

1. Pleasing the Lord and receiving reward;
2. Failing the Lord and forfeiting reward.[1]

Let me give you an example. In Paul's epistle to the Romans, he writes to those who are *"beloved of God"* and *"called saints"* (1:7). He writes to those beloved saints whose *"faith is spoken of throughout the whole world"* (1:8). This is unquestionably a letter to believers. In Romans 14:1-3, Paul writes:

> Receive the one who is weak in the faith, but not to disputes over doubtful things. For one believes he may eat all things, but he who is weak eats vegetables only. Let not him who eats despise him who does not eat, and let not him who does not eat judge him who eats, for God has received him.

What is taking place? Believers who are strong in the faith are despising believers who are weak in the faith. Believers who are weak in the faith are critically judging those believers who are strong in the faith. What a tragic situation! Christians are despising and destroying one another! What does Paul do? How is Paul going to motivate them to Christ-like living? The answer is found in Romans 14:10-12:

> But why do you judge your brother? Or why do you show contempt for your brother? For we shall all stand before the judgment seat of Christ. For it is written, "As I live," says the Lord, "every knee shall bow to Me, and every tongue shall confess to God." So then each one of us shall give account of himself to God.

Does Paul suggest that they are mere professors and not possessors of eternal life? No! Does he suggest that they stop right where they are and ask themselves the question, "Am I really born again?" No! Paul never tries to motivate believers by having them question his eternal life. He motivates them by having them question their eternal lot. He tells them they should live for the Lord because they will all have to stand before the judgment seat of Christ. He reminds them that every believer will give account of himself to God. He tells them that their life could be an honor to Christ now and throughout all eternity!

I've heard some people say, "I don't work for reward, I work for the Lord." Now that may be pretty poetry, but its terrible theology! We have already seen that Paul considered the judgment seat of Christ a justifiable motivation for Christ-like living. This same motivation can be found in the writings of the beloved Disciple John, who urged his readers to live in such a way as to receive a full reward (2 Jn. 8). Jesus Christ also considered rewards to be a justifiable motivation for

Christ-like living. He challenged his listeners to lay up treasures in heaven (Mt. 6:19-20). Jesus challenged his disciples to deny themselves and follow Him, and He sought to motivate them by reminding them that when He came back in glory they would be rewarded according to their works (Mt.16:24-27). Jesus told Peter and the apostles that those who had made sacrifices in following Him would be rewarded with the privilege of reigning with Him in the coming kingdom (Mt.19:27-30).

C. S. Lewis knew this motivation. In his sermon, entitled "The Weight of Glory," C. S. Lewis writes:

> If you asked twenty good men today what they thought the highest of virtues, nineteen of them would reply, Unselfishness. But if you had asked almost any of the great Christians of old, he would have replied, Love. You see what has happened? A negative term has been substituted for a positive, and this is of more than philological importance. The negative idea of Unselfishness carries with it the suggestion not primarily of securing good things for others, but going without them ourselves, as if our abstinence and not their happiness was the important point. I do not think this is the Christian virtue of Love. The New Testament has lots to say about self-denial, but not about self-denial as an end in itself. We are told today to deny ourselves and take up our crosses in order that we may follow Christ; and nearly every description of what we shall ultimately find if we do so contains an appeal to desire. If there lurks in most modern minds the

> notion that to desire our own good and earnestly to hope for enjoyment is a bad thing, I submit that this notion has crept in from Kant and the Stoics and is no part of the Christian faith. Indeed, if we consider the unblushing promises of reward and the staggering nature of the rewards promised in the gospels, it would seem that Our Lord finds our desires not too strong, but too weak. We are half-hearted creatures fooling about with drink and sex and ambition when infinite joy is offered us, like an ignorant child who wants to go on making mud pies in a slum because he cannot imagine what is meant by the offer of a holiday at the sea. We are far too easily pleased.[2]

It should be our desire to please God. We should find pleasure in pleasing Him! We should be acutely aware of the fact that we will give an account to God. Man tends to avoid responsibility and ignore accountability. It happened in the Garden of Eden, and it is still happening today. Will Rogers once said, "The history of North America could be written in three phases: the passing of the American Indian, the passing of the buffalo, and the passing of the buck." We want to blame others and blame circumstances when we should really accept the blame ourselves. We are responsible for the choices we make, and we will be held accountable for everything we have thought and said and done.

Even in the old days, the cowboys knew that every thought, word, and action had its consequences. That's why they had sayings like these:

"Never squat with yer spurs on!" There are consequences!

"Never miss a good chance to shut up." There are consequences!

"Always drink upstream from the herd." There are consequences!

"Lettin the cat outta the bag is a whole lot easier than puttin it back in." There are consequences!

What we think and say and do has consequences, not only in this life, but also in eternity! We desperately need this kind of teaching in our churches today. The old "You better question your salvation!" method of motivation is not biblical; nor is it effective in the lives of those who know the Scripture well enough to know that eternal life is freely, eternally, and unconditionally given to those who believe in Jesus Christ as their personal Savior. A good friend once said to me:

> Well I know that I know Christ and I know I'm going to Heaven. I want to do some things for Him, but I want to live my life. I want to enjoy my life. And after all, I realize He could discipline me, but once we get to Heaven we'll all see Christ.

He was trying to tell me something, but he was also trying to ask me something. He was asking, "What difference does it make how I live here on earth as long as I know I'm going to heaven?" This young man needed to hear about the judgment seat of Christ. He needed a motivation to live a life that was pleasing to the Lord. He needed to hear the words of our Lord when He said to His disciples:

> If anyone desires to come after Me, let him deny himself, and take up his cross daily, and follow Me. For whoever desires to save his life will lose it, but whoever loses his life for My sake will save it. For what profit is it to a man if he gains the whole world, and is himself destroyed or lost? For whoever is ashamed of Me and My words, of him will the Son of Man be ashamed when He comes in His own glory, and in His Father's, and of the holy angels. (Lk. 9:23-26)

He needed to be reminded that while we are not saved by good works (Eph. 2:8-9), we are saved unto good works (Eph. 2:10). He needed to remember that God has a unique plan for his life. He needed to understand that God has a special part for him to play. He needed to discover God's will for his life. God is going to hold every believer accountable for the time, the talents, and the treasures that He entrusts to us during our earthly life.

Prophecy is not given to *satisfy our curiosity*; prophecy is given to *stimulate our purity*! The prospect of standing before the judgment seat of Christ in the *future* is designed to stimulate the believer to live for Christ in the *present*. Therefore, it is imperative that every believer understands the importance and the impact of the judgment seat of Christ.

THE FUTURE MANIFESTATION OF THE BELIEVER

In describing what takes place at the judgment seat of Christ, Paul says, *"We must all* ***appear*** *before the judgment seat of Christ"* (2

Cor. 5:10). The translation of Paul's term as *appear* is not rich enough or full enough to give us a clear picture of what happens. This term means "to appear, to make visible, and to reveal."[3] Therefore, we will not only be present at the judgment seat, we will be revealed at the judgment seat!

The judgment seat of Christ then, is primarily a means of revealing the character and conduct of the believer's life. If this is true, then why is it true? Why does God want to reveal my life at the **bema**? Paul gives us the answer in 2 Corinthians 5:10:

> For we must all appear before the judgment seat of Christ, that each one may receive the things done in the body, according to what he has done, whether good or bad.

The reason for revealing the believer's life is in order that he might be recompensed for the things he did during his earthly life. The reason for the revelation is compensation! Believers are going to receive back exactly what is due. They will receive a just reward for everything they have done, whether good or bad.[4]

Wow! What a revelation! The sun couldn't shine any clearer on this passage, and yet the teaching on it is very cloudy. We will be recompensed for what we have done, whether good or bad. There are no exceptions. This is not going to be a mockery. This is going to be a judgment. This is not going to be a time for parading the good and passing over the bad. The inexorable principle of Galatians 6:7 rings forth a very clear sound: *"Do not be deceived, God is not mocked; whatever a man sows, that he will also reap!"*

The purpose of the judgment seat is to determine the degree and the nature of rewards for the believer. It is delightful to think that we will be rewarded for the good we have done. It is discomforting to think that we will be rewarded for the bad we have done. This raises many other questions. How will my failures and faults be judged at the **bema**? What impact will that have on my rewards? What impact will that have on my Lord? How does one reconcile this with the idea that sins confessed are removed and forgotten? Will my life be flashed on a large screen for all to see? Just what will take place at this manifestation? How will Christians be judged? What is the basis of the judgment? These questions can best be answered by an exposition of three New Testament passages illustrating the truths of the judgment seat of Christ:

1. The illustration of a builder (1 Cor. 3);
2. The illustration of an athlete (1 Cor. 9);
3. The illustration of a steward (Lk. 16).

We'll examine each of these illustrations, one at a time, in the next four chapters. For now, let me just say that the awesome threat of some fiery revivalists that our lives will be flashed on a screen for all to see cannot be supported by Scripture. But let me also mention a couple things that can be supported by Scripture:

1. No waste of time, talent or treasure will be hidden from our Lord!

2. No loving deed, obedient action, or kind words will be forgotten by our Lord!

The Lord is not so unjust as to forget any love you have shown or any work you have done in His name!

SUMMARY

We have discovered two basic purposes of the judgment seat of Christ. First of all, the **bema** should serve as ***a motivation big enough to move us.*** It should drive us to please God in our character and conduct. Secondly, the **bema** will serve as ***a manifestation clear enough to reveal us***. It will reveal our thoughts and motives, words and deeds, character and conduct. We will see ourselves as we really are.

I see two major considerations we should each personally address:

1. *Am I pleasing God?* Am I pleasing God in my family? Am I pleasing God in my church? Am I pleasing God in my friendships? Am I pleasing God in my work? Am I pleasing God in my finances? Am I pleasing God in my use of my time?

2. *Am I ready to give account to God?* Perhaps there are some things you have left undone. Perhaps there are some things you need to do. Perhaps there are some habits that need to be broken and some patterns of sin that need to be conquered. Perhaps there are some attitudes that need to be changed.

For not one of us lives to himself, and no one dies to himself. For if we live, we live to the Lord; and if we die, we die to the Lord. Therefore, whether we live or die, we are the Lord's. For to this end

Christ died and lived again, that He might be Lord of both the dead and the living. (Rom. 14:7-9)

Pause a moment and allow the Holy Spirit to convict you, challenge you, and change you.

"His Plan for Me"
—Martha Snell Nicholson

When I stand at the judgment Seat of Christ
  And He shows His plan for me,
The plan of my life as it might have been,
  Had He had His way—and I see
How I blocked Him here, and checked Him there,
  And I would not yield my will,
Will there be grief in my Savior's eyes,
  Grief though He loves me still?
Would He have me rich and I stand there poor,
  Stripped of all but His grace,
While memory runs like a hunted thing,
  Down the paths I cannot retrace.
Lord, of the years that are left to me,
  I give them to Thy hand;
Take me and break me and mold me,
  To the pattern that Thou hast planned![4]

Study Guide – Chapter 2 – Motivation and Revelation

"Prophecy is not given to satisfy our curiosity; prophecy is given to stimulate our purity!"

—Harlan D. Betz: *Setting the Stage for Eternity*

1. **Read 2 Corinthians 5:9.**

    What is your aim in life?

    What is it that drives you in your daily life?

    Do you have a passion to please Christ?

    How would a passion to please Christ be manifest in relationship to family, classmates, friends, neighbors, co-workers?

    Take some time to do a little inventory of your life.

    Are you pleasing God in your family?

    Are you pleasing God in your church?

    Are you pleasing God in your work?

    Are you pleasing God in your finances?

    Are you pleasing God in the use of your time?

2. **Read Matthew 6:19-20.**

    What are some of the things in life that you treasure?

    How can a person lay up treasures in heaven?

3. Are you ready to give an account to God?

    Do you have habits you need to change?

    Do you have addictions that need to be broken?

    Are there some things God has been urging you to do that you have left undone?

4. Discuss this quote by John Keble from *The Effect of Example:*

"The deeds we do, the words we say, into air they seem to fleet,
We count them ever past; but they shall last—
In the dread judgment they and we shall meet."

5. Have you been captured by the love of Christ? Are you excited about the prospect of His return? How can this attitude be cultivated? Are you praying, "Come, Lord Jesus!"?

6. Consider this quote by William Culbertson:

"Sometimes those of us who hold that the Lord Jesus Christ is coming again are spoken of as pessimists. I think it can truly be said that we are really the only ones who have any right to be optimistic!"

7. Reflect on Martha Snell Nicholson's poem, *His Plan for Me:*

When I stand at the judgment Seat of Christ
    And He shows His plan for me,
The plan of my life as it might have been,
    Had He had His way—and I see
How I blocked Him here, and checked Him there,
    And I would not yield my will,
Will there be grief in my Savior's eyes,
    Grief though He loves me still?
Would He have me rich and I stand there poor,
    Stripped of all but His grace,
While memory runs like a hunted thing,
    Down the paths I cannot retrace.
Lord, of the years that are left to me,
    I give them to Thy hand;
Take me and break me and mold me,
    To the pattern that Thou hast planned.[5]

---

[1] H. A. Ironside, "Salvation and Reward," *Miscellaneous Papers*, II, p. 1. Ironside appropriately distinguishes between the doctrine of rewards and the doctrine of salvation, writing, "To the casual reader of the New Testament it sometimes seems as though there is an apparent contradiction, when in one place we are distinctly told we are saved by grace alone, apart from works, whereas, in another, we are just as clearly told that we are to be rewarded according to our works. It is only as we learn the mind of the Spirit in regard to these two very different lines of teaching that the soul is set free from self-occupation and given to know the blessedness of peace with God, on the ground of pure grace, thus leaving one free to serve in the happy knowledge that the *sin question* is forever settled, but that *service* is the outflow of a grateful heart to the One who has redeemed us, and yet that He, in His wondrous loving-kindness, takes note of everything we do for Him, and will reward accordingly."

[2] C. S. Lewis, *The Weight of Glory*, (New York, New York: Simon & Shuster, 1980), pp.25-26.

[3] Geoffrey W. Bromiley, ed., *Theological Dictionary of the New Testament*, (Grand Rapids, Michigan: William B. Eerdmans Publishing Company, 1985), pp. 1244-1245.

[4] *His Plan for Me* by Martha Snell Nicholson © Moody Publishing Company. All rights reserved. Used by permission.

[5] Ibid.

CHAPTER 3

BUILDING ON THE ROCK!

Sometimes believers act like unbelievers. Sometimes churches become divided. Sometimes they even split! Sin among the saints? That's right. Carnality in the church? That's right. Paul could not speak to the Corinthian believers as spiritual, but as carnal. At a time when they should be in stages of maturity, they were still in stages of infancy. They were believers acting like unbelievers. There was jealousy and strife among them. They were focusing their attention on men, and giving their glory to men. They were arguing over who was the most important.

They were arguing over issues like this: Who is more important—Paul or Apollos? Who is more important—the evangelist or the Bible teacher? Who is more important—the one who led me to new birth in Christ or the one who helped me grow in Christ?

This is like asking, Which is more important—the sun or the rain? It is like asking, Which of our legs is more important—the right or the left? Actually, we need them both! The truly important thing is to give credit where the credit is due. The glory belongs not to the sun or the rain, but to the Creator. The glory belongs not to the right or left leg, but to the God who formed them. Even so in Corinth, the glory belongs not to Paul or Apollos, but to God.

The believers in Corinth needed to recognize that it was God who gifted the individuals that ministered unto them. Yes, these individuals deserve honor, but God deserves the glory! Certainly these individuals labored, and definitely they shall be rewarded, but God will receive the glory!

Let's pick up Paul's challenge in 1 Corinthians 3:9 where he says, *"We are God's fellow workers; you are God's field, you are God's building."*

Paul speaks of the believers as a building. Paul's emphasis is on God. Verse nine literally reads as follows: *"God's fellow-workers are we; God's field are you, God's building are you"* (Greek). The church is God's. The ultimate builder is God. The church is an exhibition of God's operations in spiritual farming and spiritual building.[1]

This metaphor is primarily designed as a blueprint for ministers. It tells them where to build. It tells them how to build. "Oh," you say, "I'm glad you told me. I will just skip this chapter and move on to the next one; after all, this message is designed for ministers, priests, and clergy, not for the average layman."

Wait just a minute. Do not set aside biblical directions simply on the basis of traditional distinctions. The division of believers into clergy and laity—meaning those who minister and those who are simply ministered unto—is not found in the biblical teaching on the church.

The Bible says that every believer is a minister! In fact, the Bible says that God has given gifted individuals to the church *"for the equipping of the believers unto the work of the ministry, unto the building up of the body of Christ"* (Eph. 4:12, Greek.).

The Bible says that every believer is a priest! The division of believers into priests and peons is not found in the biblical teaching on the church. Peter declares that every believer is a living stone *"being built up as a spiritual house, a holy priesthood"* (1 Pet. 2:5). He tells these believers that they are a *"royal priesthood"* (1 Pet. 2:9).

The Bible says that every believer is divinely gifted for ministry! Peter goes on to say that every believer has either a speaking gift or a serving gift. Please note his words:

> As each one has received a spiritual gift, use this gift in ministering to one another, as good stewards of the diversified grace of God. Whoever speaks, let it be as the oracles of God; whoever serves, let it be

> out of the strength which God abundantly provides; in order that in all ministries God might be glorified through Jesus Christ. (1 Pet. 4:10-11, Greek)

Peter, in harmony with Paul, indicates that the giving God, not the gifted believer, deserves the glory. Peter, in harmony with Paul, indicates that every believer is to be involved in the ministry. Consequently, the challenge to the builders in 1 Corinthians 3 is being issued to each of us who knows Jesus Christ as our personal Savior.

Paul's presentation of this blueprint for builders provides a very vivid picture of the judgment seat of Christ. There are three major parts in Paul's presentation—the responsibility, the reckoning, and the results.

THE RESPONSIBILITY

> According to the grace of God which was given to me, as a wise master I have laid the foundation, and another builds on it. But let each one take heed how he builds on it. For no other foundation can anyone lay than that which is laid, which is Jesus Christ. (1 Cor. 3:10-11)

What is the responsibility of every believer? Our responsibility is to build! To partner with Paul and all other believers in the building of the church!

Where are we to build? We are to build on Jesus Christ. Jesus is the solid rock. Jesus is the chief cornerstone.

If you are going to be involved in God's building program, there's something you must understand. Jesus Christ isn't simply one foundation on which you can build; He is the only foundation on which you can build!

I remember watching a building project of my children, Joshua and Sarah. They were building sandcastles. They worked tirelessly to make the walls tall and strong. They dug zealously to make the moat deep and smooth. They were determined to design castles that would last . . . castles they could come back to and play with. That next day they went running down to see their castles. Something was wrong. They had eroded away like a ball of butter under the hot Texas sun. Why? They eroded because they were sandcastles. Their castles were not built on a solid foundation. It didn't matter how zealously they worked. It didn't matter how earnestly they tried. All of their effort, energy, and work were for nothing because they didn't build on a solid foundation!

What's the point? It doesn't matter how hard you work. It doesn't matter how hard you try. It doesn't matter how sincere you are. If you don't build your life on Jesus Christ, you are not building on a solid foundation.

What are you building on? What foundation are you banking on to get into Heaven? Are you counting on your good works? Are you trusting in your baptism? Are you basing your hope on taking the Eucharist? Are you relying on your church attendance? Are you banking your hopes for eternal life on saying a church liturgy? Are you counting on getting to Heaven because you believe all roads lead to Heaven, and it really doesn't matter what you believe? Are you banking on the hope that all people go to Heaven? My friend, those are not solid foundations. Jesus Christ said, *"I am the way, the truth, and the life. No one comes to the Father except through me"* (Jn. 14:6).

Have you placed your faith in Christ's death and resurrection as the full and final payment for your sins? If not, why not trust Him now, and firmly plant yourself on the Solid Rock.

Where are we to build? We are to build on Jesus Christ. He is the Solid Rock!

How are we to build? The Bible says, "*Let each one take heed how he builds on it!*" (1 Cor. 3:10). We should build carefully. The manner in which we build, and the materials that we use, must be carefully considered. Why? Because there will come a day of reckoning.

THE RECKONING

> Now, if any one builds on this foundation with gold, silver, precious stones, wood, hay, straw, each one's work will become clear; for the Day will declare it, because it will be revealed by fire; and the fire will test each one's work, of what sort it is. (1 Cor. 3:12-13)

Like a roving reporter at the site of the newsworthy event, Paul tells us what, when, how, and why. Let's look at each of these.

What is involved in the reckoning? *"Each one's work will become clear."* Every believer's work will be clearly and plainly *revealed.* This is the same term we examined in 2 Corinthians 5:10, which says, *"We must all* ***be revealed*** *before the judgment seat of Christ!"*

When will the reckoning take place? *The Day will declare it.* This future day when the believer's work will be revealed is the day of Christ. It is the day when the believer stands before the judgment seat of Christ.

How will the reckoning take place? Each believer's work will *be revealed by fire*. The Bible says the eyes of our Lord Jesus Christ are like a *flame of fire* (Rev. 1:14; 2:18; 19:12). I believe that Jesus Christ's eyes, like a flame of fire, will test our work. As Paul says, He will *"bring to light the things hidden in the darkness and reveal the motives of men's hearts"* (1 Cor. 4:5).

Why will the reckoning take place? The reckoning is designed *to determine the quality of each believer's work*. The eyes of Jesus Christ, like a flame of fire, will penetrate, perceive, and plainly reveal the quality of our work. Gold, silver, and precious stones endure the test of the fire. Wood, hay, and straw perish in the fire.

When we stand before Christ at the **bema**, every facade will fade, and every mask will be torn away. The true character and the genuine quality of our work will be revealed:

1. Everything we have done and become that is perishable will perish;
2. Everything we have done and become that is imperishable will remain.

This gives us some insight into the importance and the impact of the judgment seat of Christ! The Bible declares the results of the judgment seat. Are you listening?

THE RESULTS

> If anyone's work which he has built on it endures, he will receive a reward. If anyone's work is burned, he

will suffer loss; but he himself will be saved, yet so as through fire. (1 Cor. 3:14-15)

The Contrasting Possibilities:

1. The Conquering Christian: his work abides, and he is *rewarded*!
2. The Carnal Christian: his work is consumed, and he *suffers loss*!

No, that is not a misprint. The Bible makes it clear that for some believers, the judgment seat of Christ will be a time of pain and loss and suffering.[2]

I can see it now. Red flags are going up all over the place. Perhaps you're thinking to yourself, What is this guy . . . some kind of heretic?

Please don't close your mind. If you are committed to Jesus Christ, you have an obligation to be open to the Scripture. These verses of Scripture have raised an issue that must be dealt with. While the concept of rewards has been passively set aside in many evangelical circles today, the concept of suffering loss has been actively set aside.

What is the biblical perspective? How should the Bible teacher answer the student who asks: "Is it possible that I shall be ashamed at the judgment seat of Christ?" Or, "Is it possible that I will experience pain, and loss, and suffering at the **bema**?"

The answers to these questions are unmistakably set forth in the Scriptures. While judgment at the **bema** is not to determine one's eternal destiny (heaven or hell), it is to determine one's eternal lot (reward or regret).

While judgment at the **bema** does not deal with the penalty of sin, it does deal with sin's effects. Paul declares that the life of every believer will be exposed at the **bema** in order that each one may receive the things done in the body, *"whether good or bad"* (2 Cor. 5:10).[3]

The good will be commended. The bad will be condemned.

The good will be commended, in that there will be a reward given for the imperishable deeds. The imperishable deeds will place the believer in the joyful position of being pleasing to God, honoring to God, praised by God, and rewarded by God.

The bad will be condemned, in that there will be the shame of failing the Lord and the heartache of forfeiting reward. Jesus warned His disciples about the danger of sinning by fearing to give of themselves to His rejected ministers. He told them that to do so would be to forfeit rewards (Mt.10:34-42). Jesus also warned his disciples about the danger of trying to live their lives for themselves and consequently being ashamed of Christ. Please observe the tragic consequences: *"For whoever is ashamed of Me and My words, of him the Son of Man will be ashamed when He comes in His own glory"* (Lk. 9:26).

Can you even begin to imagine the anguish and heartache you would feel at that day if Jesus Christ were ashamed of you? The beloved Apostle John writes,

> And now (in this present life), little children, abide in Christ in order that when He appears you may have joyous confidence and not shrink away in shame before Him at His coming. (1 Jn. 2:28, Greek)

John's declaration is in perfect harmony with Paul's. There are two distinct possibilities:

1. The conquering Christian who is confident at Christ's coming;
2. The carnal Christian who is ashamed of himself at Christ's coming.

Therefore, it is clear that one's life is either characterized by imperishable works and he is rewarded; or his life is characterized by perishable works and he suffers the pain and loss of knowing he has both failed his Lord and forfeited his reward.

I know this is not commonly taught. It is very discomforting to think that one's bad deeds will be exposed at the **bema**. But that is what the Bible teaches. It must be noted that God does not condone sin in His children now (1 Cor. 11; Heb. 12), and He will not condone it at the **bema** (1 Cor. 3; 2 Cor. 5).

At this point you may be thinking, "But a Christian can't come into judgment, can he?" The Scriptural answer is not uncertain. *"We (Christians) must all appear before the judgment seat of Christ"* (2 Cor. 5:10). This judgment will take place in spite of the fact that John assures believers that they will not come into judgment (Jn. 5:24).

How can these two passages be reconciled? It must be observed that John is speaking of judgment with respect to one's *eternal destiny* (life and eternal contact with God or death and eternal separation from God), and Paul is speaking of judgment with respect to one's *spiritual duty* (walking by faith in obedience or walking in the flesh and disobedience).[4]

The judgment seat does not deal with *where you're going.*
The judgment seat does deal with *what you've done*!
The judgment seat does not deal with *where you're going.*
The judgment seat does deal with *what you're getting*!
And it deals with what you will be able to give to our Lord!

The Bible makes it clear that believers are to judge themselves in this present life. If we fail to judge ourselves, God will judge us. The Bible says that God judges us so that we will not be condemned (1 Cor. 11:28-32). What does that mean? A believer cannot lose eternal life, so we must reject the explanations of commentators who say God's disciplinary action is to spare sinning sons of God from eternal hell. God's disciplinary action has three results (Heb. 12:5-11):

1. It prevents condemnation—by turning us back from a sinful way of life.
2. It promotes sanctification—by moving us toward Christ-likeness.
3. It prompts exaltation—by making our life an honor to Christ!

It is important to notice that though the believer's work may be consumed, he is still saved.[5]

Reaching Heaven depends on *where* you build.
Rewards in Heaven depend on *how* you build.
Reaching Heaven is dependent on *belief.*
Rewards in Heaven are dependent on *behavior.*

The Bible makes it abundantly clear that eternal life is freely given to everyone who believes in Jesus Christ as his personal Savior (Jn. 3:16, 5:24). The Bible makes it abundantly clear that salvation is a gift of God's grace: *"For by grace you have been saved through faith, and that not of yourselves; it is the gift of God; not of works, lest anyone should boast"* (Eph. 2:8-9).

The Bible also makes it abundantly clear that every one of these believers must appear before the judgment seat of Christ. The purpose of this judgment is to evaluate the quality of their work. The perishable work will be consumed. The imperishable work will remain. The works that remain count for eternity and will be rewarded.

Eternal life is a free gift.

Rewards are an earned inheritance.

Eternal life is given to the unworthy by God's grace.

Rewards are granted to the worthy by God's grace.

And so we must remember that while we are not saved by good works, we are saved unto good works: *"For we are His workmanship, created in Christ Jesus for good works, which God prepared beforehand that we should walk in them"* (Eph. 2:10).

Perhaps an illustration can clarify the real meaning of Paul's portrait of the judgment seat of Christ in 1 Corinthians 3. Arthur Betz, my brother both physically and spiritually, used the classic story of *The Three Little Pigs* to teach this passage to me. I have written a contemporary version of *The Three Little Pigs* to teach this passage to others.

Once upon a time there were three little pigs. Each of them set out to build a home. The first little pig worked long enough to pick up some straw. He found a nice location and proceeded to build a straw hut. He rejoiced in the home of his youth. It kept out the heat by day. It kept out the cold by night. Best of all, it cost him very little in terms of time or work or money. He was free to live his life for himself. The building of his home required almost nothing in terms of sacrifice. He was free to spend hours in the hog wallow behind his house.

The second pig cut down some little trees and picked up some good sticks. He found a nice location and proceeded to build a log cabin. He rejoiced in the home of his youth. It kept out the heat by day. It kept out the cold by night. Best of all, it cost him fairly little in terms of time or work or money. He was now free to live for himself. The building of his home required almost nothing in terms of sacrifice. He was free to spend hours in the cornfield behind his home.

The third little pig worked long and hard making bricks. He worked day after day mixing and forming, setting and stacking. His two brothers watched him work from their wallow and cornfield. They told him to relax and live a little. Finally, after much sacrifice in terms of time and work and money, the third pig finished his brick mansion. The other two pigs snorted at him and mocked his mansion. What did he have that they didn't? Their straw hut and log cabin kept them warm by night and cool by day.

Suddenly, there was a knock on the door of the straw hut in the middle of the night. It was not the big bad wolf of the classic version. This hideous and hungry monster was the twentieth century fox.

He said, "Little pig, little pig, let me come in."

Quickly, the pig responded, "Not by the hair of my chinny-chin-chin."

Confidently the fox replied, "Then I'll light my blow torch and burn your house down." And he did! And that little pig saw his straw hut going up in flames. He took off for his brother's log cabin squealing like a pig that had walked through a fire, with the hair burned off his chinny-chin-chin. Immediately behind him was the twentieth century fox.

The fox knocked on the door of the log cabin, and said, "Little pig, little pig, let me come in."

"Not by the hair of my chinny-chin-chin," replied the second pig.

"Then I'll light my blow torch and burn your house down," said the twentieth century fox. And he did. He lit all four corners of the log cabin. The little wood cabin caught fire and the fire began spreading rapidly. I don't know if you've ever noticed, but when logs burn, they often sizzle and crackle like bacon. Little pigs don't like that sound! When the two little pigs felt the heat of that fire, heard the sizzle of that wood, and saw the cabin going up in smoke, they took off for their brother's brick mansion. They were squealing because their hide had been singed, the hair had been burned off their chinny-chin-chins, and the fox was right behind them.

The twentieth century fox knocked on the door of the brick mansion, and howled, "Little pig, little pig, let me come in."

The third pig confidently replied, "Not by the hair of my chinny-chin-chin."

"Then I'll light my blow torch and burn your house down," cried the angry fox. He tried to light one corner, and he failed. He tried to light another corner, and he failed. He tried to light one of the brick walls, and he failed. He just couldn't burn it down.

Suddenly, a brilliant idea occurred to him. I'll climb up on the roof, slide down the chimney, and catch those three little pigs. Fortunately, the third little pig had read the classic version of this story, and he had a huge pot of water boiling at the bottom of the chimney. The three little pigs enjoyed fox soup for supper.

Notice the parallels. The first two pigs were involved in a work that could not stand the test of fire. The work of their hands perished in the fire. But, they themselves were saved; though they had the smell of smoke upon them.

The third pig, on the other hand, not only had his life at the end of the story; he also had the work of his hands! His brick mansion stood the test of the fire!

Even so, as believers, we have the opportunity of living a life that counts for eternity. We have the opportunity of doing works that can stand the test of fire.

Will the work of your hands go up in smoke? Is your *time* being consumed by the urgent things or invested in the important things? Are your *talents* being devoured by selfish pursuits, or are they being used to build up the church and reach the lost? Are your *treasures* all laid up here on earth, or are they being laid up in heaven?

Let me remind you again of the words I read over and over again on a plaque that hung on a wall in my Grandma Bahr's house. These words are indelibly fixed in my mind and they have had a powerful impact on my life: "Only one life will soon be past; only what's done for Christ will last!"

Study Guide – Chapter 3 – The Builder!

"Do not set aside biblical directions on the basis of traditional distinctions."

—Harlan D. Betz: *Setting the Stage for Eternity*

1. **Read Ephesians 4:11-16.**

2. Who are the saints being spoken of in verse 12?
   The answer to this question is found in Ephesians 1:1-11

3. According to Ephesians 4:12-16, what is the role of the saints?
   Discuss the concept of every believer being responsible for the work of ministry!

4. Discuss this quote by Pastor Norm Adamson:
   "Every person is either a missionary or a mission field."

5. **Read 1 Corinthians 3:10-15.**

6. What is involved in this concept of building?

7. Where are we to build?
   "Jesus Christ isn't simply one foundation on which you can build; He is the only foundation on which you can build. If you are not building your life on Jesus Christ, you are not building on a solid foundation."

   —Harlan D. Betz: *Setting the Stage for Eternity*

8. Why is secular humanism such a danger for people in our world today?

9. Discuss this quote:

   "The safest road to hell is the gradual one—the gentle slope, soft underfoot, without sudden turnings, without milestones, without signposts."

   —C. S. Lewis: *The Screwtape Letters*

10. Clarify the purpose of the judgment seat of Christ.

    "While the judgment seat is not to determine one's
    eternal destiny (h_______ or h____________);
    it is to determine one's
    eternal lot (r_________or r___________)."

11. Take a few moments to clarify the contrast between:
    regeneration, which by God's grace is divinely given, and
    rewards, which by God's grace are humanly earned!

12. Discuss this famous saying,

    "Only one life will soon be past; only what's done for Christ will last!"

What are you doing for Christ?

Remember, being precedes doing! Don't get so caught up in doing things for Him that you fail to be drawing closer to Him and growing more like Him!

---

[1] Archibald Robertson and Alfred Plummer, *A Critical and Exegetical Commentary on the First Epistle of St. Paul to the Corinthians* (Edinburgh: T. & T. Clark, 1911), p. 59.
[2] The Greek term **zemiow** is translated "to suffer loss." According to Arndt and Gingrich, *A Greek Lexicon*, p. 339, **zemiow** means *"1. to suffer damage or loss, forfeit, sustain injury . . . 2. be punished . . . 1 Corinthians 3:15."* "Punish," according to *Webster's New World Dictionary*, p. 1180, means *"1. to cause (a person) to undergo pain, loss, or suffering for a crime or a wrongdoing."*
[3] Some people try to soften the blow of 2 Corinthians 5:10 by noting the Critical Text's reading of **phaulon** as opposed to the Majority Text's reading of **kakon**. They go on to translate the verse as follows: "For we must all appear before the judgment seat of Christ, that each one may be recompensed for his deeds in the body according to what he has done, whether usable (good, **agathon**) or useless (**phaulon**)." This translation allows for reward for the good deeds and loss of rewards for the worthless deeds. Their emphasis is that we won't be judged for any wickedness in our character or badness in our conduct.
There are three major problems with this approach.

First of all, the Majority Text, Codex Vaticanus, and Papyrus 46 all support the use of the term **kakon** ("bad"). This is very strong manuscript support, and I believe it is the correct reading.

Secondly, even if one accepts the less likely Critical reading of **phaulon** ("worthless"), the meaning of the passage is still basically the same as if it read **kakon**; for **phaulos** (found six times in the New Testament) is used as a synonym for **kakos**; and means "evil or bad," according to *The New International Dictionary of New Testament Theology,* Volume 1, pp. 561-564.

Thirdly, with either term, there is clearly going to be a revealing and a reaping for everything that is done, whether good or bad (cf. Galatians 6:7).
[4] Romans 8:1, in its shorter reading, is also used as a supporting text for the idea that a believer will not face any judgment. The shorter reading could be explained in the same way that John 5:24 was explained (i.e., no judgment with regard to position and eternal life, but definite judgment with regard to practice and eternal lot). There is however, good reason to accept the conditional phrase following the promise of no condemnation . . . **me kata sarka peripatousin alla kata Pneuma** ("who do not walk according to the flesh, but according to the Spirit"). The majority text as a whole is united in including this phrase! It is only omitted by Codex Sinaiticus and Codex Vaticanus. This reading gives good sense, fits well with the surrounding context, and indicates there would be some condemnation for the believer who walks according to the flesh.
[5] C. I. Scofield, editor, *The Scofield Reference Bible* (New York: Oxford University Press, 1945), p. 1214. Scofield notes that, "God, in the N. T. Scriptures, offers to

the *lost,* salvation; and for the faithful service of the *saved*, rewards. The passages are easily distinguished by remembering that salvation is invariably spoken of as a free gift (e.g., John 4:10; Rom. 6:23; Eph. 2:8, 9); while rewards are earned by works (Mt.10:42; Lk. 19:17; 1 Cor. 9:24, 25; 2 Tim. 4:7, 8; Rev. 2:10; 22:12). A further distinction is that salvation is a present possession (Lk. 7:50; john 3:36; 5:24; 6:47), while rewards are a future attainment, to be given at the coming of the Lord" (Mt. 16:27; 2 Tim. 4:8; Rev. 22; 12).

CHAPTER 4

BUILDING FOR ETERNITY

We have the opportunity of living a life that counts for eternity. We have the opportunity of doing works that can stand the test of fire. The question is, Will my work stand the test of fire? Will what I have done and become be imperishable?

Before we leave the illustration of the builder, we must hammer out one more crucial issue. We have discovered that every believer's work will be tested by fire, and only those works that are imperishable will be rewarded. The crucial issue at this point is the determination of just what it means to be imperishable. What are these works of gold, silver, and precious stones that stand the test of fire? Many fine suggestions have been made, but in the final analysis they are mere conjectures. The terms *gold, silver, precious stones, wood, hay, and straw* are all appropriate materials for the metaphor of a builder. We want to go beyond the metaphor to the meaning. We want to go beyond the building to the **bema**.

Is there anything in the context of this passage that might give us a clue as to what makes a work imperishable and rewardable? I'm sure no one is surprised that 1 Corinthians 3 is followed by 1 Corinthians 4. Look at 1 Corinthians 4:1-2. This passage is still talking about God's evaluation of Christians as ministers:

> Let a man so consider us, as servants of Christ and stewards of the mysteries of God. Moreover, it is required of stewards that one be found faithful.

This passage emphasizes that every believer is a servant and steward of Christ. It also emphasizes that the major requirement of a steward is that he be found faithful! Therefore it is obvious that believers will be examined with regard to their faithfulness as servants of Christ and stewards of God.

But how is faithfulness measured? Check out 1 Corinthians 4:3-5.

> But with me it is a very small thing that I should be judged by you, or by any human court; in fact, I do not even judge myself. I know of nothing against myself, yet I am not justified by this; but He who judges me is the Lord. Therefore judge nothing before the time, until the Lord comes, who will both bring to light the hidden things of darkness and reveal the motives of men's hearts. Then each one's praise will come from God.

Paul recognized that man looks on the outward appearance, but God looks on the heart. When the Lord comes back and believers stand before Him at the **bema**, He will reveal not only what appears on the outside, but also what exists on the inside. He will *reveal the motives of men's hearts.* This revelation is the *revealing* spoken of in the 2 Corinthians 5:10 **bema** passage and in the 1 Corinthians 3:13 **bema** passage.

Here at last we discover the character of an imperishable work. It is a work that is carried out with godly *motives*!

Let's pursue this a little further. Is there anything else in the context of these passages that highlights the motives of men's hearts? As a matter of fact, a closer look at the three central passages on the judgment seat of Christ, will show that there are three crucial components of a work that is genuinely good and worthy of reward.

The Glory of God the Father

We will look first at the *tested by fire* **bema** passage. 1 Corinthians 3 tells us that Jesus is going to determine the quality of our works at the judgment seat of Christ. That passage begins by emphasizing the glory of God. First, because we are dependent upon God. *"So then neither he who plants is anything, nor he who waters, but God who gives the increase"* Second, because we belong to God. *"For we are God's fellow-workers, you are God's field, you are God's building."* Third, because we are gifted by God. The glory belongs to the giving God, not to the gifted believer.

It is true that the believer labors, and the believer will be rewarded. The believer deserves honor and will be rewarded, but God deserves the glory. Why? Because the believer was created by God and gifted by God, and anything worthy the believer does is done by the grace of God.

Everything we say and do should be said and done to bring honor and glory to God! Our motive should not be to bring attention to ourselves; our motive should be to bring attention to our God. We should shine the spotlight on Him. He is worthy of our honor and praise and glory! Paul nails this truth down a little later in this same letter. In 1 Corinthians 10:31 Paul writes, *"Therefore, whether you eat or drink or whatever you do, do all to the glory of God."* In order for a work to be imperishable, it must be done to the glory of God the Father!

The Love of God the Son

Next we turn to the *reality of accountability* **bema** passage. 2 Corinthians 5 tells us that we must all appear before the judgment seat of Christ in order that we might be compensated for everything we have done, whether good or bad.

First, Paul speaks of his present ambition to please Christ (2 Cor. 5:9). Next, he acknowledges his future revelation at the judgment seat of Christ (2 Cor. 5:10). Then he expresses his concern that the saints have an answer for those who take pride in *"appearance and not in heart"* (2 Cor. 5:12). Finally, Paul goes on to share the dynamic force that should be the impelling motive of every true servant of God. He says, *"The love of Christ compels us"* (2 Cor. 5:14).

The believer's life should be motivated by the love of Christ. We should love Him because He first loved us. We should give our life to Him because He gave His life for us. We should love others the way He loved us. In order for a work to be imperishable, it must be done because of the love of God the Son!

The Power of God the Spirit

Next we must check out the *kingdom of God* **bema** passage. Romans 14, the third major passage on the judgment seat of Christ, reminds us that every believer will one day stand before the judgment seat of Christ. Paul speaks of the division between the believers over the eating of meat offered to idols. He tells them to stop judging one another. He reminds these believers that each one of them will give account of himself at the judgment seat of Christ. He warns the strong in faith against despising the weak, and he warns the weak in faith against criticizing the strong.

Instead of bitterness and friction and unhappiness, they are to pursue the things which make for peace and the building up of one another. How can these believers stop this sinning and start seeking the kingdom of God? Paul's answer is clear, *"The kingdom of God is not eating or drinking, but righteousness and peace and joy* ***in the Holy Spirit****"* (Rom. 14:17).

If these believers really want to live their lives for the Lord, they are going to have to walk in the power of the Holy Spirit. Any attempt to serve God in our own strength and on our own power will fail the test at the judgment seat of Christ. In order for a work to be imperishable, it must be done in the power of God the Spirit.

Granted, every believer has the Holy Spirit (Rom. 8:9), but not every believer is filled with the Spirit. Every believer has the Holy Spirit, but not every believer is controlled by the Holy Spirit. I grew up on a farm just northwest of Ladora, Iowa. We had two horses the whole time I grew up on that farm. The epitome of a good horse is bridled strength. A good horse is sensitive to his rider's leadership. Trigger, our painted pony was just such a horse. But Nugget, our sorrel pony, did not have that kind of sensitivity. I'll never forget the time I was out in the pasture and I surprised Nugget. You see, Nugget didn't really care to be ridden. I surprised him when I grabbed his mane and swung up on his back. He surprised me when he reared up on his two back legs, leaving both him and me almost perpendicular to the ground. At this point my adrenaline and his were both flowing pretty fast. I had my fists tightly wrapped around his mane as he galloped straight toward a gate that was at least five feet high with barbed wire across the top. Now both Nugget and I knew that he was not going to try to jump that gate . . . or at least, I hoped we both knew that. I also knew that somehow I was going to get hurt. When we were within about six feet of that gate, he drove his hooves into the dirt and came to a sliding halt. I was still clinging to his mane, and I slid clear up his neck till my head was about even with his. At that moment he whirled to his left and began running down the fence line. The next thing I knew he turned and ran under the low branches of a huge mulberry tree, scraping me off of his back. I landed on my back on the ground, and Nugget ran out from under the tree. Then he stopped and turned his head back to look at me. It was as if he had this big smile on his face, and down deep in his heart he was laughing at me. It was as if he was thinking, "I hope that taught you a lesson. You may own me. You may even ride me; but I refuse to willingly yield to your leadership." That is the way some believers treat the Holy Spirit. We have been bought by the blood of Christ. We are to glorify God the Father. We are to yield to the control of the Holy Spirit. He wants to fill us and lead us, but many of us refuse to willingly submit to His leadership.

Believers are commanded to be filled with the Spirit (Eph. 5:15-21). That is a command that each believer will either be obeying or disobeying on a daily basis. In order to be obedient to the command to be filled with the Holy Spirit, three things must take place:

First, a believer must be yielding to the Spirit to be filled by the Spirit (Rom. 6:12-13; Gal. 5:16-25).

Second, a believer must be dealing with sin, by confessing and forsaking it, to be filled by the Spirit (1 Jn. 1:9).

Third, a believer must be obedient to the written Word of God in order to be filled with the Spirit (Col. 3:16-17).

Being filled by the Spirit is not a luxury when it comes to living an imperishable life; it is a necessity. As Dr. Stanley D. Toussaint says, "The filling of the Spirit is not the chrome trim of the Christian life, it is the chassis!"

We have discovered that in order for our life to be worthy of reward, it must be committed to the glory of God, motivated by the love of Christ, and empowered by the Holy Spirit.

Now I would like to make five observations.

1. Setting the Stage

You are setting the stage for eternity! God is going to reward believers for doing good works. For works to be "good," they must be sourced in God. The truth of this statement is easily supported for Jesus Himself declared, *"No one is good except God alone."* Consequently, it is impossible for anyone to do or become anything worthy of being called "good" apart from God. The believer whose life is hidden with Christ in God has the power and the potential to do that which is good. This potentiality can become a reality if he abides in Christ and develops an intimate relationship with God. John emphasizes this truth when he addresses his readers with this challenge:

> And now little children, abide in Christ, so that when He appears we may have joyous confidence, and not

> be ashamed before Him at His coming. (1 Jn. 2:28, Greek)

That is John's prescription for confidence at Christ's coming. Those believers who abide in Christ will have boldness at the **bema**. If you abide in Christ in this life, your work will abide before Christ at the **bema**.

2. Monitoring our Motives

God is going to reward us for those things we have thought and said and done and become that are imperishable. The key to imperishability is faithfulness. The key to faithfulness is motives. In order for a work to be imperishable, it must be done with the right motives. Just as wood, hay, and straw are consumed by fire, works done with the wrong motives will not survive the **bema**. No matter how sweet the thought, no matter how kind the words, no matter how nice the gesture, if it isn't done for the glory of God, because of a love of Christ, and in the power of the Spirit, it is not *imperishable* and it profits nothing! How is your life being lived? What are your motives?

First of all, are you living for the glory of God? Does your conduct exalt Him? Does your character magnify Him? Does your communication praise Him?

Secondly, are you controlled by the love of Christ? Is His love the driving force in your life? Are your time and energy and love being consumed by a hunger and passion for pleasures, possessions, and positions? If so, may I suggest with John that you remember from where you have fallen, repent of your sin, and return to complete obedience and intimate fellowship with our Lord (Rev. 2:4-5).

Thirdly, are you living in the power of the Holy Spirit? Is your life open to His guidance, experiencing His power, and manifesting His fruit? Are you trying to live the Christian life on your own? Do you find yourself squaring your shoulders, clenching your fists, steeling your jaw, and saying, "I'm going to do God's will," and still failing? It is frustrating, isn't it? You have the right purpose, but you don't have the right power. As the Lord said to Zerubbabel, it is *"not by might, nor by power, but by my Spirit"* (Zech. 4:6).

Jesus Christ drew His followers' attention to the importance of motives in the Sermon on the Mount. Jesus made it crystal clear that even when a person is giving, praying, and fasting, it could be a work that will be consumed by fire at the **bema**. He revealed that God would only reward the works that are carried out with pure motives (Mt. 6:1-21). God will not reward a man who does things for men's applause. Jesus says that if you do things simply for men's applause, then you better really enjoy that temporary thrill, because when the clapping ends, the reward is over. But if you do things to please God, He will reward you eternally.

Jesus was challenging those believers to put their motives to the test. I want to challenge you to put your motives to the test. Look at your own life. Look at what you are doing and what you are becoming. Ask yourself this question: "Why do I do what I do?"

Why are you doing the things you are doing? Is it to satisfy self, is it to impress men, or is it to express your love for God?

A story is told of Jesus and His disciples walking along a stony road. Jesus asked each of them to choose a stone to carry for Him. John, it is said, chose a large one while Peter chose the smallest. Jesus led them towards the top of a mountain. John was struggling to carry his heavy stone, and Peter was feeling pretty good about picking up a little stone.

By the time they reached the top of the mountain both Peter and John were tired and hungry. Jesus changed their stones into bread, and each disciple was allowed to eat the bread he held in his hand. Peter's little stone was not nearly sufficient to satisfy his hunger.

Some time later Jesus again asked the disciples to pick up a stone to carry. This time Peter chose the largest stone of all. Jesus led them quite a long way, and Peter was struggling under the weight of his very large stone.

When they arrived at a river, Jesus told them to cast their stones into the water. Peter and John did so, and the stones just sank to the bottom of the river. That was it. There was no miracle. There was no radical transformation of stones into bread. There was no food. Peter and John looked at one another in bewilderment. Then they looked to Jesus.

"For whom," asked Jesus, *"did you carry the stone?"*

For whom do you do the things you are doing? Is it to satisfy yourself? Is it to impress others? Or is it to express your love for God?

3. Future Focus

One of the reasons people tend to reject Jesus' teaching on rewards is because they think the focus will be on their failures. This is not the case. When gold ore is put to the test of fire, there is some slag that is burned off and removed, and there is some pure gold that is purified and revealed! The focus is not on the worthless slag that is burned off; the focus is on the pure gold that remains! This is the purpose of the judgment seat of Christ. The **bema** is designed to determine what we have thought and said and done and become that is of eternal value and deserving of reward! The purpose of the judgment seat of Christ is to determine the degree of rewards and honor that will come to us and to our Lord!

4. Happy in Heaven

Another reason some reject the Bible teaching about rewards is that they fear that some believers will not be happy in eternity. Granted, there will be some anguish at the judgment seat over time lost, talents wasted, and treasure buried. There will be some heartache at the **bema** over failing the Lord and some anguish over forfeiting reward. But I believe the Scripture indicates that heaven is a paid-for place, a planned place, a perfect place, and a pleasurable place, and that eternity for the believer will be a time of blessing beyond our imagination. Will every believer enjoy eternity? The answer is an unmistakable "Yes!" Will every believer experience the same rewards and blessings in heaven? The answer is an undeniable "No!" The Scripture clearly shows there will be differences in degrees of reward!

Let me share an illustration that might help clarify this issue. Imagine that there is an incredibly wealthy man who purchases tickets to a symphony and offers free symphony tickets to the world. Immediately, there will be two very distinct classes of people. There will be those who accept the tickets and those who do not accept the tickets. Even so, God purchased tickets for everyone in the world to go to heaven. God so loved the world that He gave His only-begotten Son that whosoever believes in Him would not perish but has everlasting life. And, just as in our illustration, there are immediately two classes of people—those who accept this free offer and those who do not accept it.

Now back to our illustration. Among those who accept the free tickets to the symphony, there could be many classes of people.

There could be some that accept the tickets to the symphony who have a deaf ear. They see the choreography and synchronistic movements of the conductor and the instrumentalists, but they hear no music, they hear no sounds. However, they enjoy the company, the fellowship, and the choreography. They enjoy the symphony to the fullest of their capacity.

There could be some that accept the tickets that are tone deaf. They see the choreography, they hear the beat, they hear sounds, but they hear no melody and cannot distinguish the notes. However, they enjoy the company, the fellowship, the choreography, the sound and the beat of the music. They enjoy the symphony to the fullest of their capacity.

There could be some that accept tickets to the symphony that have a normal ear.

They see the choreography, they hear the beat, they hear the melody, and they distinguish the various instruments. They enjoy the symphony to the fullest extent of their capacity.

There could be some that accept tickets to the symphony that have a trained ear. They see the choreography, they hear the beat, they hear the notes, they sense the rise and fall of the music, they recognize the change of mood in the music, and they enjoy the intricacy of the arrangement. They enjoy the symphony to the fullest extent of their capacity.

The point of the illustration is that each one enjoys the symphony to the fullest extent of his capacity to enjoy it, but each one has a different capacity. In the same way, every believer will be enjoying eternity to the fullest extent of his or her capacity; but each believer will have his own capacity. One's faithfulness in life here on earth will determine one's capacity in heaven. The judgment seat of Christ will reveal one's capacity. Every believer will be happy in eternity, but each will have differing capacities for experiencing happiness and differing capacities for honoring Christ. The greater our faithfulness in doing the right things with the right motives, the greater our capacity to enjoy the blessings of eternity!

5. Critical Consideration

What capacity will you have in eternity? What is the quality of your words and works? Are you building with gold, silver, and precious stones, or are you building with wood, hay, and straw?

Take time to consider your motives. Why do you do what you do? Is it to impress men or to express your love for God? Is it simply because you love yourself or is it because you love your Savior? Is it in your own strength or is it in the power of the Spirit? Build for eternity! Don't settle for the momentary applause of popular recognition. Go for the eternal praise of God. Don't settle for the temporary thrill of worldly pleasures. Go for the everlasting joy of pleasing Jesus Christ.

Perhaps God has your attention now more than He has for a long time. That is a good thing. Maybe this prayer, by J. Edwin Orr, can help you express your heart.

> Search me, Oh God, and know my heart today.
> Try me, Oh Savior, know my thoughts I pray.
> See if there be, some wicked way in me.

Cleanse me from every sin and set me free!
I praise thee, Lord, for cleansing me from sin.
Fulfill Thy Word and make me pure within.
Fill me with fire, where once I burned with shame.
Grant my desire to magnify Thy name!

Study Guide – Chapter 4 – Gold and Silver

"We have the opportunity of living a life that counts for eternity!"
—Harlan D. Betz: *Setting the Stage for Eternity*

1. **Read 1 Cor. 4:1-5.**

2. What is the difference between being a servant and a steward?
   1 Cor. 4:1

3. What attitude and what action are required of a servant?
   Cf. 1 Tim. 6:1-2

4. What is the major requirement of a steward? 1 Cor. 4:2

5. How are you influenced by the following pressures?
   1 Cor. 4:3
   Religious pressure . . . evaluation of other believers.
   Social pressure . . . evaluation of other people.
   Personal pressure . . . evaluation of yourself.

6. Who is the true evaluator? 1 Cor. 4:4

7. How will He evaluate us? 1Cor. 4:5
   He will reveal the ____________ of our hearts!
   In order for our work to be imperishable, we must be:
   Committed to the ______________ of God the Father!
   Motivated by the _______________ of God the Son!
   Empowered by the ______________ of God the Spirit!

8. Discuss this quote:
   "Man judges from a partial view.
   None ever yet his brother knew;
   The Eternal Eye that sees the whole,

May better read the darkened soul,
And find, to outward sense denied,
The flower upon its inmost side!"
— John Greenleaf Whittier: *The Pressed Gentian*

9. Take some time to consider your motives.
Why do you do what you do?
Is it to impress men or is it to express your love for God?
Is it because you love your self or because you love your Savior?
Is it in your own strength or in the power of the Spirit?

10. Consider these words:
"He has sounded forth the trumpet that shall never call retreat
He is sifting out the hearts of men before His judgment seat."
— Julia Ward: *Battle Hymn of the Republic*

11. What is your goal in life?
"If you aim for nothing, you will probably hit it!"
— Dr. Howard G. Hendricks

12. Consider this final challenge:
"Don't settle for the momentary applause of popular recognition; go for the eternal praise of God.

Don't settle for the temporary thrill of worldly pleasures; go for the everlasting joy of pleasing Christ!"
—Harlan D. Betz: *Setting the Stage for Eternity*

CHAPTER 5

RUNNING THE RACE!

When I was a junior high student at Ladora, Iowa, I entered a 100-yard dash. The starter's gun went off, and I was clearly among the first out of the blocks and headed down the track. I could feel the air as it blew past my face. It was evident that I was clearly in the lead at the 50-yard mark. Some of my family were there to watch the race. I was excited to have them there to see me run. I looked over at the stands trying to find my

Dad and Mom to see if they were seeing how well I was doing. Unfortunately, while my eyes were searching for them, other runners had their eyes fixed on the finish line, and they passed me by. It was a lesson I would never forget. Keep your eyes focused on the finish line!

The Bible compares the Christian life to a race. The Bible challenges us to run that race with endurance. The Bible challenges us to finish that race! The Bible challenges us to keep our eyes fixed on Jesus! The Apostle Paul challenges us to win that race. The Apostle Paul compares the believer at the judgment seat of Christ to a runner in the Olympic Games.

The Olympic Games are familiar to all of us. Athletes compete for gold, silver, and bronze medals. The games are not new. They date back to the glorious days of Ancient Greece. As a student at the University of Iowa, I majored in Classical Greek. I studied the Greek language, the Greek culture, the Greek theatre, the Greek authors, the Greek gods, and the history of the Greek civilization. One of the most fascinating subjects of my studies was the Greek Games.[1]

The Panhellenic Games were the most exciting and enjoyable events of the Grecian calendar. Time was measured by the Games . . . a four year interval being an Olympiad. The Games were religious festivals, but they were more. They were like a sacred festival, a national fair, a trade mart, and a national athletic competition all wrapped into one.

There were four great Panhellenic Games:[2]

1. The Olympic Games held every four years at Olympia;
2. The Pythian Games held every four years at Delphi;
3. The Isthmian Games held every two years at Corinth;
4. The Nemean Games held every two years at Argolis.

The most famous and important of all Panhellenic Games were the Olympics. An Olympic festival commenced with two days of religious ceremonies, followed by five days of competition. During the pre-game ceremonies an animal was slaughtered and sacrificed as an offering to Zeus. The athletes swore that they had trained according to the rules and that they would compete according to the rules. The judges swore that they would be just and fair in their decisions.[3]

The opening event for these games was the Four-Horse Chariot Race. It took place in the Hippodrome, and consisted of professional charioteers, powerful horses, colliding chariots, and a few finishers. The victor's crown in the chariot race went not to the driver, but to the owner of the chariot and the horses. Victory in a chariot race brought great prestige, and the owners were among the most respected people in their cities.

The sports field in front of the altar of Zeus was the arena for the *pankration*, a martial arts type of contest that consisted of boxing, strangling, kicking, and wrestling.

Most of the events took place in the magnificent stadium (so named because its length was one *stadion*, 606 feet).[4] The stadium was surrounded by banks of earth and later by stone seats for the spectators. This was the place to watch the individual athletes competing in running, jumping, throwing, boxing and wrestling.

The event that brought the greatest glory and honor to the contestant was the *pentathlon*.[5] This event had five parts:

1. Running the length of the stadium,
2. Long jumping,
3. Discus throwing,
4. Javelin throwing,
5. Wrestling match (for the two highest scoring athletes).

The official prize for the winner at an event was a garland crown cut from a tree or plant that was sacred to the God for whom the games were dedicated.[6] The Nemean games at Argolis in the valley of Nemea were held in honor of Zeus, and the wreath was made of fresh wild celery. The Isthmian games at Corinth were held in honor of Poseidon, and the wreath was made from a sacred pine tree. The Pythian Games at Delphi were dedicated to Apollo, and the wreath was constructed from the sweet laurel. The Olympic Games at Olympia were dedicated to the honor of Zeus, and the victors' crowns were made of branches from the sacred wild olive tree. The official prize (the crown of leaves) was awarded to each victorious athlete in front of a **bema** where the judges and other dignitaries were seated.

While the official prize was only a simple crown of leaves, the ultimate rewards in fame and honor were tremendous. The following are some of the phenomenal rewards that often accompanied a victor's crown of leaves.[7]

1. The victorious athlete's family and friends would celebrate his victory immediately following the event.
2. He would make a triumphal return to his hometown where citizens would welcome him as a hero. He would be paraded through the town.
3. Banquets were held in his honor, musicians sang his praise, and sculptors preserved his strength and beauty in marble busts or statues that were often erected in public places.
4. Poets and writers recorded his feats of skill and courage. Often a poet, such as Pindar, would write a

poem that would praise the athlete for his victory and glory.[8]

5. Occasionally, the victor would be exempt from taxation and given free meals.

6. Some cities would give their victor box seats for all public events.

7. In Athens, and other cities as well, the winners were given large sums of money.

Paul compares the believer in the Christian life to an athlete in the Games (1 Cor. 9:24-27). This comparison was especially appropriate for the Corinthians. It provided a highly visible and truly powerful illustration of the judgment seat of Christ. We will examine that passage in order to gain further insight into the judgment seat of Christ.

First, let's review the four major truths we have discovered in 2 Corinthians 5:9-10:

1. Every believer's presence is required at the **bema**;
2. Every believer's character and conduct will be revealed at the **bema**;
3. Every believer's character and conduct will be rewarded at the **bema**;
4. Every believer's life should be motivated by the **bema**.

THE RACE

> Do you not know that those who run in a stadium all run but only one receives the victor's prize? Run in such a way that you may win. (1 Cor.9:24, Greek.)

Paul's first point is very clear: entering a race does not guarantee winning it!

Now this truth should be obvious, but when translated to the Christian life it is often missed. Somehow it gets lost in the shuffle. God wants us to know that we are not guaranteed a victorious Christian life and rewards at the **bema** just because we have taken the initial step of entering the Christian life by faith.

Paul goes on to illustrate this truth in the verses that follow our passage. He writes with a purpose:

> Moreover, brethren, I do not want you to be unaware that all our fathers were under the cloud, all passed through the sea, all were baptized into Moses in the cloud and in the sea, all ate the same spiritual food, and all drank the same spiritual drink. For they drank of that spiritual Rock that followed them, and that Rock was Christ. (1 Cor. 10:1-4)

These people had entered the race. There were over a million of them![9] They were all believers, and they enjoyed many spiritual privileges:

1. All were supernaturally guided by the cloud;
2. All were supernaturally delivered through the Red Sea;
3. All were supernaturally identified with Moses;
4. All were supernaturally fed with manna from Heaven;
5. All were supernaturally watered from a rock.

Christ was that rock. Christ was with them and ministering to them. They all enjoyed many spiritual privileges. They all had entered the race.

> But with most of them God was not well pleased, for their bodies were scattered in the wilderness. Now these things became our examples, to the intent that we should not lust after evil things as they also lusted. And do not become idolaters, as were some of them. As it is written, "The people sat down to eat and drink, and rose up to play." Nor let us commit sexual immorality, as some of them did, and in one day twenty-three thousand fell; nor let us tempt Christ, as some of them also tempted, and were destroyed by serpents; nor complain, as some of them also complained, and were destroyed by the destroyer. (1 Cor. 10:5-10)

All of them were supernaturally guided and delivered and fed by God. However, with most of them God was not well pleased. That is probably one of the greatest understatements in the Bible. Think of it! Over one million believers, age twenty and older, entered that desert, and only two of them entered the Promised Land!

Spiritual privileges do not guarantee spiritual victory. Entering a race does not guarantee winning it! Therefore, fellow believers, it is very important that we run to win! Will only one believer be rewarded at the **bema**? No. Paul, like a good Southerner, writes it this way, *"Run in such a way that y'all may win"* (1 Cor. 9:24b, Greek.). Your competition is not other believers. Your struggle is not against other runners. Your struggle is against your own sinful flesh. Your adversary is the devil. Your enemy is a love for the world. You could be defeated by the lust of the eyes, the lust of the flesh, or the boastful pride of life. But by the grace of God, and in the power of the Spirit, you can be victorious. You can win!

Paul's first point: *Don't settle for entrance . . . run to win!*

THE REQUIREMENTS

> And everyone who competes exercises self-control in all things. They then do it to receive a perishable wreath, but we do it to obtain an imperishable crown. (1 Cor. 9:25, Greek)

The term Paul uses for "the competitor" is *o agonizomenos.* We derive our word "agonize" from this Greek term. This very descriptive term pictures a man who struggles against opposition, or strives to obtain something, or strains his every nerve in his endeavor.[10] The competitor, Paul says, exercises self-control in all things.

Gymnastic training was a vital part of every Greek boy's education. As the time for the games (*agones*) drew near, this training was intensified in gymnasia and palaestra all over Greece. Rich citizens contributed large sums of money toward the expenses of the athletes.[11]

The athletes who competed in the Games during Paul's day had to commit ten months to training. During that time, they had to exercise strict self-control. Exercise, workouts, drink, diet, and sleep were all carefully monitored and controlled. The athlete could not allow himself the luxury of easy workouts, fatty foods, strong alcoholic drinks, or late nights. Those who really wanted to win disciplined themselves and refrained from indulging in many pleasures and activities that other people pursued.

Paul switches briefly from comparison to contrast. Those athletes sacrifice, deny themselves, and exercise self-control simply to receive a perishable prize. Believers are to sacrifice, deny themselves, and exercise self-control for an imperishable prize!

Now I don't know about you, but that intrigues me. Jim Elliot, missionary and martyr to the Auca Indians, once said, "He is no fool who gives up what he cannot keep to gain what he cannot lose." Think about it. He was right. If we want to be victorious, we must exercise self-control!

Paul's second point: *Don't settle for passing pleasures . . . run for eternal rewards.*

THE RESULTS

> Therefore I run in this way, not without aim; I box in this way, not beating the air; but I buffet my body and make it my slave, lest after I have preached to others, I myself should become disqualified. (1 Cor. 9:26-27, Greek)

I learned early in my years of Bible study that whenever you come across a *therefore,* you should try to find out what it is *there for*. Usually it looks back to what was just said and uses that previous statement as the basis for what is going to be said.

In this case, it points back to the basis for Paul's aim in his running, Paul's purpose in his boxing, and Paul's discipline of his body. Why does he do it? Paul runs with aim, boxes with purpose, and disciplines his body because he doesn't want to settle for entrance, he wants to win. He doesn't want to settle for passing pleasures; he wants to earn an eternal reward. Therefore, because of those desires, Paul says he runs with aim, boxes with purpose, and buffets his body.

He runs with aim. He sheds any extra weight. He starts when the gun goes off. He stays on track. He fixes his eyes on the goal. He runs to win! He doesn't waste his time and energy waving to the people in the grandstands, hoping they'll notice how well he's running. He fixes his eyes on Jesus.

He boxes with purpose. He is not just shadow boxing. He is not just putting on a show. He knows he is in a spiritual battle.

He buffets his body and makes it his slave. He doesn't bow to his body. He doesn't give in to every urge and craving and lust of his body. He disciplines his body. He keeps it under control. He presents it as a living sacrifice to God.

Why such rigorous self-discipline? Why such sacrifices of time? Why such denial of fleshly pleasures? Because he realizes that even after preaching to others, he could be disqualified. Judges in the Games sat at a bench called the **bema**. If any athlete broke a rule, one or more of the judges would cry out, *"Adokimos!"* ("Disqualified"). Paul was determined to live in such a way that he would not be disqualified.

What does Paul mean? Is he afraid he'll be mastered by the sinful desires of his flesh and be barred from Heaven and the Kingdom of God? No! Entrance into Heaven and the Kingdom of God does not depend on the man who runs, but on God who gives that gift to the believer. Paul makes this quite clear in Ephesians 2:8-9: *"For by grace you have been saved through faith, and that not of yourselves; it is the gift of God; not of works, lest anyone should boast."*

What is Paul saying? He wants more than to run. He wants to win. He wants more than entrance. He wants an abundant entrance. He wants more than this life has to offer. He wants eternal rewards.

> Entrance to Heaven is a gift to be received.
> Rewards in Heaven are joys to be won!

Therefore, Paul was willing to exercise self-control. He was willing to deny himself temporal and physical pleasures that got in the way of eternal and spiritual prizes. He was willing to sacrifice:

1. The right to marital joys for the sake of Jesus (1 Cor. 7);
2. The right to personal liberties for the sake of believers (1 Cor. 8);
3. The right to financial support for the sake of the gospel (1 Cor. 9).

Surely Paul would have enjoyed those rights. But he was willing to exercise rigorous self-control, because he did not want to be disqualified.

Jesus called for this same kind of commitment when He said:

> If anyone desires to come after Me, let him deny himself, and take up his cross daily, and follow Me.

> For whoever desires to save his life will lose it, but whoever loses his life for My sake will save it. (Lk. 9:23-24)

Future recognition demands present renunciation! That renunciation would be manifest in the following ways:

> We must have the discipline to say "no" to pleasures that keep us from living totally for Christ.
> We must have the discipline to say "no" to possessions that keep us from living totally for Him.
> We must have the discipline to say "no" to positions that keep us from living totally for Christ.
> We must have the discipline to sacrifice our desires in order to carry out God's desires.

How about it? Are you running to win? Will you receive eternal rewards, or will you be disqualified? Now you might be thinking that you are free from concern in this area. "After all," you might be thinking, "I've taught Sunday School for five years," or "I've worked in the church for ten years." Hold it! Look at verse 27 again. Look a little closer this time: *"I buffet my body and make it my slave, lest possibly after I have preached to others, I myself should be disqualified."* You see, Paul realized that even he, a preacher and an apostle, could be disqualified! The term "preached" comes from *kerusso*, and means "to make known, to preach, to proclaim as a herald."[12] The herald called the contestants to the race in the Games. The herald announced the rules.

Think of the horror of teaching someone to forgive and being disqualified for not forgiving. Think of the heartache of teaching someone to love and being disqualified for not loving. Think of the disappointment of teaching someone to resist temptation and being disqualified for yielding to temptation. Think of the anguish of encouraging someone else to be faithful, and then being disqualified for unfaithfulness yourself! Don't be disqualified, run in a way that pleases God!

I'll never forget an Olympic event that took place a few years ago. Several runners with bodies that could have been sculpted by Michelangelo were in their starting blocks. The starter fired his gun and the runners took off—all competing for the title of "World's Fastest Man." Carl Lewis had been unbeatable; but this time, to the shock of the world, a Canadian sprinter by the name of Ben Johnson did what he could never do before. He beat Carl Lewis and won the gold medal. However, the world was to be shocked again. Ben Johnson tested positive for steroids, was disqualified by the Olympic judges, and was stripped of his medal. He was disqualified! Ben Johnson had other awards that he had won in other races at other times, but he does not have that gold medal because he was disqualified in that race.

Paul did not want to disobey God in any action or displease God in any attitude that would disqualify him from receiving a reward for what he was doing.

Paul's third point: *Don't be disqualified, run in a way that pleases God!*

Paul was keenly aware of the danger of being disqualified. He goes on to demonstrate that spiritual privileges are not a guarantee of spiritual victory (2 Corinthians 10:1-10). Over a million believers enjoyed those supernatural privileges. All but two were laid low in the wilderness! Consequently, Paul concludes this section with a word of warning and a word of comfort.

Paul issues a word of warning: *"Let him who thinks he stands take heed lest he fall"* (1 Cor. 10:12).

Paul was a believer. Paul was an apostle. Paul was a preacher. Yet he could fall. He could be disqualified. So could I. So could you. The warning echoes: I could fail, I could fall, and I could be disqualified. Will you be disqualified? Are you willing to go before God right now and say with David:

> Search me, O God, and know my heart. Put me to the test and know my secret thoughts. And see if I'm living in a way that results in grief, and guide me in a way that results in eternal good. (Psa. 139:23-24, Hebrew)

Paul shares a word of comfort:

> No temptation has overtaken you except such as is common to man; but God is faithful, who will not allow you to be tempted beyond what you are able, but with the temptation will also make the way of escape, that you may be able to bear it. (1 Cor. 10:13)

Perhaps you are very discouraged. Perhaps you genuinely want to go God's way, but you don't do it. The pressures seem to be more than you can bear. You can't seem to bring some area of your life under control. Well, Paul has good news for us. God wants to help!

God knows our weaknesses. He knows our limits. He will not allow us to face more pressure than we can bear with His help. He will not allow the temptation to be more than we can handle with His help. God is waiting for us to call on Him. We can turn to Him for strength to stand, and we can call on Him for forgiveness when we fall (Heb. 4:14-16).

He is our strength to help us stand.
He is our power to help us persevere.
He is our enabler to help us endure.

By God's grace, and in His mighty power, we can resist the devil and draw near to God (Jas. 4:7-8). By God's grace, and in His mighty power, we can be victorious over sinfulness, stubbornness, and selfishness.

We're living in a day when people are claiming their lives and their rights for themselves:

"Have it your way."
"Get all the gusto you can get."
"Look out for number one."

We need to remember that *future recognition demands present renunciation.*

A marathon runner in the Olympics had collapsed on the ground when he was being interviewed; he had fallen on the cross-country course and injured himself. In spite of the injury, he had gotten up and pushed himself on. As he became wearier and the pain of his injury increased, he fell several more times, yet he did not quit. The race had been won, the winners had been recognized, and most of the people had left before this wounded and bleeding athlete even entered the grandstand. But some of the members of the press had noted his early fall and injuries and they had become aware that he was refusing to give up. This athlete, wounded and winded, literally dragged himself across the finish line, and collapsed.

The members of the press asked him why he didn't just quit as he had no chance of winning . . . the victors had already been recognized. The exhausted athlete explained that he was from a small country and he felt not only rewarded to be able to run for his country, he also felt responsible to run for his country. And then he said, "They didn't send me halfway around the world just to enter this race, they sent me here to finish this race, and I did!"

This brave athlete forgot his personal injuries and discomfort and pushed himself on to finish his race. Will you?

The Bible challenges us to run with endurance the race that is set before us. Will you be able to say to God the Father, as Jesus did, *"I accomplished the work you gave me to do!"*? Will you be able to say with the Apostle Paul, *"I have fought the good fight, I have finished the race, and I have kept the faith!"*?

The call is clear.

Don't settle for entrance; run to win.
Don't settle for passing pleasures; run for eternal rewards.
Don't be disqualified; run in a way that pleases God.

The Alabama Crimson Tide football team was up by six points. The two-minute warning had sounded. A couple more plays had been run, and the game was nearly over. Legendary

Coach Bear Bryant told his quarterback to run out the clock. When the team got in the huddle the quarterback explained to his teammates that Coach Bryant told him to run out the clock. But then the quarterback said, "That is just what the other team expects us to do. Let's surprise them and Coach." The quarterback called a pass play. The ball was snapped; the quarterback stepped back and threw a pass. A speedy cornerback knifed in, intercepted the pass, and headed down the sideline for a sure touchdown and the defeat of Alabama. Well, the quarterback knew he was in huge trouble. He took off after that cornerback and somehow managed to knock him out of bounds at the five-yard line as the time ran out.

After the game the opposing coach queried Bear Bryant. "What's this business about your quarterback not being a runner? He caught my fastest defender." Bear Bryant explained, "Well, your man was running for six points. My man was running for his life!"

What are you running for? Who are you running for?
Don't try to keep your life for yourself.
Give up your life to God. Jesus did. Paul did.
Are you ready to give up your life to God?
Sacrifice willingly. It will be worth it all!

God will richly reward and eternally bless those who run well and finish the race. Their reward will magnify Christ!

How much light will you shine upon Him?

Will your life be like a match providing a flicker of light that others can see Christ dimly from a few inches?

Will your life be like a flashlight providing a flow of light that others can see Christ moderately from a few feet?

Will your life be like a beacon providing a flood of light that others can see Christ clearly for miles?

Let your light so shine before men that they may see Jesus Christ in you and glorify your Father who is in Heaven!

Study Guide – Chapter 5 – The Athlete

"Future recognition demands present renunciation."

—Harlan D. Betz: *Setting the Stage for Eternity*

"God is waiting for us to call on Him. We can turn to Him for strength to stand, and we can call on Him for forgiveness when we fall."

—Harlan D. Betz: *Setting the Stage for Eternity*

1. **Read 1 Corinthians 9:24-27**.

2. What are some events or contests you have entered that you have not won? Did you do your best?

3. Reflect on how you are running spiritually.
"Don't settle for entrance; run to win!"

4. What are you willing to settle for?
You can settle for just getting there; or you can seek to be growing here!
You can settle for being called a child, or you can seek to be called good and faithful!

5. Reflect on the following statement:

"In heaven, to be even the least is a great thing, where all will be great; for all shall be called the children of God!"

—Thomas A. Kempis

6. **Read 2 Timothy 2:1-7.**

7. What does this passage teach us about the Christian as a soldier?
What are some things that can entangle believers in today's world?
"Don't settle for passing pleasures; run for eternal rewards."

8. What does this passage teach us about the athlete?
"Don't be disqualified; run in a way that pleases God!"

9. **Read 1 Corinthians 10:1-10.**

10. What can we learn from the warning in 1 Corinthians 10:12?
Can you name some Bible characters who seemed strong but still fell?

11. What encouraging principles can you find in Corinthians 10:13 about:
the commonness of the temptation or trial?
the faithfulness of God?
the stress level of the trouble or trial?
the success potential of the believer?

12. Consider your present living and your eternal lot.
How much will your life magnify Christ? Phil. 1:20.
How much light will you shine on Him? Mt. 5:16.

[1] There are several sources one can look to for information about the Greek Games. All encyclopedias and most books on Ancient or Classical Greece will give you some basic information on the games. The *Encyclopedia Britannica* has articles on "Classical Games" and "Olympic Games." Funk and Wagnall's' *Microsoft Encarta* has an article on "Olympian Games." C. M. Bowra and the editors of TIME-LIFE Books published an easy to read book on *Classical Greece*. The Greek term for the games was *agones*.
[2] C. M. Bowra and The Editors of TIME-LIFE Books, *Classical Greece*, (New York: TIME Incorporated, 1965), p. 125
[3] *Encyclopedia Britannica*, "Olympic Games" (Chicago: William Benton Publisher, 1969), Vol. 16, p. 944.
"The management of the athletics was in the hands of Elean officials, the *Hellanodikai*, whose fairness to all concerned was a byword in Greece." *Encyclopedia Britannica*, "Classical Games," Vol. 9, p. 1119.
[4] The Greek term for an Olympic event is *"athla,"* from which we get our term "athlete."
[5] Umberto Albini, ed. et. al., "GREECE: The People" from *The Illustrated Library of the World and Its Peoples*, vol. 28 (New York: Greystone Press, 1964), p. 51.
[6] *Encyclopedia Britannica*, "Classical Games," Vol. 9, pp. 1119-1120.
[7] The winners awards are spoken of on page 134 and 135 of Bowra's *Classical Greece*; on page 51 of Umberto Albini's "GREECE: The People," where he notes that "To the average citizen, a victory in the Olympic Games symbolized man's closest approach to the qualities of the gods." and on page 944 of the *Encyclopedia Britannica*, Vol. 16, where the editor notes that "The greatest honor then to be attained by any Greek was the winning of the simple branch of wild olive given to the victor in the games. Kings competed alongside commoners . . . winners became national heroes . . ."
[8] W. H. Auden, *The Portable GREEK READER* (New York; The Viking Press, 1967), pp. 243-249. This book contains "Two Odes" to victorious athletes written by Pindar. One ode is entitled Pythia 10, the other ode is entitled Nemea 6. These are exquisite examples of the honor and praise given to victorious athletes.
[9] Numbers 1:45-46 indicates that there were 603,550 fighting men who had come out of Egypt in the exodus. If each of these men had a wife, that would be 1,207,100 people. This figure, which is already over one million, does not count those men who were too old to be fighting men, nor the wives of those older men, nor does it count the teenagers and children of those fighting men. According to Exodus 1:7-10, one of the Egyptians concerns was that these Israelites were fruitful, increased, multiplied. Therefore, it is clear that they had many children.

There could have easily been over three million Israelites who left Egypt, crossed the Red Sea, and wandered in the wilderness.

[10] Arndt and Gingrich, *A Greek-English Lexicon*, p.15.

[11] Umberto Albini, *The World and Its Peoples*, "GREECE: The People," p. 51.

[12] Geoffrey W. Bromiley, *Theological Dictionary of the New Testament*, Grand Rapids, Michigan: William B. Eerdmans Publishing Company, 1985), pp. 430-435.

CHAPTER 6

PLANNING FOR THE FUTURE

Did you ever grow up believing something with all your heart and later find out that it wasn't true? Something had been told to you and you accepted it, never really questioning it. Later you found out that it wasn't even true.

Unfortunately, this is often a reality in the Christian world. You hear a passage explained or taught, and then without question, without hesitation, without reservation, and even without investigation, you just accept it. Then later you hear it taught again, and it is presented in a totally different way. Or, perhaps you decide to seriously study the passage on your own. You say to yourself, "I'm going to erase all the things I've heard before. I'm going to take away those blinders that so many people have on when they study the Scripture." Suddenly you find yourself coming to a new understanding of the passage.

I'm going to ask you to do that right now. Please take away those blinders. Allow God to show you something new. Allow the Holy Spirit to shed new light and insight on this passage. How exciting it is to sit down, get into the Word, and discover some new truths!

Are you ready to learn some new truths? Are you willing to gain some new insight? Let's look at Luke 15. Uh-oh! The blinders are already on. You already know what it is about . . . the prodigal son. You've heard it a hundred times. You don't need to study this passage. You know that the son takes off and lives in the squalor of immorality and poverty. You know that he finally realizes that he is a sinner. You know that he wants to be saved. You know that he comes home where his father is waiting for him.

And what is the point of this passage? You already know what it is. It is very simple. All of us like the prodigal have gone astray, and God the Father wants us to come to Him in faith to be forgiven and justified.

That is very interesting, but is that what it really says? Let's check it out. *"A certain man had two sons"* (Lk. 15:11). This father had **two sons**. If the father represents God, and I believe he does, then He is pictured here as having **two** children. Both of them are God's children. Both of them are believers! That changes things already. Now perhaps you're thinking, I have never heard it taught that way before. Well, I haven't taught you anything yet. All I did was to say what the passage said: *"A certain man had two sons."*

The younger one said to his father, *"Father, give me the portion of goods that falls to me."* What he is saying is, "I no longer want to live by your direction and guidance. I want to take everything that's coming to me and go my own way."

The father gives him his share of the wealth, and the son goes his own way. After falling into immorality and poverty, he realizes that he was a lot better off when he was under the direction and care of his father. Jesus tells it this way:

> But when he came to his senses, he said, "How many of my father's hired servants have bread enough and to spare, and I perish with hunger! I will arise and go to my father, and I will say to him, "Father, I have sinned against heaven and before you, and I am no longer worthy to be called your son. Make me like one of your hired servants."
>
> And he arose and came to his father. But when he was still a great way off, his father saw him and had compassion, and ran and (embraced him) and kissed him.
>
> And the son said to him, "Father, I have sinned against heaven and in your sight; and am no longer worthy to be called your son."
>
> But the father said to his servants, "Bring out the best robe and put it on him, and put a ring on his hand and sandals on his feet. And bring the fatted calf here and kill it, and let us eat and be merry; for this my son was dead, and is alive again;

> he was lost and is found." And they began to be merry. (Lk. 15:17-24)

Was he dead? When did he die? I missed that part of the story. He didn't die, but he wasn't really living. He was destroying himself. Just like a fish out of water, a believer in sin exists, but he is not really living.

The prodigal came back just as we need to come back. When we fall into sin we need to recognize it, we need to repent, and we need to come back. Our Heavenly Father is waiting for us. He longs to embrace us.

God loves you. If you are a believer who has gone away from God, please be assured He is waiting for you to come back. He will welcome you to Himself. There is a song that David Baker wrote about this subject:

> Welcome back to Jesus. It's great to have you home. The brothers and the sisters have been here all along. We've been waiting for you brother, and now we're close to tears . . . to see you coming home again, the answer to our prayers.

What happened with the older brother? Jesus tells us:

> Now his older son was in the field. And as he came and drew near to the house, he heard music and dancing. So he called one of the servants and asked what these things meant. And he said to him, "Your brother has come, and because he has received him safe and sound, your father has killed the fatted calf." (Lk. 15:25-27)

What is the older son's response? He is angry! Why?

> But he was angry, and would not go in. Therefore his father came out and pleaded with him. So he answered and said to his father, "Lo, these many years I have been serving you; and I never transgressed your commandment at any time; and yet you have never given me a young goat, that I might make merry with my friends; but as soon as this son of yours came, who has devoured your livelihood with harlots, you killed the fatted calf for him." (Lk. 15:28-30)

Now look at his father's response:

> And he said to him, "Son, you are always with me, and all that I have is yours. It was right that we should make merry and be glad, for your brother was dead and is alive again, and was lost and is found." (Lk. 15:31-32)

He is saying to his older son, "Relax. Think. I love you! I know you've been faithful. You'll be rewarded. You have a rich inheritance coming to you. All that I have is yours. But rejoice with me in this as well. He's my son. He's your brother. Sure he's immature. Yes, he sinned. Yes, he wasted his inheritance. But he's still part of our family. And it's good to have him back in fellowship with us."

THE SETTING

Having just finished telling the parable of the prodigal son, Jesus Christ begins telling the parable of the unrighteous steward. Why does He do this? He does it because He wants the disciples to have a deeper understanding of their responsibility as sons of the Heavenly Father.

Every son of God is a steward of God. And these disciples need insight and instruction in order that they might have a deeper understanding of the responsibilities and rewards of faithful stewardship. Information simply touched on in the parable of the prodigal son will be clearly taught in the parable of the unrighteous steward.

The prodigal son was a faithless steward. He went out from his father's guidance. He went his own way. He wasted his future. The older son was a faithful steward. He stayed under his father's guidance. He served his father faithfully. All that his father had was his for the future. With these seed thoughts in mind, let's look at the story.

THE STORY

> He also said to His disciples, "There was a certain rich man who had a steward, and an accusation was brought to him that this man was squandering his possessions. So he called him and said to him, 'What is this I hear about you? Give an account of your stewardship, for you can no longer be steward.'
>
> Then the steward said within himself, 'What shall I do? For my master is taking the stewardship away from me? I cannot dig; I am ashamed to beg. I

> have resolved what to do, that when I am put out of the stewardship, they may receive me into their houses.'
>
> So he called every one of his master's debtors to him, and said to the first, 'How much do you owe my master?' And he said, 'One hundred measures of oil.' So he said to him, 'Take your bill, and sit down quickly and write fifty.'
>
> Then he said to another, 'And how much do you owe?' So he said, 'One hundred measures of wheat.' He said to him, 'Take your bill, and write eighty.'
>
> So the master commended the unjust steward because he had dealt shrewdly. For the sons of this age are more shrewd in their generation than the sons of light.
>
> And I say to you, make friends for yourselves by unrighteous mammon, that when you fail, they may receive you into an everlasting home." (Lk. 16:1-9)

THE PEOPLE (1-2)

Let's look at the people. The rich man is the owner, possibly a wealthy landowner. The steward is in charge of the affairs and finances of the rich man. The debtors are those who have borrowed from the rich man and are indebted to him.

THE PROBLEM (3)

The steward is undisciplined. The steward was *squandering* his possessions. This is the same word we saw back in Luke 15 when the prodigal son went off to the city and *squandered* his inheritance. The prodigal son was undisciplined and unwise in the way he was using his portion of his father's wealth. The steward was demonstrating a similar character flaw. He was not disciplined or wise in the way he was handling his master's finances. Consequently, the rich man fired the steward, told him to get things in order, and directed him to prepare a final account.

The steward tries to figure out what he is going to do since he has just a little bit of time to get things in order and to get ready for the next phase of his life.

THE PLAN (4-7)

The steward comes up with a plan. He summoned each of his master's debtors, and he met with each one of them individually. He asked each of them how much they owed to his master. Then he cut down the amount they owed. It is possible that he was forgiving the interest and reducing their debt to the lowest possible amount—the principle. At any rate (no pun intended), the debtors probably said something like this: "Thank you! Thank you very much. If there is ever anything I can do for you, just tell me. I am eternally grateful to you. My home and my heart will always be open to you."

The steward cut down their debt and captured their hearts.

THE PRAISE (8)

When his master got the books and looked at what the steward had done, he praised the unrighteous steward because he had acted shrewdly. He did not praise his principles. He did praise his planning. The steward was very clever. The steward had acted shrewdly. The steward had acted with foresight.

For example, let's say you heard about a bank robber who dug underground, came up inside a bank vault, and took millions of dollars. And no one knew anything had happened until the next day. We might say that the robber was very shrewd. We are not praising his principles; we are praising his plan. This steward had a very clever plan! He displayed a cunning insight into people's hearts. He also displayed a very careful foresight into his own future. That is what is praised here.

Notice the next comment in verse eight: *". . . for the sons of this world are more shrewd in their generation than the sons of light."* The sons of this world (unbelievers) are more shrewd in material affairs than the sons of light (believers) are in spiritual affairs. Unbelievers take far more pains to have abundance on earth than believers do to have abundance in heaven! Think about it.

THE POINTS (9-13)

1. Invest in eternal things. (9)

You see, that unjust steward was fired, and he did not have a job waiting for him, but he did have several places he could go. From home to home they said, "Come to our house. Our house is your house."

He was welcome because he had cut their debts and captured their hearts, and now they wanted to help him! He didn't want to dig, he didn't want to beg, and he didn't have to. He was warmly welcomed, gladly fed, and generously helped by those he had helped.

He was unjust in what he did because it was not in the best interest of his master. But it was his right and responsibility to manage his master's affairs, and he managed them in his own best interest! He used that last bit of time very wisely for himself.

Jesus Christ says, *"Make friends for yourselves by unrighteous mammon."* Jesus is referring to material financial wealth as the mammon of unrighteousness. Jesus is not saying to buy friends with money. He is saying to make friends with money. What is the difference?

Notice what he says as He goes on, *". . . that when it fails, they may receive you into eternal dwellings."* He is telling us to invest in eternal things while we still have the opportunity! He is telling us to use our money not to control people, nor to manipulate people, but to help people. He is telling us not to invest money simply to help people temporally, but to invest money in such a way that it will help them eternally. What does He mean? How can we invest our money in a manner that helps people eternally?

Investing money in efforts that will help people come to know Christ as their own personal Savior will help them eternally. Investing money in efforts that will help people grow in Christ-likeness will help people eternally!

We must invest our money in people and ministries that are involved in sharing the gospel and in teaching the Bible. God's Word will last forever, and people's souls will last forever. We need to invest money in getting God's Word to people. We need to invest money in people and ministries that transform lives by evangelism (bringing them the gospel) and by edification (teaching them the Bible).

Then what happens? God places those changed lives on our account! He credits us with having a part in their spiritual transformation! This truth is highlighted in Philippians 4:10-17. Paul is expressing his appreciation to the Philippians for their graciousness in supporting him and his ministry. Because of their gifts Paul was able to lead many to faith in Christ as their own personal Savior, he was able to plant several churches, and he was able to build up the saints and equip them with the Word. Now look carefully at verse 17 . . . *"Not that I seek the gift, but I seek the fruit that abounds to your account."* Did you see that? This is very important.

Do you understand what this passage of Scripture is saying? It is saying that since the Philippian believers supported Paul's ministry, the people who were brought to Christ, the churches that were planted, and the lives that were transformed and equipped through Paul's ministry would be written down on their account!

In the same way, when you support efforts to evangelize the lost and to edify the saved, those lives that are transformed as a result of those efforts are written down on your account!

2. Be faithful in little things. (10-12)

Jesus anchors this second point in verses 10 to 12:

> He who is faithful in what is least will be faithful with much. He who is faithful in that which is of little

> significance (money) will be faithful in that which is of great significance (ministry). (Lk. 16:10)

If you are not faithful with temporal riches, why would God entrust you with true riches. God gives you temporal riches as a test, and if you are faithful, He will give you eternal riches as a reward. (Lk. 16:11)

And if you have not been faithful in the use of that which is another's, who will give you that which is your own? Those who are faithful in their stewardship opportunities in this life will have ownership privileges in eternity. (Lk. 16:12)

Invest in eternal things. Be faithful in little things.

3. Place God over financial things. (13)

Jesus highlights the third point in verse thirteen:

> No servant can serve two masters; for either he will hate the one and love the other, or else he will be loyal to one and despise the other. You cannot serve God and mammon (money).

Place God over financial things. You cannot serve two masters! You will either hate one and love the other, or hold to one and despise the other. If you are trying to serve God and money at the same time, then you have a conflict of interest.

God says, "Give," and money says, "Keep."

God says, "Scatter," and money says, "Gather."

God says, "Reach out to others," and money says, "Keep it for yourself."

God says, "Give me your life and time," money says "Give me your life and time."

You cannot serve God and money. Two masters claim you. One is a righteous master (God), and one is an unrighteous master (gold). They are both claiming your heart. I ask you right now to look into your heart and to allow God to look into your heart.

Ask yourself some questions: Who is your master? What controls your passions? Is it gold or is it God? Is your major passion the accumulation of wealth, possessions, clothes, cars, boats, houses, stocks, and land, or is your major passion to lay up treasure in heaven by serving and pleasing God?

Are you like the Pharisees in verses fourteen and fifteen? They were lovers of money. They loved what God loathed. They esteemed what God despised. They considered admirable those things that God considered abominable.

Have you allowed your heart to be captured by things that seem humanly and temporally important but are spiritually and eternally insignificant?

THE SIGNIFICANCE

As we wrap up this chapter, I would like to share several more applications. I see five things that link the steward in Luke 16 to a believer in his life and his accountability at the judgment seat of Christ.

1. Believers have been entrusted with a treasure which is not their own.

> As each one has received a (spiritual) gift, use it in serving one another as good stewards of the manifold grace of God. If you have a speaking gift,

> speak the words of God. If you have a serving gift, serve by the strength which God supplies, so that in all things God may be glorified through Jesus Christ. (1 Pet. 4:10-11, Greek)

Just like the steward, you have been entrusted with a treasure that is not your own. As a believer you have either a serving kind of gift or a speaking kind of gift. Whatever your gift is, it is an entrustment. It's a treasure and it's not your own. You have been given life. You have been given the Bible. You have been given time. You have been entrusted with a treasure that is not your own.

2. Believers must give an account of their stewardship.

Like the steward, we must give an account. In Romans 14:12 we are told that *". . . each one of us shall give account of himself to God."* What we do here on earth does matter. One day we will have to give an account for every thought, every word, every attitude, and every action. A day of reckoning is coming! We will be held accountable for our stewardship of the time, talents, and treasures God placed at our disposal.

3. Believers have a limited time to set the stage for their next phase of life.

Just like the steward, we have a limited time to set the stage for our next phase of life. James says our life is like a vapor that appears for a little while and then vanishes (Jas. 4:14). Moses says our life is soon gone (Psa. 90:9-10). The Bible says it is appointed unto men to die, and after that comes the judgment (Heb. 9:27). We should have a sense of urgency in getting things in order, because we are setting the stage for eternity. *"For we must all appear before the judgment seat of Christ, that each one may receive the things done in the body, according to what he has done, whether good or bad"* (2 Cor. 5:10). Right now, you are setting the stage for all of eternity.

4. Believers will be judged on the basis of faithfulness.

Like the steward, we will be judged on the basis of faithfulness. He who is faithful in a very little thing is faithful also in much. As Paul said in 1 Corinthians 4:2, *"Moreover, it is required of stewards, that one be found faithful"* (1 Cor. 4:2, Greek). The requirement is not to be successful in man's eyes, but rather to be faithful in God's eyes. That is true success! We may know the most famous Christians, but we don't know the most faithful Christians. Only God knows that. The rest of us will find out at the judgment seat of Christ.

5. Believers will be rewarded for their faithfulness.

1 Corinthians 4:5 says the Lord will *". . . bring to light the hidden things of darkness and reveal the motives of (men's) hearts. Then each man's praise will come from God."*

In the previous chapter we considered the fact that, just like an athlete in the Olympic Games, we could be disqualified in some races because of some failure on our part. It is important for us to understand that just because we fall or fail, does not mean we cannot get back on our feet and get back on track and finish the race well! You may fall, but you can come back! I grew up on a dairy farm north and west of the little town of Ladora, Iowa. We always had horses. I learned an old, time-worn truth in those days. Whenever you fall off a horse, you just have to get back in the saddle again!

Whenever we fall morally or fail spiritually, we can get back in the saddle again. God is ready to hear our confession, honor our repentance, and give us new opportunities to serve Him! David fell and came back. Jonah ran away and came back. Peter denied Christ and came back. John Mark turned back and came back!

"God is not unjust (so as) to forget your work and labor of love which you have shown toward His name, in that you have ministered to the saints and do minister" (Heb. 6:10). Not even a cup of cold water given in the name of Christ will go unrewarded. Anything you do out of a love for Christ, in the power of the Spirit, to the glory of God will be rewarded!

There is an Indian legend about three men crossing the desert by camel at night. As they were crossing the desert a voice came out of the darkness. The voice commanded them to dismount, pick up some pebbles, and put them in their pocket. Then the voice said, "At the coming of the sun, you will be both glad and sorry."

The travelers did as they were told, and later as the sun came up, they remembered what the voice had said, "At the coming of the sun, you will be both glad and sorry." They reached into their pockets and pulled out not pebbles, but diamonds! They were both glad and sorry. Glad they took as many as they did and sorry that they did not take more.

In effect, it is as though God is speaking to you right now, and He is saying something like this: "I am giving you pebbles of opportunity. At the coming of the Son, you will be both glad and sorry . . . glad you used the opportunities that you did and sorry you did not use more."

Be faithful in using the opportunities that God gives to you, and those whose lives are touched by your generosity and ministry will be like diamonds of joy for you and like diamonds of praise to God throughout eternity!

Study Guide – Chapter 6 – Finances

"Unbelievers do more to have an abundance on earth than believers do to have an abundance in heaven!"

—Harlan D. Betz: *Setting the Stage for Eternity*

1. Name at least two things that are wrong with this quote:
   "Money is the root of all evil."
   Check out 1 Tim. 6:10.

2. Discuss this quote from the Wall Street Journal:
   "Money is an article which may be used as a universal passport to everywhere except heaven, and as a universal provider of everything except happiness."

3. Where is your source of security?
   "That money talks I'll not deny,
   I heard it once: It said, "Goodbye."
   —Richard Armour

4. Who are you serving?
   "Money is a terrible master but an excellent servant."
   —P.T. Barnum

5. **Look at 1 Peter 4:10-11.**
   What gifts has God entrusted to you?
   Do you have a speaking gift?
   Do you have some serving gift?

6. **Reflect on Romans 14:10-12.**
   Are you prepared to give an account of your stewardship?

Are there some ways your time could be used more faithfully?
Are there some ways your money could be used more faithfully?
Are there some ways your skills could be used more faithfully?

7. Can you think of a time when you were faithful in a little thing and as a result, you were entrusted with some greater thing?

8. **Consider Matthew 6:19-21.**

Are you investing in eternal things?

What do your checkbook register and your credit card bill say about your heart?

Discuss this quote:

> "Where your pleasure is, there is your treasure.
> Where your treasure is, there is your heart.
> Where your heart is, there is your happiness."
>
> —St. Augustine

9. **Read 1 John 3:16-18.**

10. Discuss these comments on money:

> "The Bible is very clear on the point that if we have enough money to live well, and do not share with others in need, it is questionable whether God's love is in us at all."
>
> —George Sweeting
>
> "How we use our money demonstrates the reality of our love for God. In some ways it proves our love more conclusively than depth of knowledge, length of prayers, or prominence of service. These things can be feigned, but the use of our possessions shows us up for what we actually are."
>
> —Charles Caldwell Ryrie: *Balancing the Christian Life*

CHAPTER 7

THE CROWN REWARDS

The greater the risk, the greater the reward! There is a story of a West Texas oilman who threw a big party for his daughter's graduation from the University of Texas. The celebration took place out at his ranch. The biggest surprise was when the college students saw the twenty-five huge alligators in the Olympic-size pool. The oilman said he was going to offer the choice of 250,000 dollars or 250 acres of his ranch to the person who would swim the length of the pool. Great risk, great reward! Nobody even budged for about five minutes, and then suddenly a young man was seen diving into the pool, frantically avoiding the alligators and swiftly swimming the length of the pool. The oilman went up to him and asked him if he wanted the 250 acres of land. The young man said, "No, that's not what I want." Then you'll be content to take the quarter million dollars? The young man said, "No, that's not all I want." Well then, said the oilman, "What else do you want?" "I want five minutes alone with the guy who pushed me into that pool!"

Those who first flew took great risks. Those who first submerged to the ocean depths took great risks. Those who first split the atom took great risks. Those who first performed a heart transplant took great risks. Those who invested money in drilling for oil took great risks. Those who invested money in microchips took great risks. Why? Because the greater the risk, the greater the reward.

Jesus' most often stated principle was this: He who tries to save life for himself will lose it, but he who gives up his life to God will find it. The risk is great. God is asking us to give up our life to Him! The reward is even greater. God is offering us the reward of experiencing life as He designed it to be, life at its highest and most fulfilling level. Is it worth the risk? Absolutely! Who wouldn't want to experience a life that is abundant in its blessings, eternal in its joys, and fulfilling in its quests?

Are you interested in finding out more about the abundant life God really wants us to experience now and throughout eternity? I am too, and that is why I invested so many years in a study of the nature of rewards at the judgment seat of Christ.

One major category of rewards is the crown rewards. I want to invite you to join me in an examination of the Biblical texts that highlight the crown rewards. Most people know very little about the crown rewards. This is revealed in questions, some of them facetious, such as these:

What are the crown rewards? How does a person win a crown reward? What if you win more than one crown? Will they stack up on top of each other like checkers? Will you need some type of duffel bag to carry them around? Will there be trophy cases in heaven in which to display one's crowns?

A good friend of mine once said, "I really couldn't care less if I win any crowns. Why should I want to win them? What difference does it make? So what if you win several crowns, and I don't win any? They'll all be cast at Jesus' feet, and then we'll all be the same throughout eternity. After all, if you get to heaven, what more could you want?"

Those are good questions. They are very practical. They are also extremely important. The answer to those questions lies in a clear understanding of the nature of the crown rewards.

Paul lays the groundwork for this study in 1 Corinthians 9:24-27. He says this:

> Do you not know that those who run in a stadium all run, but (only) one receives the prize? Run in such a way that you may obtain it. And every one who competes for the prize exercises self-control in all things. They (the athletes) do it to obtain a perishable wreath, but we (believers) exercise self-control to obtain an imperishable crown.

There are two observations from this passage and one principle not spelled out in this passage that I want to mention.

> First, these crowns must be won.
> Second, these crowns are eternal.
> Third, these crowns bring glory to God.

The New Testament reveals four distinct crowns that are to be awarded to victorious believers at the judgment seat of Christ. We are going to investigate those crown rewards.

1. THE CROWN OF REJOICING

Paul makes reference to the crown of rejoicing in 1 Thessalonians 2:19-20. Paul asks a rhetorical question, and then he answers it. The question: *"What is our hope or joy or crown of rejoicing?"* The answer: *"Is it not even you?"* Paul tells these Thessalonian believers that they are his hope and joy and crown of rejoicing. They will be his crown of rejoicing in eternity . . . as he says, *"Is it not even you, in the presence of our Lord Jesus Christ at His coming?"* And they are his glory and joy at the time he is writing them this letter . . . as he says, *"For you are our glory and joy."*

Why would Paul refer to these believers in Thessalonica as his glory and joy and crown of rejoicing? The answer is found in the first chapter of this letter to the Thessalonians. Paul referred to them as his crown of rejoicing because of the incredible joy he experienced in knowing their lives have been forever impacted by Christ and the personal joy of knowing God used him as an instrument to bring about this eternal spiritual transformation in their lives! Some of them came to know Jesus Christ through Paul's ministry. Some of them have grown and matured through Paul's ministry. In addition to that, the Thessalonians were involved in ministering to other believers (they set forth a godly example to believers), and they were involved in a mission to reach the lost (they sounded forth the gospel).

Paul is able to glory and rejoice and boast in those changed lives! Why? Because God used him to bring about those changes.

Paul is not exalting himself. He knows he can only boast in his weakness (2 Cor. 11:30). He makes it very clear that if anyone wants to boast, he should boast in the Lord (1 Cor. 1:31). But, he also realizes that although he is just an earthen vessel, Christ lives in him (Gal. 2:20), and Christ is delighted to manifest the surpassing power of His greatness in earthen vessels (2 Cor. 4:7)!

Paul's basis for boasting and his ground for glorying is that the Lord Jesus Christ worked in him and through him to bring about a radical, eternal, spiritual transformation in the lives of the Thessalonians. Paul was just an earthen vessel, but he was also an empowered vessel. In another letter, Paul calls the Philippians his joy and crown for the same reason (Phil. 4:1).

What a thrilling anticipation it is to imagine standing before the Lord with those people whose lives you have touched. This reward is not limited to apostles or to those who are involved in a full-time ministry. Every believer has been called to minister! We are all called by God to minister to one another by loving one another, encouraging one another, and praying for one another. Every believer has a mission. We are all called by God to reach out to the lost by living for God, loving other believers, sharing the good news of God's love with those who do not yet know the Lord as their own personal Savior.

The joy of having an intimate fellowship with our Lord is phenomenal. The joy of helping others come to know Him or grow to love Him is a joy that is incredibly phenomenal! It is hard for me to even begin to describe the joy I have experienced in knowing God has used me to encourage someone who was discouraged, to show compassion to someone who had suffered loss, to have a part in someone's spiritual growth, to serve as a model for someone, and to help someone come to know Christ as their own personal Savior.

Do you want your life to count for eternity? Do you want to experience a joy that is indescribable and eternal? Become a fit vessel for His use, a wick for His lamp, an instrument in His hands, and a reflection of His heart. Let Christ eternally impact others through you! Do you want the crown of rejoicing? Let Christ see through your eyes, hear through your ears, touch with your hands, model with your life, encourage with your words, and love with your heart.

The people whose lives are challenged and changed by the Christ in you will be your crown of rejoicing!

So what? What does this mean to you and me? It should impact our attitudes and our actions. The crown of rejoicing is given to believers who eternally impact the lives of others for the sake of Christ. Those whose lives have been challenged and changed by the Christ in you will be your crown of rejoicing!

Are you involved in the great mission of sharing God's love with the lost? Are you involved in the great ministry of encouraging and helping other believers? Would you be willing to commit yourself to these two God-given tasks? Those whose lives have been challenged and changed by the Christ in you will bring joy to your heart eternally.

The impact of the crown of rejoicing is captured by Ray Boltz in his incredibly powerful song, "Thank You for Giving to the Lord."

Thank You for Giving to the Lord
(Words and Music by Ray Boltz)

I dreamed I went to heaven and You were there with me.
We walked upon the streets of gold beside the crystal sea.
We heard the angels singing, and then someone called your name.
You turned and saw this young man and he was smiling as he came.
And he said, "Friend you may not know me now." Then he said, "But wait,
You used to teach my Sunday School when I was only eight.
And every week you would say a prayer before the class would start.
And one day when you said that prayer I asked Jesus in my heart."
Thank you for giving to the Lord.
I am a life that was changed.
Thank you for giving to the Lord.
I am so glad you gave.

Then another man stood before you and said, "Remember the time
A missionary came to your church and his pictures made you cry?
You didn't have much money but you gave it anyway.
Jesus took the gift you gave and that's why I am here today."
    Thank you for giving to the Lord.
    I am a life that was changed.
    Thank you for giving to the Lord.
    I am so glad you gave.
One by one they came far as the eye could see.
Each life somehow touched by your generosity.
Little things that you had done, sacrifices made.
Unnoticed on the earth, in heaven now proclaimed.
And I know up in heaven you're not supposed to cry.
But I am almost sure there were tears in your eyes.
As Jesus took your hand and you stood before the Lord.
He said, "My child look around you. Great is your reward."
    Thank you for giving to the Lord.
    I am a life that was changed.
    Thank you for giving to the Lord.
    I am so glad you gave.[1]

Those people whose lives are challenged and changed by the Christ in you will be your crown of rejoicing!

2. THE CROWN OF RIGHTEOUSNESS

When I was a student at the University of Iowa, I adopted Philippians 1:20 as my life verse "*. . . and this is my earnest expectation and my hope, that in nothing I shall be ashamed, but with all boldness, as always, so now also, Christ will be magnified in my body, whether by life or by death!*" I will be the first to tell you that Christ hasn't always been magnified by my life. But, thankfully, God the Father forgives me when I fail, and He gives me the opportunity and the grace to become increasingly conformed to the righteous character of His Son!

The crown of rejoicing is related to our ministry. The crown of righteousness is related to our character! Paul mentions this crown in Second Timothy chapter four, verses seven and eight:

> I have fought the good fight, I have finished the course, I have kept the faith; In the future there is laid up for me the crown of righteousness, which the Lord, the righteous Judge, will award to me on that day; and not only to me, but also to all who have loved His appearing.

Righteousness is a character quality of God. He is right and just! He is pure and free from sin. He is *"holy, holy, holy"* (Isa. 6:3)! *"The heavens declare His righteousness"* (Psa. 97:6). The Bible declares that Jesus is *"righteous and true"* (Rev. 3:7; 10:6). The Bible states that *"His righteousness endures forever"* (Psa. 111:3). In contrast to the righteousness of God is the sinfulness of man. The Bible makes it clear that there is none righteous, not even one (Jer. 9:17; Rom. 3:10). The Old Testament prophet Isaiah puts it this way: *"Only in the Lord is righteousness"* (Isa. 45:24). The Apostle Paul, under the inspiration of God, tells the Roman Christians that all men have sinned and come short of the righteous standard of God (Rom. 3:23).

There are two kinds of righteousness spoken of concerning mankind.

The first is an imputed righteousness. This righteousness is God's righteousness placed on man's account by God's grace and through man's faith. This is the gift of righteousness that comes through faith in Jesus Christ. This is a positional righteousness. This is spelled out in detail in the third, fourth, and fifth chapters of Romans. Abraham is the key example of one who believed God, and it was reckoned to him as righteousness. Jesus, who committed no sin, became sin for us that we might become the righteousness of God (2 Cor. 5:21). Jesus is our righteousness (1 Cor. 1:30).

The second is a cultivated righteousness. It is cultivated by God's grace through man's pursuit. This righteousness is manifested in faithfulness, obedience, and conformity to the divine standard. This is a practical righteousness. This is spelled out in detail in the sixth, seventh, and eighth chapters of Romans. Jesus challenged His followers to hunger and thirst for righteousness. Jesus, our good shepherd, *"leads us in paths of righteousness"* (Psa. 23:3). God called us to Himself that we might be conformed to the image of His Son (Rom. 8:29). This is our *"holy calling"* (2 Tim. 1:9). We were chosen that we might be holy and blameless (Eph. 1:4; Col. 1:22). Our love for God and others must grow in knowledge and discernment so that we might be filled with the fruit of righteousness (Phil. 1:11). By God's grace, we can mature into and manifest the righteous character of Christ! The crown of righteousness is awarded to the believer who cultivates this practical righteousness.

The crown of righteousness is not be confused with the gift of righteousness.

The gift of righteousness is freely imputed to a man's account at that moment when he trusts in Jesus Christ as his own personal Savior (Rom. 3:21-23). The crown of righteousness is awarded to the one who through yielding his life to God becomes righteous in his character and conduct (Rom. 6:13).

The crown of righteousness is a crown, which consists of righteousness. The crown of righteousness is the capacity to reflect the righteousness and purity and holiness of Christ. It comes as a result of faithfulness. A faithfulness that is grounded in Christ's coming and works itself out in a love for His appearing.[2]

Listen to this plea from the heart of the beloved Apostle John:

> And now little children, abide in Him, that when He appears, we may have confidence and not be ashamed before Him at His coming. If you know that He is righteous, you know that every one who practices righteousness is born of Him. …
>
> Beloved, now we are children of God, and it has not yet been revealed what we shall be, but we know that when He is revealed, we shall be like Him, for we shall see Him as He is. And every one who has this hope in Him purifies himself, just as He is pure. (1 Jn. 2:28-29; 3:2-3)

That passage, like every prophetic passage, is not designed simply to help us know, it is designed to help us grow! Prophecy is not revealed to satisfy our curiosity, it is revealed to stimulate our purity. John explains how Christ's appearing should affect us. It should cause us to seek to purify ourselves! When Christ returns, every believer will be like Him. We will all be children of God. We will all have eternal life. We will all be free from sin. In this sense we will all bear a likeness to Christ . . . a family likeness. But some believers, John tells us, will bear far more than a family likeness. Some will bear a special likeness to Jesus Christ. They will reflect the very righteousness and purity of Christ.

Right now I hope you are saying, "That's what I want!" I hope you have a passion for purity. But let me remind you that you can't have the product without the process. The process, John says, involves abiding in Christ and purifying yourself. If you abide in Christ, your character and conduct will gradually but surely conform more and more into a reflection of the righteousness of Christ. Consequently, you will be eager for His return and you will be living in the light of His coming. You will be able to say with the Apostle Paul, *"There is laid up for me the crown of righteousness."* If, on the other hand, you fail to abide in Christ, you will be ashamed of yourself at Christ's return.

Harry Ironside is right on target in speaking of this crown:

> Nothing is so conducive to a life of integrity before God and uprightness before men as an abiding sense in the soul of the near coming of the Lord. He who truly waits for God's Son from Heaven will be found serving the living and true God day by day.

> To profess to hold the doctrine of the pre-millennial coming of Christ is one thing. To be really held by it is quite another. He whose life is unrighteous, whose spirit is worldly, whose outlook on life is carnal and selfish, has never yet learned to love His appearing. Nor will such ever obtain the crown of righteousness in that day. It is alone for those who, esteeming the reproach of Christ greater riches than all earth's boasted treasures, live now in view of then, because, like Moses, they "have respect unto the recompense of the reward." [3]

Those believers who abide in Christ and thereby purify themselves will be transformed. Their image will reflect the righteousness of Christ. They will look forward with great anticipation to Christ's return. John presents only two options: be conformed to this world and be ashamed, or be transformed by God's Word and be awarded. John goes on to describe the reward for this practical righteousness:

> Let us be glad and rejoice give Him glory, for the marriage of the Lamb has come and His bride has made herself ready. And to her it was granted to be arrayed in fine linen, clean and bright, for the fine linen is the righteous acts of the saints. (Rev. 19:7-8)

How does a person cultivate this practical righteousness? The process that leads to practical righteousness is called sanctification. To be sanctified is to be set apart from sin and set apart to the Savior. The call to holiness is clearly set out in the New Testament. God calls us to be holy as He is holy (1

Pet. 1:15). The Bible charges us to constantly pursue holiness (Heb. 12:14). The Bible challenges us to continually put on righteousness (2 Tim. 2:22). The Bible commands us to put on the Lord Jesus Christ and make no provision for the flesh (Rom. 13:14).

For most people, the concept of holiness is a very negative concept. Far too many people associate holiness with somberness and sadness. They think being holy means living an isolated, out of touch, monk-like life. They think being holy means living an austere, burdensome life that is so heavenly minded that it is of no earthly good. They think a life of holiness is the opposite of a life of happiness.

The story is told of a little girl who was visiting her grandparents' farm. Her grandpa and grandma were very legalistic, pharisaic, and negative. They gave her the impression that God was a cosmic killjoy. The outworking of their religion seemed to take the fun out of life. The little girl, numbed by the negativity and reeling under the rules, decided she needed to get out of the house and get some fresh air. As she was walking by the corral, she noticed the old mule with his long face and his head hung down. She looked at the old mule and said, "What's wrong mule, have you got religion too!"

This is a false understanding of God and a false understanding of holiness. A holy person doesn't have to have a face so long they could suck marbles out of a gopher hole! The truth is that holiness is inseparably linked to happiness! It is the unholy life that blinds us and binds us. It is the unholy life that deceives us and dominates us.

James describes what I call "The LSD Cycle" . . . in which <u>L</u>ust leads to <u>S</u>in which leads to <u>D</u>eath. The unholy life results in the inability to think rightly, the bondage of addicting sins, and the heartache of damaged lives. Living a life of holiness results in the clarity of guilt-free thinking, freedom from slavery to sin, the joy of helping others, and the pleasure of honoring God.

God honors holiness with gladness! The Bible says, *"You have loved righteousness and hated lawlessness; therefore God, your God, has anointed You with the oil of gladness above Your companions!"* (Heb. 1:9).

Nancy Leigh DeMoss asks:

> Why do we make holiness out to be some austere obligation or burden to be borne, when the fact is that to be holy is to be clean, to be free from the weight and burden of sin? Why would we cling to our sin any more than a leper would refuse to part with his oozing sores, given the opportunity to be cleansed from leprosy? To pursue holiness is to move toward joy—joy infinitely greater than any earthly delights can offer.[4]

The crown of righteousness is a reward for living a holy life. The crown of righteousness is given to believers who live in the light of Christ's return and reflect the light of Christ's righteousness.

What practical steps can I take to obtain the crown of righteousness?

1. Cultivate a love for God.

We are to love God with all our heart, all our soul, and all our mind (Mt. 2:37-39). Love for God will be manifest in a hunger to feed on His Word and a desire to be in His presence. Love for God should cause us to long to be fitted for the kingdom and the holy city. Love for God will cause us to "abhor that which is evil and cling to that which is good" (Rom. 12:9). We cannot have both a love for God and a love for sin at the same time. Holiness and worldliness cannot abide in the same heart.

If we genuinely love God we will seek to be holy as He who called us is holy (1 Peter 1:15). We will want our life to reflect the beauty and purity of our Heavenly Father. We will want the world to know what He is like. We will let our light shine so that others will glorify our Father who is in Heaven!

2. Cultivate a passion for Christ-likeness.

God's desire is that we be conformed to the image of Christ (Rom. 8:29). The Apostle Paul had a consuming passion to press toward the prize of becoming like Christ (Phil. 3:12-14). Becoming Christ-like involves a passion for the development of purity. Christ wants His bride to be without spot or wrinkle. The Psalmist asks, *"How can a person be pure?"* Then he answers, *"By reading and heeding the Word of God"* (Psa.119:9, 11). Becoming Christ-like involves a passion for the enjoyment of intimacy with God. We cannot experience intimacy with God unless we have clean hands and a pure heart (Psa. 24:3-4).

3. Commit yourself to walking in the Spirit.

We cannot be what God wants us to be on our own. God never gives us a command to obey without giving us the resources to obey it. God has given every believer the Holy Spirit. By submitting to God's will and drawing on God's power, we can cultivate a holy life! It is imperative that we yield our will to the Holy Spirit's leading. God commands us to be controlled by the Spirit (Eph. 5:18; 1 Th. 5:19; Gal. 5:16). We must allow our will to be swallowed up by God's will. God's will is revealed in God's Word. The old hymn writer put it this way, "I'll go where you want me to go, dear Lord. I'll be what you want me to be. I'll do what you want me to do." Yielding to God is saying yes to His call and His commands. It is walking in the Spirit. It is walking in obedience to the Word. It is walking in newness of life!

4. Confess and forsake all sin.

Charles Spurgeon gave this warning: "Those who tolerate sin in what they think to be little things will soon indulge it in greater matters."[5] The Bible gives us this word of encouragement: *"If we confess our sins, God is faithful and just to forgive us our sins and to cleanse us from all unrighteousness"* (1 Jn. 1:9). The believer who confesses and forsakes sin will prosper (Prov. 28:13).

The Bible says, *"Make no provision for the flesh, to fulfill its lusts"* (Rom. 13:14). John Ruskin said, "No one can ask honestly or happily to be delivered from temptation unless he has honestly and firmly determined to do the best he can to keep out of it." Thomas Secker wrote, "To pray against temptation, and yet to rush into occasion, is to thrust your fingers into the fire, and then pray they might not be burnt."

Why is it that we are so hesitant to burn the bridges to sin? Robert Robinson recognized this problem as evidenced by these words from his hymn: "Prone to wander, Lord I feel it, prone to leave the God I love." The Apostle Paul admitted failing to do what he knew was right and finding himself doing what he knew was wrong (Rom. 7). How can we act righteously when we dwell in a body of sinful flesh? We need to have our minds set on Christ and our wills steeled by the Spirit (Rom. 8). Only then can we put off the deeds of the flesh and walk in holiness.

God's Word is a lamp to our feet and a light to the path of holiness. Jesus said God's Word is the truth, and He prayed that His followers would be sanctified by obedience to the Word (Jn. 17:17). Unfortunately, instead of using the Word as our guide, we have used the world as our guide, and consequently we have compromised our standards. Instead of loving God and confronting worldliness, we are loving the world and compromising godliness. Instead of having lives characterized by a biblical tone, we have lives characterized by a comfort zone. We just stay comfortably removed from the world and slide down the moral and spiritual tubes with the world—keeping ourselves a safe, comfortable distance behind.

Nancy Leigh DeMoss says it well:

> Somehow the evangelical world has managed to redefine sin; we have come to view it as normal acceptable behavior—something perhaps to be tamed or controlled, but not to be eradicated or put to death. We have sunk to such lows that we can not only sin thoughtlessly, but astonishingly, we can even laugh at sin and be entertained by it![6]

What is keeping you from a life of holiness? What battles are you losing?

Are you losing the battle for holiness in your mind? Is your thought life out of control? Are you struggling with sensual lust and sexually immoral thoughts? Remember the old saying: "Garbage in, garbage out." What are you feeding your mind? Perhaps you need to change your input. Far too much of today's entertainment is filled with sexual immorality and vulgar language. God challenges us to take every thought into captivity to the obedience of Christ! (2 Cor. 10:5) Are you willing to cut out movies, magazines, novels, and television shows that do little more than glamorize adultery and legitimize sexual immorality? Are you addicted to pornography? This secret sin can be piped into the depths of your soul through the internet, videos, and magazines. Pornography pollutes the mind, promotes lust, and prevents satisfaction. Are you willing to confess your sin to someone who can help? Are you willing to be held accountable? Are you willing to change your behavior?

Are you losing the battle for holiness in your relationships? Are you lying to your marriage partner? Are you deceiving your friends? Are you spending time alone with a person who is married to someone else? Are you flirting with disaster and playing with fire in your relationships? Are you willing to cut off relationships that are unhealthy and could lead to immorality? Are you willing to stick with guidelines that keep you out of compromising situations?

Are you losing the battle for holiness in your finances? Are you letting the little things slide? Are you cutting corners and making excuses for doing things the way the world does them? Are your buying and spending habits out of control? Are you refusing to say no to yourself? Are you trying to find satisfaction in things? Are you spending an inordinate amount of money on things that are peripheral? Are you going into debt? Are you using credit cards to purchase things you don't have money to buy? Would you be willing to ask God to help you cultivate contentment? Would you make a commitment to thank God every day for some of His blessings? Are you fudging on your numbers, lying on your reports, and giving only partial truths? Are you willing to commit yourself to purity and whole truths in your finances?

Are you losing the battle for holiness in your failure to care for your body? Are you eating too much, exercising too little, and working too long? Would you commit yourself to taking better care of your body, which is the temple of the Holy Spirit?

Are you losing the battle for holiness in your attitude? Are you self-willed, self-pitying, self-indulgent, and self-centered? Are you envious, jealous, angry, bitter, wrathful, vengeful, and impatient? Are you critical and judgmental? Ask God to help you to focus on things that are lovely, pure, and just. Ask God to help you think about things that are virtuous and of good report. Ask God to help you set your mind on Christ.

Are you losing the battle for holiness with your tongue? Are you caustic and condemning? Are you spreading gossip, sowing discord, and tearing others down? Are you destroying others with your words? Are you making promises you do not keep? Ask God to help you control your tongue. Make a commitment to think before you speak. Ask yourself if what you are about to say is going to be uplifting and gracious (Eph. 4:29).

Do you have a passion for purity? I want to have a passion for purity. I am asking God to give me an attraction to holiness and revulsion to sin. I want to experience the joy and gladness that comes from purity in my life and intimacy with my God! Won't you join me in this quest? The crown of righteousness comes as a reward for abiding in Christ. It is the result of Christ's power in an abiding earthen vessel.

Almeda J. Pearce expresses my prayer:

> When He shall come, resplendent in His glory, To take His own from out this vale of night, O may I know the joy at His appearing, Only at morn to walk with Him in white! When He shall call, from earth's remotest corners, all who have stood triumphant in His might, O to be worthy then to stand beside them, and in that morn to walk with Him in white![7]

The crown of righteousness is given to those believers who live a holy life! The crown of righteousness is given to those believers who live in the light of Christ's return and reflect the light of Christ's righteousness. Fight the good fight, finish the course, keep the faith, and God will crown you with righteousness!

3. THE CROWN OF LIFE

Although I grew up in a Christian home, and although my parents saw to it that I was involved in a Bible teaching church and attended a Bible teaching camp, in some ways my spiritual journey was rather slow.[8]

I was seven years old when I trusted in Christ as my own personal Savior out at my Great-Uncle Dale's farm just south of Ladora, Iowa. My dad and mom opened a Bible and reviewed the truths of John 3:16 with me, placing my name in the verse. This is how they read it to me: "For God so loved Harlan that He gave His only begotten Son that if Harlan believes in Him Harlan would not perish, but would have everlasting life!" For the first time in my life, I came to realize that it was not enough to know that Jesus died for the sins of the world; I needed to know that He died for my sins. It was not enough to know about Jesus; I needed to personally trust in Him. I did not understand then, at age seven, many of the things I understand now, but I did know I was a sinner. I did know that God loved me so much He sent His Son to die in my place and pay for my sins. I did know that Jesus rose from the dead. Right then and there, in that old farmhouse, I placed my faith in Jesus Christ as my own personal Savior. At that very moment, I was born again, freed from the penalty of my sins, and guaranteed eternal life. I was thrilled to receive such a phenomenal free gift and to have such an incredible personal Savior.

It wasn't until six years later, at the age of thirteen, that I began to understand that there was more to Christianity than receiving the free gift of eternal life, loving Christ as my Savior, and having the blessed assurance that I would spend eternity with Him. At the beginning of my teen years, I was beginning to understand that coming to Christ as my Savior was just the foundation of the Christian life. God wanted me to build on that foundation. I had come to Christ for salvation, but now I needed to follow after Christ in discipleship. My thinking was something like this . . . since Jesus had given His life for me; I should live my life for Him. Consequently, at thirteen years of age, I was baptized as a public testimony of my faith in Christ as my Savior and as a public symbol of my commitment to follow Christ as my example. I wanted to be the kind of person God wanted me to be and I wanted to do the things God wanted me to do.

It was another six years before the next major transition took place in my spiritual journey. As I look back on my high school years, I realize now that I was mentored by my brother, Arthur, and I was held accountable for my spiritual life by my sister, Charma. God brought Norm Adamson to our little country church. Norm was a young pastor who had a great love for God, a great enthusiasm for ministry, and a great love for people. Pastor Adamson had a huge impact on my life. He took over where my brother left off when my brother went to college. Pastor Adamson showed me what it was like to love God enough to live for Him. He challenged me to begin memorizing chapters of the Bible and books of the Bible. He challenged me to make a difference in this world for Christ.

God brought two other men into my life through the ministry of East Iowa Bible Camp—Dr. Stanley Toussaint and Dr. Don Hillis. Both of these men had a genuine love for God and a compassionate heart for people. Dr. Toussaint had an incredible grasp of God's Word, a wonderful ability to exposit it, and a keen sense of humor. Dr. Hillis had a genuine burden for the lost and for the fulfillment of the great commission. There at East Iowa Bible Camp, at the end of a week sitting under the ministry of these two men, the young people who were present were challenged to totally surrender their lives to God. I was sitting there in that screened-in tabernacle in the woods of East Iowa. The weight of the challenge was heavy upon me. The Holy Spirit was working in my heart. I knew Jesus was my Savior. I knew I was committed to living a life that was good and honorable and glorifying to Christ, but this was something more. This call was for a total surrender of my life to God. This was presenting my body as a living sacrifice. This was saying, "Here am I, Lord; I am at your disposal. Let Your will be done in my life! I will be what you want me to be, do what you want me to do, say what you want me to say, and go where you want me to go."

This decision could not be taken lightly! I remember thinking that this might mean a painful separation from my family. I remember thinking this might mean being a foreign missionary. I remember thinking this might mean going to the darkest place in the world. I remember thinking this might mean physical death. I was wrestling in my mind as to whether I was truly ready and willing to make this commitment. Was I ready for total surrender? Was my family too precious to me? Were my plans too precious to me? Was my life too precious to me? Would I let Jesus bore my ear with an awl? Was I really ready to become his bondslave?[9] Dr. Hillis asked those of us who were willing to surrender our lives to God to take a public stand.

My heart was pounding and my mind was racing as I wrestled with making a decision I knew would change my life forever. God in His grace spoke to me through Dr. Hillis and calmed some of my greatest fears. I was thinking . . . could I be miserable and disappointed with God's will for my life? Dr. Hillis said, "God's plans are for welfare and not calamity. God wants to give you a future and a hope." I was thinking . . . would my life be snuffed out like that of Jim Elliott? (He was killed by the very people he tried to reach with the gospel.) Dr

Hillis said, "The safest place in the world is the center of God's will. The man of God is indestructible until God's will for his life is finished." When I was starting to lean towards saying "Yes!" to God, I started thinking . . . Are you crazy? You're just eighteen years old. How can you make that kind of decision? How could you be so foolish as to give up your life? Dr. Hillis said, "The wise man of the ages is the man who determines the direction in which God is moving and moves in that direction!" Dr. Toussaint had said, "God honors those who honor Him!"

I don't remember if the piano and organ were both playing, but I do remember the song:

> All to Jesus I surrender, all to Him I freely give,
> I will ever love and trust Him in His presence fully live.
> I surrender all. I surrender all.
> All to Thee my blessed Savior, I surrender all.

I decided to get up and walk to the front of the tabernacle. I determined that my life would, from that moment on, belong to my Lord! That was one of the best decisions I ever made. It impacted my life on a daily basis, and it changed the course of my life during my freshman year in college. But that is another story!

Do you love God enough to live for Him? That is what this crown reward is all about. James refers to the crown of life when he writes: *"Blessed is the man who endures temptation; for when he has been approved, he will receive the crown of life which the Lord has promised to those who love Him"* (Jas. 1:12). The Lord Himself spoke of the crown of life in Revelation 2:10, saying, *"Be faithful unto death, and I will give you the crown of life."*

The crown of life is awarded to those believers who love the Lord enough to live for Him. The crown of life is given to those who love the Lord enough to live for Him even when enduring hardship! The crown of life is promised to those who are faithful in life and faithful until death. It is being promised to believers who are ready and willing to endure whatever suffering comes because of a commitment to love God and be faithful to the Lord.

The trials a committed believer faces can come in a great variety of ways. It could be criticism, antagonism, or ostracism. It could be rejection, persecution, or accusation. It could be poverty, mockery, or bribery. It could be physical, emotional, or financial. In every case, the choices are clear:

1. Faithful in time of suffering or faithless in time of suffering;
2. Standing firm under trials or falling flat under trials;
3. Holding up when tempted or folding up when tempted;
4. Living for our Savior or living for ourselves.

The key to understanding the crown of life is found in one of Christ's most famous sayings:

> If anyone desires to come after Me, let him deny himself, and take up his cross daily, and follow Me. For whoever desires to save his life will lose it, but whoever loses his life for My sake will save it. (Lk. 9:23-24)

Jesus is telling us how we can experience life at its fullest, life as God really designed it to be. And that is exactly what we all want—this crowning experience of life. But the path to this pinnacle seems risky. Jesus is asking us to give up our lives to Him. It would be a great risk if it were not God who was doing the asking. We know that God wants what is best for us. God is working for our good and His glory!

Paul puts it this way:

> I beseech you therefore, brethren, by the mercies of God, that you present your bodies a living sacrifice, holy, acceptable to God, which is your reasonable service. And do not be conformed to this world, but be transformed by the renewing of your mind, that you may prove what is that good and acceptable and perfect will of God! (Rom. 12:1-2)

This is a call for a voluntary submission of our lives to Christ. It involves a total surrender. It is a call for a living sacrifice. The question often asked is this: "What is the biggest problem with a living sacrifice?" The answer: "It keeps crawling off the altar!" This highlights a very important truth. Although total surrender is a once-in-a-lifetime, all-for-a-lifetime decision, it requires a daily yielding and daily surrendering of our wills to the will of our Father! Our natural tendency will be to crawl off the altar.

C.S. Lewis reminds us that . . .

> Those Divine demands which sound to our natural ears most like those of a despot and least like a lover,

> in fact marshal us where we should want to go if we knew what we wanted. [10]

Ultimately, surrender to God is the way to fulfillment and joy and peace and life—life as it was divinely designed to be experienced. Instead of being conformed to the world, we must be transformed by the Word! Our minds must be renewed by the Word of God. A mind that is renewed by the Word will result in a life that is lived for the Lord! The crown of life is being promised to those who love the Lord enough to live their life for Him!

> A life lived for self is lost;
> A life lived for God is saved.
> A life lived for self is destroyed by sin;
> A life lived for God is delivered from sin.
> A life lived for self is disappointing to God;
> A life lived for God is delightful to God.
> A life lived for self is devoid of rewards;
> A life lived for God is deserving of rewards.

Once again it must be pointed out that the crowns are rewards and not gifts. The crown of life is distinct from the gift of life. Every believer has received the gift of life, but not every believer will receive the crown of life. The gift of life is received freely (Eph. 2:8-9). The crown of life is earned sacrificially (Jas. 1:12). The Scriptures clearly distinguish between the possession of eternal life as a gift to be received (Jn. 3:16) and the full, rich experience of eternal life as a goal to be pursued (1 Tim. 6:12-19)!

The believer who is willing to die to self and live for God is going to experience a richness, a fullness, and an abundance that other believers won't ever experience. The believer who gives his life to God is going to know Jesus Christ in a way that other believers won't ever know Him. Paul was aware of this concept. He understood Jesus' enigmatic saying about losing your life to save it. Listen to Paul's testimony:

> But what things were gain to me, these I counted as loss for Christ. Yet indeed I also count all things loss for the excellence of the knowledge of Christ Jesus my Lord, for whom I have suffered the loss of all things, and count them but rubbish, that I may gain Christ and be found in Him, not having my own righteousness, which is from the law, but that which is through faith in Christ, the righteousness which is from God by faith; that I may know Him and the power of His resurrection, and the fellowship of His sufferings, being conformed to His death. (Phil. 3:7-10)

The crown of life involves the capacity to enjoy the height of life's potential and to experience the depth of the Christ-like life, both in this life and in the life to come!

The believer who does not live for the Lord is much like a fish out of water. That fish may be alive, but it is not really experiencing life. It is experiencing death because it is dying. A believer who lives his life for himself is experiencing death. On the other hand, the believer who is willing to die to sin and live for the Savior will experience an extraordinarily abundant life.

George Duffield issues the challenge with these words:

> Stand up; stand up for Jesus, the strife will not be long;
> This day the noise of battle, the next the victor's song;
> To him that overcometh, a crown of life shall be;
> He with the King of glory shall reign eternally.

Let me ask a few questions based on that song. Are you standing up for Jesus, or are you sinking down in sin? Are you engaged in this spiritual battle, or are you entangled in the affairs of this life? Are you loving the Lord, or are you loving the world? Are you overcoming by surrendering all, or are you being overcome by seeking all?

Jesus wants us to be without spot or wrinkle, holy and blameless, a pure and righteous bride (Eph. 5:25-27). Paul wrote to the Corinthian believers and said,

> I am jealous for you with godly jealousy. For I have betrothed you to one husband, that I may present you as a chaste virgin to Christ. But I fear, lest somehow, as the serpent deceived Eve by his craftiness, so your minds may be corrupted from the simplicity that is in Christ. (2 Cor. 11:2-3)

Unfortunately, for many Christians there will not be a crown of life because they love the world more than they love the Lord. Vance Havner's word picture captures the problem: "The world and the professing church first flirted with each other, and then fell in love, and now the wedding is upon us!"

Do you love the Lord? What has captured your heart? What is it that you long for and live for? Do you have a passionate love for Christ? Do you have a passion for intimacy with your Lord? Or has your heart been captured by a longing for the things this world has to offer . . . the lust of the flesh, the lust of the eyes, and the boastful pride of life? The Bible says you cannot love the Lord and love the world at the same time. Have you been led astray from the simplicity and purity of devotion to Christ? Do you love the Lord enough to live for Him?

Are you willing to say to the Lord what songwriter Frances Havergal said?

> Take my life and let it be, consecrated Lord to Thee.
> Take my silver and my gold, not a mite would I withhold.
> Take my lips and let them move at the impulse of your love.
> Take my feet and let them be swift and beautiful for Thee.
> Take my love, my God, I pour, at your feet its treasure store.

The crown of life will be given to those believers who love the Lord enough to live their life for Him. Will you totally surrender your life to God? If you love the Lord that much, He will reward you with the crown of life. And one day you will be able to fall down and lay your crown at the feet of Jesus!

4. THE CROWN OF GLORY

Every year, millions of people watch about sixty football players compete to win the superbowl. Every one of those players is a Super Bowl competitor, but only some win the prize. Every one of these athletes has the opportunity to compete, but only half of them are victorious. Those athletes either experience the thrill of victory or the agony of defeat. In a similar way, the Bible says Christians are competing for a prize. Every believer is to run the Christian race, but only some will receive the prize. We are to run in such a way that we all can win.

And why do those Super Bowl football players compete? It is for the pride and glory of being victors in a game. It is for the rings and money and glory that come from winning a game.

But think about it . . . the rings and the money could be lost or stolen, and the glory and fame are not lasting? Most people don't even know most of the players who played in the Super Bowl three years ago. The rewards that come from winning the Super Bowl are passing. The rewards a believer receives for being victorious in living the Christian life are permanent! Jesus said, *"Do not lay up for yourselves treasures on earth, where moth and rust destroy and where thieves break in and steal; but lay up for yourselves treasures in heaven, where neither moth nor rust destroys and where thieves do not break in and steal. For where your treasure is, there your heart will be also."*

Don't settle for passing prizes; go for permanent prizes! Don't settle for receiving the praise of man; go for the praise of God. Don't settle for the honor of men; seek the glory of God!

The Westminster catechism reminds us that the chief end of man is to enjoy God and to glorify Him forever! The highest duty of man is to glorify God in our character and in our conduct. Paul challenges us with these words, *"Do all to the glory of God!"* John reminds us that God is worthy of *"honor and glory and blessing"* (Rev. 4:11, 5:12-14). The Psalmist tells us that *"the heavens declare the glory of God!"* (Ps.19:1).

What is this glory? The terms for glory and honor are often used synonymously. Glory involves radiating character and conduct that is worthy of praise. Honor involves recognizing goodness and glory by giving position and praise. Glory is something that is manifested, and glory is something that is merited.

Who has this glory? God manifested His glory in creation, in the incarnation, and in the transfiguration. God merits glory because of who He is and because of what He has done. Ephesians 1 tells us that God the Father chose us to the praise of His glory, God the Son redeemed us to the praise of His glory, and God the Spirit sealed us to the praise of His glory!

God is worthy of the highest position and the greatest praise! Jesus Christ is said to be the radiance of His Father's glory, the exact representation of His Father's nature (Heb. 1:3).

Who can share this glory? Incredibly, this glory is shared and manifested through believers (1 Pet. 5:1-4). Think of it . . . a believer manifesting the imperishable radiance of God and meriting the incomparable praise of God! Just as Jesus is the radiance of His Father's glory and the express image of His Father's nature, even so believers are to reflect the radiance of Jesus' glory and the express image of Jesus' nature!

How do you get the crown of glory?

1. You must be enlightened by Christ (2 Cor 3:18).

This requires focusing on Christ and His Word. The Bible gives us the illustration of a man who looks in a mirror and then either deals with what he sees or just ignores it and goes on with life. We must take the time to look into the mirror of God's Word (Jas. 1:22-25) and the mirror of Christ's face (Heb. 12:1-2). Fix your eyes upon Jesus. Look at Him. Learn from Him. Live for Him!

2. You must be energized by Christ (Col. 1:27).

This requires being empowered by Christ. Imagine an empty pair of gloves at a piano. They could no nothing. Now imagine those gloves on the hands of Paderewski. They could play a difficult, classical piece. Without Christ, we can do nothing. He wants to fill our lives and empower us to bring glory and honor to His Father. We do not have to try to live this Christian life in our own strength. We can be energized by Christ! Adopt David's attitude: *"The battle is the Lord's!"*

3. You must be embraced by Christ (2 Cor. 5:14).

This requires responding to the love of Christ. He cannot embrace you if you run away from Him. He cannot embrace you if you turn your back on Him. Christ gave His life for you. He loves you as you are, but He doesn't want you to stay that way! He has great hopes for what you can be. He not only sees your present value, but He also sees your future potential. We should love Him because He loves us!

Some of you have fallen in love. You have been loved by another person, and that love has motivated you to do things you would have never done otherwise.

Consider Alice Gray's words from *Stories from the Heart:*

"The Treasure"

The cheerful girl with bouncy curls was almost five. Waiting with her mother at the checkout stand, she saw them—a circle of glistening white pearls in a pink foil box.

"Oh please, Mommy. Can I have them? Please, Mommy, please!"

Quickly the mother checked the back of the little foil box and then looked back into the pleading blue eyes of her little girl's upturned face.

"A dollar ninety-five. That's almost two dollars. If you really want them, I'll think of some extra chores for you and in no time you can save enough money to buy them for yourself. Your birthday's only a week away and you might get another crisp dollar bill from grandma."

As soon as Jenny got home, she emptied her penny bank and counted out 17 pennies. After dinner, she did more than her share of chores and she went to the neighbor and asked Mrs. McJames if she could pick dandelions for tens cents. On her birthday, grandma did give her another new dollar bill and at last she had enough money to buy the necklace.

Jenny loved her pearls. They made her feel all dressed up and grown up. She wore them everywhere—Sunday school, kindergarten, even to bed. The only time she took them off was when she went swimming or had a bubble bath. Mother said if they got wet, they might turn her neck green.

Jenny had a very loving daddy and every night when she was ready for bed, he would stop whatever he was doing and come upstairs to read her a story. One night when he finished the story, he asked Jenny, "Do you love me?"

"Oh yes, daddy. You know that I love you."

"Then give me your pearls."

"Oh daddy, not my pearls. But you can have Princess—the white horse from my collection—the one with the pink tail. Remember, daddy? The one you gave me; she's my favorite."

That's okay, honey. Daddy loves you. Good night." And he brushed her cheek with a kiss.

About a week later, after the story time, Jenny's daddy asked again, "Do you love me?"

"Daddy, you know I love you."

"Then give me your pearls."

Oh daddy, not my pearls. But you can have my baby doll—the brand new one I got for my birthday. She is so beautiful and you can have the yellow blanket that matches her sleeper."

"That's okay. Sleep well. God bless you, little one. Daddy loves you." And as always, he brushed her cheek with a gentle kiss.

A few nights later when her daddy came in, Jenny was sitting on her bed with her legs crossed Indian-style. As he came close, he noticed her chin was trembling and one silent tear rolled down her cheek.

"What is it, Jenny? What's the matter?"

Jenny didn't say anything but lifted her little hand up to her daddy. And when she opened it, there was her little pearl necklace. With a little quiver, she finally said, "Here daddy. It's for you."

With tears gathering in his own eyes, Jenny's kind daddy reached out with one hand to take the dime-store necklace, and with the other hand he reached into his pocket and pulled out a blue velvet case with a strand of genuine pearls and gave them to Jenny. He had them all the time. He was just waiting for her to give up the dime-store stuff so he could give her genuine treasure.[11]

So like our Heavenly Father. Do you realize the incredible love that God has for you? He is offering you something far better than the earthly goods you are hanging onto. Do you love Him more than temporary treasures and passing pleasures? What is it that you are refusing to give up?

Are you willing to give up your time to God?
Are you willing to give up your talents to God?
Are you willing to give up your treasures to God?
Are you willing to give up your preferences to God?
Are you willing to give up your bitterness to God?
Are you willing to give up your hurts to God?
Are you willing to give up your will to God?
Are you willing to give up your pearls to God?

Jesus loves you. His love should constrain you, move you, and motivate you. Love Christ because He first loved you (1 Jn. 4:19). Obey Christ because you love Him (Jn. 14:21). Let His love radically transform your life!

4. You must be engaged by Christ (1 Thess. 2:10-12).

This requires walking worthy of His calling—walking in Jesus' footsteps. That means walking in love, walking in wisdom, walking in truth, and walking in the Spirit. Your walk gives weight to your words!

You were not saved by good works, but you were saved unto good works. As a believer, you cannot afford to be entangled in the affairs of this world. You must be engaged in the tasks Christ has for you to do. You must be pressing toward the prize of the high calling of God in Christ Jesus.

5. You must be embattled with Christ (Rom. 8:16-17).

This does not mean we go out looking for a fight. This means we are in a spiritual warfare. The flesh wars against the spirit; darkness wars against the light; Satan wars against believers (Eph. 6:10-13). The Bible tells us that Satan is like a roaring lion seeking whom he may devour (1 Pet. 5:8). Satan wants to steal your faith, kill your hope, and destroy your love (Jn 10:10). The Bible teaches that in this world we will have tribulation (Jn. 16:33). The Bible tells us that it is given unto us, not only to believe in Christ, but also to suffer for His sake (1 Pet. 2:21; 1 Pet. 4:12-13).

Those who share the sufferings of Christ now will share the glory of Christ eternally! The crown of glory is given to those who suffer justly in following Christ.

> Therefore we do not lose heart. Even though our outward man is perishing, yet the inward man is being renewed day by day. For our light affliction, which but

for a moment, is working for us a far more exceeding and eternal weight of glory. (2 Cor 4:16-17)

The crown of glory is reserved for those believers whose lives are transformed in such a way that they manifest the radiance of Christ's character and the righteousness of Christ's conduct.

At this point, you may be asking, "Is there any hope for me? Is there really any chance that I could reflect Christ's radiance?" On the basis of God's Word, I'm delighted to tell you that there is hope. The Bible says that as a believer you have Christ in you, and He is the hope of glory (Col. 1:24-29)! Christ can work in you and through you to transform you into His image! Focus on Christ as your teacher and your transformer.

F. Howard Oakley reveals the hope of reflecting the radiance of Christ's glory in this poem:

If sunrise's golden glories and sunset's golden gleams
Are reflected light on airborne dust, suspended in sunlight beams,
Each sunrise holds a promise, each sunset proves a plan:
The light of heaven that transforms dust can also transform man.
Dust of earth by nature, if from world set free,
I can reflect the character of Him who shines on me
A son of dust and nothing in the darkness of the night,
But looking up on Jesus' face I can reflect His light.
The transformation's simple: reflecting what I see,
I'm changed to the character of Him who shines on me![12]

Choice Gleanings carried an anonymous quote that provides a poignant challenge to every believer:

> God does not reveal Himself hurriedly to the man on the jump. He does not unveil His heart to the one who wants only a curious casual glance. He does not manifest His glory to the spiritual tourist, but to the one who comes up to Him on the mount. The reflected glory on Moses' face as he came forth from his forty days of communion with God was not produced by a snapshot, but by a time exposure.

The crown of glory is reserved for believers whose lives are transformed in such a way that they manifest the radiance of Christ's character and the righteousness of Christ's conduct.

Isaiah says to the Lord, *"We are the clay, You are our potter."* Are you willing to get on The Potter's wheel? Are you willing to place yourself in The Potter's hands? Are you willing to say with Adelaid Pollard:

> Have Thine own way, Lord! Have Thine own way!
> Thou art the Potter, I am the clay.
> Mold me and make me after Thy will
> While I am waiting, yielded and still.
> Have Thine own way, Lord, Have Thine own way!
> Hold o'er my being absolute sway.
> Fill with Thy Spirit till all shall see
> Christ only always, living in me!

Will you give your life into The Potter's hands? Pray this prayer with Darlene Zschech:

I'm captured by Your holy calling.
Set me apart, I know You're drawing me to Yourself.
Lead me, dear Lord, I pray.
Take me, mold me, use me, fill me.
I give my life to The Potter's hand![13]

One other prophetic passage must be considered in light of the crown rewards. God gave the beloved Apostle John a glimpse into the future. John pictured believers casting their crowns before the throne of the Lord God and saying, *"You are worthy, our Lord and our God, to receive glory and honor and power; for You created all things, and because of Your will they existed and were created"* (Rev. 4:11). These believers will have the pleasure of enjoying His presence, the joy of worshipping His person, and the thrill of being His possession. They will fall down before the throne of the Lord God, and in recognition of His awesome power and His preeminent worthiness, they will cast their crowns at His feet. As they do so, they will cry out, *"You are worthy, O Lord, to receive glory and honor and power."*

The crowns are obviously symbolic of glory, honor, and power. These victorious saints are acknowledging the fact that anything good they have become and everything good they have done has been accomplished by the strength which God supplied. They are also acknowledging that anything good they have become and everything good they have done has been done out of a love for Christ and for the glory of God. Consequently, they glorify God by casting their crowns at His feet. Their very lives . . . their character and conduct, their attitude and actions, their reflection and their rewards . . . are a crowning glory to their Lord and God!

Thank You, dear Heavenly Father, for giving us this insight into the future. Thank You for preparing a future for us that is far greater than anything we have ever seen or heard. Give us a heart for the lost. Give us the joy of loving them and seeing them come to You. Give us a heart for the church and for our fellow believers. Give us the joy of building into their lives and seeing them conform to Your image. Inspire us to stay in Your presence and tap into Your power so that we might manifest the Christ-like character and conduct that is worthy of our calling and worthy of these crowns! We long to cast ourselves at Your feet, and we want that moment to be the commencement of an eternity of intimacy with You and worship of You! We want to crown You with many crowns!

Amen!

Study Guide – Chapter 7 – The Crown Rewards

"God is offering us the reward of experiencing life as He designed it to be—life at its highest and most fulfilling level."

—Harlan D. Betz: *Setting the Stage for Eternity*

The Crown of Rejoicing

"Those whose lives have been challenged and changed by the Christ in you will be your crown of rejoicing."

—Harlan D. Betz: *Setting the Stage for Eternity*

1. Take a moment to reflect on the following:

Just for a moment, reflect on the past.

Who have you reached with the gospel?

Who have you encouraged and built up?

Now, for a moment, think about the present.

Who are you befriending that does not yet know Christ?

Who are you loving and encouraging spiritually?

Now think for a moment about the future.

Whose lives could you be reaching with the love of Christ?

Whose lives could you be encouraging to grow in Christ?

2. Spend some time in prayer and ask God to guide you in making the following lists:

Make a list of three people you could try to reach with the gospel.

Make a list of three people you believe God wants you to disciple.

The Crown of Righteousness

"The crown of righteousness is given to those believers who live in the light of Christ's return and reflect the light of Christ's righteousness." —Harlan D. Betz: *Setting the Stage for Eternity*

3. Positional righteousness. Do you have a personal relationship with Jesus Christ? Have you come to the point where you have placed your faith in His death and resurrection as the full and final payment for all your sins?

Would you like to share the story of how you came to have a personal relationship with Christ?

4. Practical righteousness. Have you given yourself to a pursuit of holiness?

"Holiness and worldliness cannot abide in the same heart!"

"Instead of loving God and confronting worldliness,
we are loving the world and compromising godliness."

"Instead of having lives characterized by a biblical tone,
we have lives characterized by a comfort zone!"

—Harlan D. Betz: *Setting the Stage for Eternity*

What is the danger of tolerating little sins?

Why is it that we are so hesitant to burn the bridges to sin?

What is keeping you from living a life of holiness? Is it your reading, your viewing, your thinking, your relationships, your finances, your attitude, your tongue, your body, your desires?

"Pornography pollutes the mind, promotes lust, and prevents satisfaction." —Harlan D. Betz: *Setting the Stage for Eternity*

The Crown of Life

"The crown of life is promised to those who love the Lord enough to live for Him."

—Harlan D. Betz: *Setting the Stage for Eternity*

5. **Study Romans 12:1-2.**

What are some mercies of God that all believers have experienced?

What are some mercies of God that you personally have experienced?

What does it mean to present our bodies a living sacrifice?

Contrast conformation to the world with transformation by the Word.

6. Take some time to reflect on your own spiritual journey.

Has the glorious light of the gospel shined unto you?

Who was influential in this process? When and where did it take place?

Have you given public testimony of your faith? Have you been baptized after having trusted in Christ as our own personal Savior?

Have you given your life to Christ? Are you His willing servant?

Who is mentoring you? Who are you discipling?

The Crown of Glory

"The crown of glory is given to those believers whose lives are transformed in such a way that they manifest the radiance of Christ's character and the righteousness of Christ's conduct."

—Harlan D. Betz: *Setting the Stage for Eternity*

7. You must be enlightened by Christ (2 Cor. 3:1).
What does John 14:6 tell us about finding the truth?
What does John 17:17 tell us about finding the truth?
What does Hebrews 4:12 tell us about finding the truth?

8. You must be energized by Christ (Col. 1:27).
What does Philippians 4:13 tell us about being energized?
What does Philippians 2:13 tell us about being energized?
What does Galatians 2:20 tell us about being energized.
What does John 15:5 teach us about being energized?

9. You must be embraced by Christ (2 Cor. 5:14).
What does 1 John 4:19 reveal about the love of Christ?
What does John 14:21 reveal about a true love for Christ?

10. You must be engaged by Christ (1 Thess. 2:10-12).
What does God expect of us according to Ephesians 2:10?
What does God expect of us according to Titus 2:11-14?
What does God expect of us according to Philippians 1:9-11?
What does God expect of us according to 1 Corinthians 10:31?

11. You must be embattled with Christ (Romans 8:16-17).
Who is our battle against according to Ephesians 6:10-13?
What armor is available to us according to Ephesians 6:14-20?
How is this battle to be fought according to 2 Corinthians 10:3-5 and James 5:7?

---

[1] "Thank You" by Ray Boltz © Gaither Music Company/ASCAP 1988.
[2] Kittel and Friedrich, *Theological Dictionary*, VII, 629.
[3] Ironside, *"Salvation and Reward,"* II, 16.
[4] DeMoss, Nancy Leigh, *Holiness* (Moody Publishers: Chicago, 2004), p. 42.
[5] Charles Spurgeon, *1000 Devotional Thoughts* (Grand Rapids: Baker, 1976), p. 204.
[6] DeMoss, loc.cit.
[7] "When He Shall Come" © 1934, 1962, Almeda J. Pearce.
[8] When I speak of my spiritual journey, I am describing it as I experienced it. I am absolutely convinced that our God is a sovereign God. He is the blessed controller of all things. I am so very grateful that He chose to reach out to me. There is no question about how my spiritual journey started. It started with God. It started with His choice and His grace. The Bible is very clear in stating that God is sovereign (see Romans 9). The Bible is also clear in stating that man has the ability to choose and that man is responsible for the choices he makes (see Romans 10). In today's intellectual climate, many people want to be able to rationally and logically explain every aspect of the Christian life. This cannot be done. The mind of man cannot comprehend how God can be sovereign and man can still be held accountable for the choices that he makes. We cannot reconcile God's sovereignty and man's responsibility with our finite minds. The Bible makes it clear in Romans 11:33 that God's judgments are unsearchable and God's ways are unfathomable. We need to guard against the peril of the pendulum which would cause us to emphasize one of these truths at the expense of the other. They are both true. I have prepared a summary of Calvinism and Arminianism which are at opposite ends of the spectrum and a chart of what I call Biblicism, which I believe is a more balanced Biblical view. It is appendix 10. I have created a TULIP acronym (which is often used for Calvinist view) for the more balanced Biblical view.
[9] Exodus 21:1-6 illustrates what it means to be a bondservant of the Lord!
[10] C. S. Lewis, *The Problem of Pain* (London: Collins Clear-Type Press, 1940), p. 41.
[11] Excerpted from *Stories from the Heart*, Second Collection © 1997, 2001 by Alice Gray. www.alicegray.com
[12] "The Light of Heaven" by Howard F. Oakley.
[13] Excerpted from "The Potter's Hands" by Darlene Zschech © 1997, Darlene Zscech/Hillsongs Australia.

CHAPTER 8

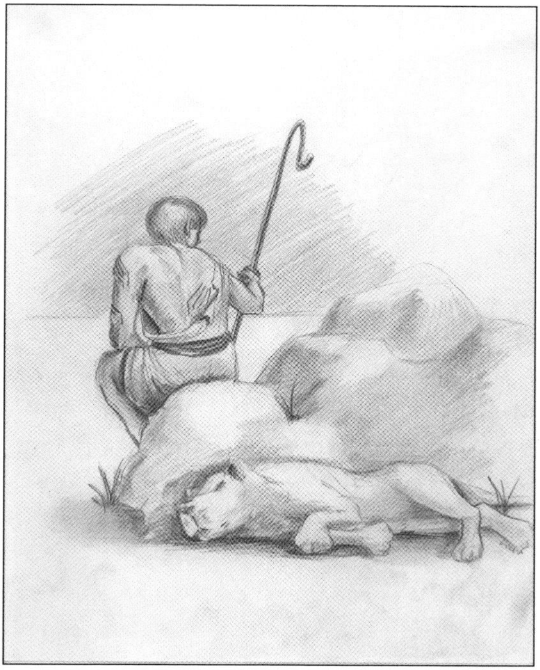

THE IDENTITY OF THE OVERCOMER

One night Joshua, Sarah, Sharon, and I gathered around the fireplace in our living room to read a true story. It was a story about a man who had gone up to Alaska to hunt.

This man shot a caribou, left it where it fell, and went on a little further. He was approximately two hours away from his cabin. He decided that it was time for him to start making his way back to the caribou.

When he was within about thirty feet of where he had left the caribou, he saw a huge grizzly charging him! He picked up his rifle and fired a shot. He was quite sure he hit the grizzly, but he knew he hadn't stopped it. He tried to shoot again, but that big grizzly was coming down on top of him and the gun was knocked out of his hands. He was pretty sure he'd shot the grizzly twice.

The grizzly clamped its jaws over his head. His jaw was broken, his scalp was ripped, and one of his eyes was deeply punctured. He reached his right hand up inside the grizzly's jaw and tried to force it open so he could pull his head out. His right arm was crushed.

The grizzly backed off and bit into the hunter's legs, deeply wounding and lacerating both of his legs. The hunter continued to pound at the grizzly with his left hand.

Finally, after what seemed an eternity but was probably only a small amount of time, the grizzly slumped to the ground, dead from the shots the hunter had fired.

THE BATTLE IS RAGING

As I read that story, I realized how painfully aware that hunter was of the battle. That grizzly was trying to destroy him. The hunter was very much aware that his life was in grave danger.

I began to think about the fact that those who are believers in our Lord Jesus Christ are involved in a battle—just as real and even more dangerous. As the Bible says, *"The devil walks about like a roaring lion, seeking whom he may devour."* Believers are involved in a spiritual battle with Satan. Jesus once said, *"The thief does not come except to steal, and to kill, and to destroy."* As a believer in Jesus Christ, are you aware that Satan is trying to steal the faith out of your spiritual life, kill the hope that is in your heart, and destroy the love you have for the Lord? He is trying to put you on a detour that takes you away from being genuinely devoted to Jesus Christ.

How is he doing that? According to the Bible, Satan has a strategy for your defeat (Eph. 6:10-13). He will mislead you with false impressions. He will entrap you with false allurements. He will distract you from the invisible and permanent by appealing to you with things that are visible and passing.

Satan's Lures

The beloved Apostle John warns us about three of Satan's lures in First John chapter two, verses fifteen to seventeen.

First of all, there is **the lust of the flesh** that Satan puts before us. Pleasure! We're living in a world that longs for it, lusts for it, and is driven by it. We're living in a world that is filling up with sexual immorality, homosexuality, and immorality of all kinds as people live for pleasure. Pleasure is their god. If it feels good, they'll do it. If they want it, they'll go for it. "Eat, drink, and be merry" is the theme of their lives and the focus of their pursuits! Unfortunately, many believers have gone down that path. The lust of the flesh—the inordinate desire for pleasure.

Second, there's **the lust of the eyes**. Possessions! Satan places things before us in this area, and we find ourselves pursuing things that will pass away . . . things that moth and rust corrupt, things that thieves can break in and steal, things that can take our time and money and focus and priorities away from God. Maybe it's a house, maybe it's a boat, maybe it's a car, maybe it's money, maybe it's land, maybe it's clothes. You know what it is that you're constantly pursuing. Satan's got you—the lust of the eyes and the consuming desire for possessions.

And finally, there's **the pride of life**. Prestige! This is a lust and hunger for power, position, and fame. It is the pride that wells up within each of us. It is a desire to be exalted. It's a self-seeking hunger for personal power, importance, and glory. It sometimes causes people to walk over other people in order to get where they want to be. Many believers, when they really look in the mirror, see a person who is a lover of self instead of a lover of God. The pride of life—the compelling desire for prestige.

There's nothing wrong with some of these things in their place. But for many believers they have come out of place. Pleasures, possessions, and prestige have taken the place that Jesus Christ should have in their lives. Have you been sidetracked? Are you losing the battle? Satan's lures are like a riptide. They take away your footing, and they pull you under.

God's Desire

God does not want you to be pulled under. He wants you to resist Satan. He wants you to be victorious in your Christian life and triumphant in this spiritual battle. He wants you to become like His Son! He wants you to be an overcomer!

The Greek word *nikaw* is translated "to overcome." It means to be victorious, to prevail, and to conquer. It is used in reference to a battle, to an athletic contest, and to a legal action. In Scripture, it describes overcoming someone, overcoming the world, overcoming the devil, overcoming the earthly part of man, and overcoming evil with good.[1]

Jesus Christ offers several very special rewards to the overcomers in the book of Revelation. Before we look at the overcomer rewards, we must investigate the identity of the overcomer. It is important that we take a moment to consider the concept of the overcomer as it is defined in 1 John 5:4-5. In this epistle, John makes it clear that *"whatever is born of God overcomes the world. And this is the victory that has overcome the world—our faith."* The key to the overcoming life is our faith.

John tells us that he who overcomes the world is he who believes that Jesus is the Son of God. It is by faith that we are born of God and being born of God is, in itself, a victory over Satan and the world. Overcoming in 1 John is associated with faith! The key to the overcoming life is faith. We overcame the world initially, at the moment we placed our faith in Christ and were born again.

Zane Hodges writes:

> It hardly needs to be said that initial victory does not guarantee subsequent victory in Christian living. John's point is that the victory achieved by the very fact of the new birth makes obedience to God's commands an achievable goal. His readers should not regard these commands as impossibly burdensome, but doable with God's help. Neither here nor in Revelation 2 and 3 are believers regarded as automatic "overcomers" in Christian experience. The seeds of victory are found in our new birth; but as the whole New Testament testifies, these must be nurtured until they ripen into mature, victorious living.[2]

The key to overcoming is faith active in obedience. This is reinforced in the book of Revelation. Unfortunately, there is some confusion over the meaning of the term "overcomer" in the book of Revelation.

VIEW ONE: EVERY BELIEVER IS AN OVERCOMER

Some commentators propose that every true believer is an overcomer.[3] This proposal has four serious problems:

First: Salvation is not by works. In order to be considered an overcomer in Revelation 2 and 3, the believer must be obedient, persevering, faithful, and victorious. If one has to be an overcomer in order to be a true believer, then one has to be obedient, persevering, and faithful in order to be a true believer. If this is the case, then the inspired truths of Ephesians 2:8-9 are wrong! That cannot be. God's Word is true. God's Word says that salvation is *"not of works!"*

Second: Commands are not meaningless. Obedience is not automatic. Christ's challenges to the individuals in these churches are genuine. His warnings are real. If every true believer were an overcomer, then obedience would have to be automatic. If this was the case, Christ's commands would be superfluous, Christ's warnings would be useless, and Christ's promises would be meaningless. In reality, Christ's commands are critical, Christ's warnings are needed, and Christ's promises are motivational. Because of them, many individual believers will choose to deny self, resist temptation, and walk in a manner worthy of their calling. The promises to the overcomer are not to *"them* (plural) *who overcome,"* but to *"him* (individual) *who overcomes"* (Rev. 2:7, 17, 26; 3:5, 12, 21). An obedient response to these commands is not universal and automatic; it is individual and conditional.

Third: Victory is not guaranteed. The status of the overcomer is not a privilege to be received; it is a position to be achieved. Spiritual blessings are not a guarantee of spiritual victory (1 Cor. 10:1-13). Entering the kingdom is not a guarantee of inheriting the kingdom (Lk. 19:11-27). Victory in the spiritual life is not presented as a guarantee, but as a goal (1 Cor. 9:24-27). Each individual in the church is challenged to overcome.

Fourth: Losing is not winning. G. H. Lang makes this point very clear when he writes:

> The assertion that all believers are overcomers is so plainly contrary to fact and to Scripture that one wonders it ever has been made. It involves the false position that no believer can be a backslider. It avoids and nullifies the solemn warnings and urgent pleadings of the Spirit addressed to believers, and by depriving the Christian of these, leaves him dangerously exposed to the perils they reveal.
>
> In the house of the high priest, Peter was defeated by the fear of man. Is he the last? Ananias and Sapphira were defeated by the love of money and pride of reputation. Were they the last? Demas forsook Paul, being overcome by the love of this present world. Was

he the last? In the Corinthian church some were conquered by carnal lusts. Were they the last? Peter re-entered the battle and fought to the end. Ananias and his wife were cut off in their defeat. So were some of the Corinthian believers. We do not know that Demas won through finally.

If all Christians were conquerors, how shall it be possible at the close of the age that *"the love of many (the majority) will grow cold"* (Matt. 24:12)? Overcomers are to receive crowns; but if all overcome, how can any be warned lest he lose his crown (Rev. 3:11)?[4]

VIEW TWO: THE VICTORIOUS BELIEVER IS AN OVERCOMER

I have become convinced before God in the study of the Scripture that the overcomer is a believer who lives by faith and is victorious over sin, self, and Satan.[5]

The letters in Revelation chapters two and three are addressed to churches. Throughout the New Testament, the church is a body of believers:

called out by God,
redeemed by the Son,
sealed by the Spirit.

These letters do not deal with unbelievers and their need for regeneration. They deal with believers and their need for sanctification.

Jesus is warning these believers to persevere under pressure. Jesus is challenging these believers to remain strong and pure and faithful.

By God's grace and through their faith, believers can be obedient and triumphant. Or, in their flesh and in selfish disobedience, they could fall and fail to receive the rewards He offers. Theodore Epp shares this very helpful insight:

> Faith is the key to the overcoming life. The potential is laid up in our hearts the moment we trust in Christ, and it is the purpose of God that we should go on from triumph to triumph in our daily walk. [6]

Theodore Epp goes on to point out:

> The fact that overcoming is made practical through faith is presented by Paul in Colossians 2. He told the believers in Colossae that though he was absent in body he was, nevertheless, with them in spirit, rejoicing in their steadfast faith in Christ. Then he admonished them in these words: *"As ye have therefore received Christ Jesus the Lord, so walk ye in Him"* (v. 6). Note the words "as" and "so." How do we receive Him? By faith! This is the way we appropriate Christ. So, as we receive Christ by faith, the same faith principle is to be operative throughout our lives. We are to go ahead and walk in Christ, rooted and built up in Him and established in the faith as we have been taught. An added thought is given in Romans 8:13 where Paul says, *"But if ye through the Spirit do mortify the deeds of the body, ye shall live."* We have all the practical power needed in this wonderful salvation Christ provided. With the Spirit of God dwelling in us there is no need and no excuse to fail in obtaining God's objective in us.[7]

All believers have been enlisted as soldiers of Jesus Christ. We are involved in a spiritual battle:

A battle between light and darkness.

A battle between flesh and spirit.

A battle between God and Satan.

We cannot remain neutral. Our Lord Jesus Christ said, *"He who is not with Me is against Me"* (Matt. 12:30). James wrote, *"Whoever therefore wants to be a friend of the world makes himself an enemy of God"* (Jas. 4:4).

Service as a soldier does not guarantee success as a soldier (2 Tim. 2:3-4). Consequently, in order for a believer to be an overcomer, that believer must overcome temptation, trials, and tests. In order for a believer to be an overcomer, that believer must be victorious in his determination to be obedient to God's Word.

It is very clear throughout the New Testament that some believers will be overcomers and other believers will be overcome (Revelation 2-3). Some believers will be spiritual, and others will be carnal (1 Cor. 2:15-3:3). Some believers will be joint heirs with Christ, and others will only be heirs of God (Rom. 8:16-17). The distinction between those believers who are faithful and those believers who are not faithful is abundantly evident in the New Testament.[8]

Jesus, in His parables, refers to the victorious believer as good and faithful and wise, as opposed to bad, unfaithful, and foolish. The servant who uses his time, talents, and treasures for the Lord will be rewarded with God's gracious recognition (*"Well done!"*) and with God's gracious reward (*"Enter into the joy of the Lord!"* and *"Be in authority with Me"*).[9]

John, in the book of Revelation, refers to the faithful believer as a *nikaw* (an overcomer). The believer who overcomes and merits the commendations given to the seven churches will be honored and rewarded with a greater capacity to enjoy and experience the joys of eternal life.[10]

The author of Hebrews refers to the faithful believer as part of the *metochoi* (partakers). The author of Hebrews warns believers of five dangers: the danger of drifting (2:1-4), the danger of disbelief (3:7-14), the danger of degeneration 5:11-14), the danger of despising (10:26-34), and the danger of departing (12:25-29). Those believers who heed these warnings and remain faithful will be considered *metochoi* (partakers). The *metochoi* are close associates of Christ. The *metochoi* are intimately identified with Christ in His person and in His position![11]

Esau was caught up in this spiritual battle. Esau exchanged his birthright for a mess of pottage! He sacrificed God-given privileges for man-made pottage. He bartered away his future position for his present satisfaction. He bartered away his eternal treasure in order to experience temporal pleasure. Eric Sauer says, "Thus miserably does sin pay her servants!" and continues:

> Therefore take heed of the warning of this passage in Hebrews! So much hangs in the balance: glorious eternal gain or irretrievable loss.
>
> In that disastrous moment Esau, at the cost of his future, had chosen satisfaction for the present. The mess of pottage pleased him for the moment. But finally the great disappointment came.

Thus he experienced in his own life the principle of the word of the Lord. *"He that loveth his own life shall lose it"* (Jn. 12:25). *"For what is a man profited, if he shall gain the whole world, and lose (damage) his own life?"* (Matt. 16:26).

The Apostle Paul makes it very clear that the warrior must be willing to lay down his own life. A true warrior—a soldier for Christ, cannot allow himself to get entangled in the affairs of this life (2 Tim. 2:3-4). The Pauline epistles and the letter to the Hebrews show many similarities in thought and sometimes also of expression. Just as Paul, in various places in his epistles, uses the picture of the racecourse in the arena of faith, so also the writer of Hebrews does here at the very beginning of this chapter [Hebrews 12]. It is in the light of these opening words on the race and the joy set before the runner that the reference to the "birthright" ought to be read. Both are great possibilities; but both are forfeitable as regards the fullness of their eternal possession and enjoyment. Therefore the unreserved devotion of all our life and spiritual energy is needed in order to attain the full prize, the "crown," the "joy set before us" (cf. Heb. 12:2), the "birthright" in its God-appointed, all-embracing, threefold totality as special abundance of riches, heavenly priesthood, and glorified kingship.[12]

Let me speak personally to you for just a moment. How are you doing in the battle? I know the flesh wages war against the Spirit. I know Satan wants to pull you under. Don't give in!

Don't give up! Walk in the Spirit and you can be an overcomer.

If you don't overcome temptation, temptation will overcome you! George Sweeting is right on target when he says, "Unfortunately 'resisting temptation' has gone out of style and 'doing what comes naturally' has become the in thing!"

Far too many people willingly accept the approach to life expressed by Oscar Wilde, who said, "I can resist anything except temptation."

D. L. Moody points out that "When Christians find themselves exposed to temptation, they should pray to God to uphold them. When they are tempted, they should not be discouraged. It is not a sin to be tempted; the sin is to fall into temptation."

Martin Luther noted that a believer cannot avoid being tempted, but he can avoid falling into sin. Luther put it this way: "You cannot keep the birds of the air from flying over your head, but you can keep them from nesting in your hair!"

Charles Haddon Spurgeon told his students, "Learn to say no; it will be of more use to you than to be able to read Latin."

Alexander MacLaren notes that "The temptation once yielded to gains power. The crack in the embankment which lets a drop, or two, ooze through is soon a hole which lets out a flood."

Someone rightly said, "If you would master temptation, you must first let Christ master you." Johnny Cash learned this lesson. Johnny said, "Every once in a while I meet a youngster who knows I used to be a drug addict, as he is now. He asks what he can do to kick the habit. I tell him what I've learned. 'Give God's temple, your body, back to Him. The alternative is death!'"

Adrian Rogers' words still ring in my ears, "Sin will take you farther than you want to go, keep you longer than you want to stay, and cost you more than you want to pay!" He is absolutely right.

It is far better to struggle to resist the temptation to sin than to struggle to free yourself from the trap of sin. Paul tells the Roman Christians to "Put on the Lord Jesus Christ and make no provision for the flesh, to fulfill its lusts" (Rom. 13:12). I heard about some kids whose pet cat died. They went out in their back yard and buried it all but the tail. The next day they went out, dug it up, played with it, and then buried it again, all but the tail. Then the next day they went out and dug it up to play with it again. That is the way some people are with temptation. They are not truly committed to forsake the sin. They want to keep it within reach. Someone said, "Most people who flee from temptation leave a forwarding address." They are making provision for the flesh!

What will it be for you? You will be tempted! Will you stand or fall? Will you be overcome, or will you overcome?

George Duffield, Jr. adds these words of encouragement:

Stand up, stand up for Jesus, The trumpet call obey;
Forth to the mighty conflict, In this His glorious day,
Ye that are men now serve Him. Against unnumbered foes;
Let courage rise with danger, And strength to strength oppose.
Stand up, stand up for Jesus, The strife will not be long;
This day the noise of battle, The next, the victor's song;
To him who overcometh, A crown of life shall be;
He with the King of glory Shall reign eternally.

By God's grace and through the power of the Holy Spirit, you can walk by faith, and you can walk in obedience. By trusting in Christ and by obeying His Word, you can be an overcomer. Jesus Christ has some special rewards for you if you are triumphant in this spiritual warfare.

John H. Sammis wrote it this way:

When we walk with the Lord in the light of His Word,
What a glory He sheds on our way!
While we do His good will He abides with us still,
And with all who will trust and obey.

Not a burden we bear, not a sorrow we share,
But our toil He doth richly repay;
Not a grief nor a loss, not a frown nor a cross,
But is blest if we trust and obey.

But we never can prove the delights of His love
Until all on the altar we lay;
For the favor He shows and the joy He bestows
Are for them who will trust and obey.

Study Guide – Chapter 8 – Temptation

"If you don't overcome temptation, temptation will overcome you!"

—Harlan D. Betz: *Setting the Stage for Eternity*

1. **Take time to study 1 John 2:15-17.**
   Which area is your greatest battleground?

2. Discuss the difference between temptation and sin.
   "Temptation is the tempter looking through the keyhole into the room where you are living; sin is drawing back the bolt and making it possible for him to enter."

   —J. Wilbur Chapman

3. Does temptation ruin our hearts or does temptation reveal our hearts?
   "Temptations discover what we are."

   —Thomas A. Kempis

   "No one knows how bad he is until he has tried to be good."

   —C. S. Lewis: *Screwtape Letters*

4. Does temptation get less tempting as a person grow older?
   "The long dull monotonous years of middle-aged prosperity or middle-aged adversity are excellent campaigning weather (for the devil)."

   —C. S. Lewis: *Screwtape Letters*

5. **Read James 1:13-15.**
   What is the progression related to temptation?

6. Discuss this quote by Alexander Maclaren:

"The temptation once yielded to gains power. The crack in the embankment which lets a drop, or two, ooze through is soon a hole which lets out a flood."

7. **Read Matthew 26:41.**

What is the role of prayer in relation to temptation?

Consider these quotes:

"When Christians find themselves exposed to temptation they should pray to God to uphold them, and when they are tempted they should not be discouraged. It is not a sin to be tempted; the sin is to fall into temptation."

—D. L. Moody

"To pray against temptation, and yet to rush into occasion, is to thrust your fingers into the fire, and then pray they might not be burnt."

—Thomas Secker

8. What is the key to victory over temptation?

"If you would master temptation, you must first let Christ master you."

—Anonymous

"Learn to say no; it will be of more use to you than to be able to read Latin."

—Charles Haddon Spurgeon

"Every once in a while I meet a youngster who knows I used to be a drug addict, as he is now. He asks what he can do to kick the habit. I tell him what I've learned. 'Give God's temple, your body, back to Him. The alternative is death!'"

—Johnny Cash

---

[1] Arndt and Gingrich, *A Greek-English Lexicon*, p. 541.
[2] Zane Hodges, *The Epistles of John* (Irving, Texas: Grace Evangelical Society, 1999), pp. 216-217.
[3] This view is proposed by Lehman Strauss, *The Book of Revelation* (Neptune, New Jersey: Loizeaux Brothers, 1964), p. 108; William R. Newell, *The Book of Revelation* (Chicago: Moody Press, n.d.), p. 42; James E. Rosscup, *"The Overcomer of the Apocalypse,"* GTJ3 (Fall 1982), 261-286.
[4] G. H. Lang, *The Revelation of Jesus Christ* (London: Oliphants, 1945), pp. 91-92.
[5] This view is also supported by the following: Donald G. Barnhouse, *Messages to the Seven Churches* (Philadelphia: Eternity Book Service, 1953), p. 38. Richard Reagan Benedict, "The use of Nikaw in the Letters to the Seven Churches of Revelation" (Th.M. thesis, Dallas Theological Seminary, 1966), pp. 43-46. Joseph A Seiss, *Letters to the Seven Churches* (Grand Rapids, Michigan: Baker Book House, 1956), pp. 224-225.
[6] Ibid. *Practical Studies*, p. 202.
[7] Theodore H. Epp, *Practical Studies in Revelation* (2 Vols. Lincoln, Nebraska: Back to the Bible Publishers, 1969), I, p. 201.
[8] The Bible clearly points out that a believer can be good or bad, wise or foolish, faithful or lazy. Just as entrance in a race does not guarantee winning it (1 Cor. 9:24-27), even so entrance into the kingdom does not guarantee inheritance in the kingdom (Luke 19:11-28). Enlistment as a soldier does not guarantee effectiveness as a soldier (2 Tim. 2:1-5). The calling to be a servant does not guarantee the development of the character of a servant (1 Pet. 5:1-4). Therefore, believers must be challenged to "not let sin reign in their mortal bodies" (Rom. 6:12-13), to "run in such a way that they may win" (1 Cor. 9:24), to "walk worthy of their calling" (Eph. 4:1), and to "press toward the prize of the upward call of God in Christ Jesus" (Phil. 3:13-14).
[9] Matthew 24:45-5, faithful *(pistos)* and sensible *(phronimos)* vs. evil/wicked (k*akos*); Matthew 25:1-13, wise *(phronimos)* vs. foolish *(moros)*; 25:14-30, good *(agathos)* & faithful *(pistos)* vs. wicked *(poneros)* & lazy *(okneros)*; Luke 19 11-28, good *(agathos)* vs. wicked *(kakos)*.
[10] The promises to the overcomers in Revelation will be investigated in chapter nine of this dissertation.
[11] Cf., Eric Sauer, *In The Arena of Faith* (Grand Rapids, Michigan: William B. Eerdmans Publishing Company, 1955), pp. 125-166. The book of Hebrews speaks of birthrights *(ta prototokia)*, which involve a position of authority, priestly service, and a double portion of the inheritance. A believer who fails to heed the warnings of God and fails to be faithful will forfeit the enjoyment of the full possession of his firstborn rights and privileges. This would be an immense loss. Sauer makes this insightful comment: *"The believer, although belonging to the church of the firstborn, may*

practically deny his birthright. Instead of riches inward poverty, instead of priesthood practical separation from God, instead of kingship actual slavery!"

[12] Erich Sauer, *In The Arena of Faith*, pp. 156-157.

CHAPTER 9

THE OVERCOMER REWARDS

Henry Morrison and his wife were on their way home from a lifetime of service as missionaries in Africa. They were on the same ocean liner as President Teddy Roosevelt, who was returning from a big game hunting expedition.

The missionary couple was amazed at the attention, the publicity, and the fanfare given the President and his entourage. When the ocean liner docked in New York, a band was there to greet him, the mayor was there to welcome him, and the reporters were there to publicize his return.

In sharp contrast, the missionary couple had no band there to greet them, no public official there to welcome them, and no publicity about their return. They disembarked from the ship unnoticed and unheralded. Henry could not seem to get over how the President had received such acclaim when he came home after just a short time of recreation, while he and his wife received no notice or applause when they came home after four decades of missionary service. He was discouraged, and he was disappointed.

Then, silently, but surely, the still small voice of God came to his mind, "Henry, you're not home yet!" The One whom he loved and served would recognize him and reward him when he got home to heaven!

We need to remember the very important truth spoken of in the old spiritual: *This world is not my home, I'm just a passin' through; my treasures are laid up somewhere beyond the blue.* The Bible says, *"And let us not grow weary while doing good, for in due season we shall reap, if we do not lose heart"* (Gal. 6:9). This is a challenge to keep on keeping on! It is a challenge to never give up! This is a reminder that God recognizes our good work and God will reward our good work. There may be some rewards in this life, but the ultimate rewards will come in eternity!

Everyone faces difficulties and disappointments. Everyone experiences hurts and heartaches. Every believer wages war with the world, the flesh, and the devil. God is encouraging us to hold up instead of fold up. He is challenging us to keep on doing good. God is encouraging us to never give up when we are doing what He wants done. It may be hard. It may take its toll. It may require blood, sweat, and tears, but if it's something God wants, it is worth the perseverance and the sacrifice because one day God will richly reward those who did not give up.

The anticipation of Christ's return and the motivation of Christ's rewards encourage us to stand for righteousness instead of falling in selfishness. Satan tries to steal our faith, kill our hope, and destroy our love. The world seeks to control us with the lust of pleasure, consume us with a love of possessions, and capture us with the pride of prestige. Satan wants to lead our minds astray from the simplicity and purity of devotion to Christ! But we can overcome! In all these things we can be more than conquerors! Nothing can separate us from the love of God which is in Christ Jesus our Lord. We love Him because He first loved us. The love we have for Christ motivates us to persevere under pressure. The love we have for Christ encourages us to keep on keeping on!

Will we go unrewarded for such steadfast love? Is God unjust so as to forget our work and the love we have shown toward Him? No! Absolutely not! The Bible says:

> For God is not unjust (so as) to forget your work and the labor of love which you have shown toward His name . . . (Heb. 6:10)

> Finally, there is laid up for me the crown of righteousness, which the Lord, the righteous Judge, will give to me on that Day; and not to me only but also to all who have loved His appearing. (2 Tim. 4:8)

God will recognize and reward those who overcome![1]

Having considered the identity of the overcomer, it is now appropriate for us to take a closer look at the rewards promised to the overcomers. These rewards are spelled out in the letters to the seven churches in the book of the Revelation of Jesus Christ.

1. THE TREE OF LIFE

The first church our Lord addresses is the church at Ephesus. He points out that the believers in Ephesus have kept their first beliefs but left their first love. They are sound in doctrine but sick in devotion.

Is that you? Are you sound in doctrine but sick in devotion? Have you fallen into cold orthodoxy? Are your dispensations all right and your dispositions all wrong? Are you legalizing others instead of loving others? Are you passionate and on fire for Christ, or are you only passionate and on fire for yourself?

The Great Physician's prescription is three-fold:

- Remember from where you've fallen;
- Repent of wrong loves;
- Return your love to Jesus Christ.

To the believers who follow this challenge and overcome this sick condition, the Lord promises the privilege of eating of the tree of life, saying, *"To him who overcomes I will give to eat from the tree of life, which is in the midst of the Paradise of God"* (Rev. 2:7).

William Hendriksen comments on this promise:

> The expression, "to him that overcomes," means "to the conqueror." It is the same word used in 6:2: "and he came forth conquering and to conquer." The conqueror is the man who fights against sin, the devil, and his whole dominion, and in his love for Christ perseveres to the very end. To such a conqueror is promised something better than the food offered to the idols, which the heathen at their licentious festivals probably tried to tempt church members. The conqueror would be given to eat of the tree of life . . .[2]

What is the tree of life? This term is first found in Genesis 3:22 and 24. There we discover that it had qualities that would sustain life and that Adam and Eve were cut off from the tree of life after they sinned. The only other uses of this phrase in the Old Testament are found in the book of Proverbs. Solomon tells us that wisdom is a tree of life to those who take hold of her (3:18); the fruit of the righteous is a tree of life (11:30); a desire fulfilled is a tree of life (13:12); and a healing tongue is a tree of life (15:4). These phrases all indicate that the tree of life is the result of a life that is lived skillfully in the fear of the Lord and in fellowship with the Lord. This corresponds with the meaning of the tree of life in the book of Revelation. There we see that the tree of life is granted as a reward to those believers who walk in fellowship with the Lord and keep the commandments of the Lord.

Leon Morris speaks of the tree of life as a special reward for the believer who, in obedience to Christ, is a triumphant overcomer:

> To the man who perseveres through to final victory Christ says He will give to eat of the tree of life (Rev. 22:2, 14, 19). After Adam's sin the way to the tree of life was cut off and guarded by cherubim (Gen. 3:24). Now it is given by Christ to His triumphant follower. But it is not to be taken for granted. Only some have the right to it (Rev. 22:14), and it may be taken away. (Rev. 22:19)[3]

The meaning of the "tree of life" in Revelation 2:7 can best be understood in the light of the three other uses of this phrase in the book of Revelation. The tree of life is referred to in Revelation 22:2, 14-19.

First, God reveals a phenomenal picture of the New Heaven, the New Earth, and the New Jerusalem in Revelation 21 and 22. In Revelation 22:1-2, John describes the tree of life as a literal tree that bears literal fruit. John writes:

> And he showed me a pure river of water of life, clear as crystal, proceeding from the throne of God and of the Lamb. In the middle of its street, and on either side of the river, was the tree of life, which bore twelve fruits, each tree yielding its fruit every month. The leaves of the tree were for the healing of the nations.

Next, in Revelation 22:14, John points out that the right to eat of the tree of life is reserved for those who are keeping the commandments of God:

> Blessed are those who do His commandments, that they may have the right to the tree of life, and may enter through the gates into the city.[4]

Therefore, the right to eat of the tree of life is only granted to those believers who are triumphant in their Christian life. The tree of life is a conditionally earned reward that is granted to those who have not only believed in Christ for eternal life, but have also followed Christ in the costly service of discipleship.

Finally, in Revelation 22:19, John is guided by the Holy Spirit to warn his readers that if anyone takes away from the Word of God as revealed in the book of Revelation, God will take away that person's opportunity to eat the fruit of the tree of life.

Eating in the Scripture is often used as a symbol for fellowship.[5] Consequently it is natural to understand the privilege of eating the tree of life as a symbol of the overcomer partaking in a very special fellowship with our Lord Jesus Christ throughout eternity. The privilege of eating of the tree of life means that all the possibilities of the complete and glorious life are open to the overcomer. Thus the overcomer will be granted this greater capacity to enjoy eternal life. To be granted the privilege of eating of the tree of life is to be granted unrestricted access to all that is good in the world to come.[6]

Eating the fruit from the tree of life has nothing to do with obtaining or sustaining eternal life. It has everything to do with experiencing and enjoying eternal life. The water of life, regeneration, is gifted—it is free and without cost to those who simply believe in Jesus Christ as their own personal Savior. The tree of life, reward, is granted—it is merited and awarded to those believers who overcome by doing God's commandments.

While gathered with His disciples in the Upper Room the night before He was betrayed, denied, and crucified, Jesus made this striking statement, *"He who has My commandments and keeps them, it is he who loves Me."* The manifestation of love for Christ is obedience to His commands!

The right to eat of the tree of life is a special privilege promised only to those believers who overcome by obedience to the commandments of God. To be granted the privilege of eating of the tree of life is to be granted the privilege of enjoying and experiencing access to spiritual resources not available to believers who failed to overcome.[7] Partaking of the tree of life is a precious promise and a glorious privilege for the victorious believer!

Have you left your first love? Has your love for Christ grown cold? If so, you need to remember from where you have fallen, repent of your lack of love, and return to that vital and vibrant love for Christ. Draw close to Him. Look at His life. Listen to His Word. Remember His love. As a friend of mine likes to say, "If this doesn't fire you up, your wood is wet." You see, the more you know Christ, the more you will love Him. The more you love Christ, the more you will want to obey Him. Our love for Christ should cause us to be on fire for Him!

The story is told of a fireman that responded to a fire alarm at an old country church. The pastor took that opportunity to say to the fireman, "I've never seen you at church before." The fireman responded, "I've never seen your church on fire before!" Ouch! That hurts. Is that what people would say of you? Are you on fire for Christ, or have you left your first love? If you are on fire for Him, you will be granted the special privilege of eating of the tree of life! Cultivate a passionate love for Christ!

2. NO SECOND DEATH . . . THE CROWN OF LIFE

The second church our Lord addresses is the church at Smyrna. The believers at Smyrna were experiencing pressures and poverty and persecution.

Jesus predicted that things were going to get worse. Some of them would be imprisoned and executed. Jesus tells them to exercise faith instead of fear. He encourages them not to bail out or give up or back down.

To those who overcome, that is, to those who exercise faith and stay true to God, there will be a reward. As Christ said, *"Be faithful until death, and I will give you the crown of life. . . . He who overcomes shall not be hurt by the second death"* (Rev. 2:10-11).

The promise to the overcomers in Smyrna is given in two aspects:

> On one hand they shall not be hurt by the second death (Rev. 2:11).
>
> On the other hand, they shall be given a crown of life (Rev. 2:10).

How are these promises to be understood? The meaning of "the second death" must be determined before the promise can be understood.

The second death is unmistakably equated with the lake of fire (Rev. 20:6, 14; 21:8). Therefore one aspect of this promise is that the lake of fire will not hurt the overcomer. Does this imply that the Christian who fails to overcome the tests and trials of the world will be hurt by the second death? No, it does not.

This promise can best be understood if classed as a figure of speech known as "litotes."[8] Litotes is the affirmation of a fact by denying its opposite. Bullinger explains that litotes *is used for the purpose of emphasis; to call our attention, not to the smallness of the thing thus lessened, but to the importance of that which is put in contrast to it.*[9]

The lesser part of this promise is that the overcomer will not be harmed by the second death. This would be the weaker or inferior expression because it is true of all Christians, whether overcomers or not. John negates being harmed by the second death with an emphatic double negative, and thereby fixes the reader's attention on the stronger and opposite expression, *"and I will give you the crown of life."* His point is that the overcomer has far more awaiting him than a mere escape from the second death. In fact, the overcomer is going to be granted the crown of life. Reagan Benedict's explanation of the crown of life is worth quoting in full:

> The overcomer will experience life at its best and life at its fullest. He'll experience the height of life's potential. There will be special privileges and joys that he will experience that will not be available to others. As Jesus Christ once said, "I have come that you might have life and that you might have it abundantly." (Jn. 10:10)[10]

The crown of life is a richer, deeper, fuller capacity to enjoy life now and throughout eternity that is given to those believers who give their life to God. This reward has already been investigated in chapter seven.

Do you have abundant life? If you have been trying to grab life for yourself, then you don't have it. If you've been trying to get all the gusto, you don't have it. You see, the abundant life comes from giving one's life to God (Lk. 9:24). As you give your life to God you begin to experience a depth and a richness of life that is not available elsewhere. One day when you get to heaven, God will give you the crown of life, and you will enjoy a superlative experience of really living throughout eternity.

I was reminded of this truth when my wife and I drove to the base of Amicalola Falls in the Blue Ridge Mountains of Georgia. At the base all we could see was a little pool and a small creek. We could have settled for that, but it would have been rather disappointing. We chose to hike four tenths of a mile up a trail along the creek. Along that trail we found some people sitting on benches beside the trail. They were not sure they were going to go on. We pressed on and came to a lookout point where we could see the water cascading down the rock cliffs about 300 yards on up the mountain. It was an incredible sight—well worth the four tenths of a mile hike up the side of that mountain. We could have stopped there . . . many people did. Most turned around and went back down the mountain. Sharon and I chose to press on—we climbed some 175 feet higher up the mountain, and that brought us to a bridge that crossed the cascading waters and looked right into the face of the falls, about thirty feet in front of us. The climb was strenuous, but the view was spectacular. Once again we could have turned back and gone back to the base of the mountain. Many people did turn back. Instead, we chose to climb another 425 feet higher to the top of the mountain. Our heart rates were up, our lungs were fighting for more air, and our legs were starting to feel like rubber. We occasionally had to stop a moment to catch our breath and to rest our legs. Finally, after a tremendously steep climb, we reached the top of Amicalola Falls. We were weary, but the view was wonderful. We had expended our energy, but we were rewarded with the thrill of victory. We had reached the pinnacle, and if we had not climbed to the top, we would never have realized the true depth of the falls or the amazing beauty of the valley below.

In a similar way, we can try to grab life for ourselves by taking the easy way out, but the results will be disappointing and we will be giving up the joy of life we are trying to gain. On the other hand, we could love God enough to live our life for Him, and in doing so, we would discover a depth and a beauty that others will never experience.

Every day we have new opportunities to love God and live for God, and every day we can choose to give our life to Him and climb higher, or we can choose to turn back and take the easy way out. If we are willing to give our life to Him, sacrifice for Him, and draw close to Him, we will be rewarded with a depth of life with God, a joy of intimacy with God, and a thrill of victory with God that is beyond our imagination.

The more we invest, the greater the return. The more we sacrifice, the greater the satisfaction. A greater love for God results in a deeper intimacy with God and a greater impact for God.

Jesus used a parable of soils to teach this truth. It was a simple story about a farmer sowing grain on soil that was like roadway, soil that was rocky, soil that was thorny, and soil that was good.

The roadway pictured the heart of the unbeliever. Satan blinded his mind lest the glorious light of the gospel would shine unto him. The other three soils pictured the hearts of believers. In each of the last three soils, the seed took root. In each of the last three soils the seed came to life. In each of the last three soils there was the possibility of producing fruit. But clearly there were degrees of fruitfulness.

Jesus makes it clear, in His story of the vine and the branches, that believers could produce no fruit, some fruit, more fruit, or much fruit. The more properly our hearts are prepared, the more fruitful our lives will be. The more we give our lives to God in this life, the greater our capacity to honor Him in the next. Those who experience a depth of life and closeness to Christ now by giving their lives to God will experience a depth of life and closeness to Christ in eternity that is given only by God.

Right now you, as a believer in Jesus Christ, are determining your capacity to enjoy life and your capacity to glorify Christ throughout eternity. What are you bringing to Christ in this life? Does He just get your leftover time, your half-hearted energy, and your spare change? The more you give to Him in this life in terms of your time, your talent and your treasure, the more you will be able to enjoy eternity and glorify God!

As a believer in Christ, you'll enjoy eternal life to the fullest of your capacity. Yes, you'll be full and running over. But what will your capacity be?

How much will you be able to reflect what Jesus Christ is really like?

How much will you be able to enjoy what Jesus Christ really wants to offer?

How much will you be able to glorify God?

3. HIDDEN MANNA

The third church our Lord addresses is the church in Pergamum, the chief seat of imperial worship. Its believers were strangers and pilgrims in a crooked and perverse world.

Some of the believers in Pergamum were resisting Satan, holding fast to the name of Christ, and standing firm for the faith of Christ. Other believers in Pergamum were falling away from the faith, paying attention to deceitful spirits and doctrines of demons.

The false teachings that infiltrated this church were twofold:

- Some held to the teachings of Balaam (leading others astray in immorality and idolatry).
- Some held to the teachings of the Nicolaitans (lording over others in power and pride).

Wrong beliefs inevitably lead to wrong behavior! Some of the believers in Pergamum had accepted these false teachings. Christ makes it very clear that their friendship with these teachings has put them at enmity with Him. Christ gives them a very solemn warning:

> Repent, or else I will come to you quickly, and I will fight against them with the sword of My mouth. (Rev. 2:16)

Christ promises those who overcome these doctrinal and moral compromises two very special rewards . . . hidden manna and a white stone with a new name on it.

The first reward He promises the overcomer is that He will give him *"hidden manna"* (Rev. 2:17). In Exodus 16, manna was provided for the Israelites' physical sustenance. In John 6, Jesus Christ declares that He is the *"true manna."* Earlier in the Gospel according to John, Jesus Christ had told the disciples, *"I have food to eat that you do not know about"* (Jn. 4:32). His statement puzzled the disciples, and Jesus explained what He meant. He said, *"My food is to do the will of Him who sent me and to accomplish His work"* (Jn. 4:34).

Some of the believers in Pergamum were trying to live by bread alone instead of by the Word of God. They were not feeding on the living and abiding Word of God.

Hidden manna pictures the life-sustaining nourishment of intimacy and fellowship with Christ that comes from spending time in the Word and standing firm in the truth.

As you think about the manna, there is something that is important to notice. It was divinely produced, but it was humanly gathered. You only had the amount of manna that you gathered. If you didn't gather any, you didn't have any. Even so, these believers are promised hidden manna, the privilege of feasting on heavenly food not available to others, if they are willing to gather it.

Are you standing firm in the truth or are you being tossed to and fro by every wind of doctrine?

Are you feeding on the Word of God or are you feeding on the reasoning of relativism and the philosophy of humanism?

If you want intimacy and fellowship with Christ, you must spend time in His Word and stand firm in His truth!

4. A WHITE STONE WITH A NEW NAME

The overcomers in Pergamum were also promised *". . . a white stone, and on the stone a new name written which no one knows except him who receives it"* (Rev. 2:17).

Two things stand out in a surface look at this reward.

First of all, the name is recorded on a stone. It is not on wood, hay, stubble, or parchment, nor is it simply spoken. It is recorded on a white stone, a precious stone, as a lasting record. The nature of the reward emphasizes permanence.

Secondly, the stone is white. Isaiah uses *white* to describe the purity of a person whose sins have been forgiven (Isa. 1:18). John uses *white* to describe the holiness of Jesus Christ (Rev. 1:14). The color of the reward emphasizes purity.

This reward has puzzled Bible commentators for centuries and is subject to many plausible explanations.[11] While it is impossible to be certain of the correct interpretation of this promise, several suggestions are worth considering.

Moses Stuart suggests that:

> . . . the **conqueror** in the Christian warfare will not only be admitted to partake of the manna in the most holy place, but he will wear a diadem on which the unknown and unutterable name is inscribed. In other words: the conqueror shall be advanced to the dignity, honor, and privilege of the high priest of the sanctuary–not on earth, but in heaven. The **new name** which he shall bear in his miter shall designate him as the consecrated

> servant of the **new Regent** of the universe, to all the privileges and honors conferred upon those who held such a rank.[12]

A historical look at the white stone gives us further insight.[13]

A white stone was used as a mark of acquittal. When someone was brought to trial and was declared not guilty, he was given a white stone. These overcomers could be declared "not guilty" of the doctrinal and moral compromise creeping into their church.

A white stone was used as a token of friendship. It was known as the *tessara hospitalis.* Two friends about to part would break a white stone into two pieces. Each one would inscribe his name upon a piece and give it to his friend. That white stone served as a lasting reminder of their friendship and commitment to one another. The overcomers at Pergamum chose friendship with God over friendship with false teaching, and they will receive a white stone with a new name written on it by God.

A white stone was used as a medal of honor. It was given to honor a Roman soldier who was victorious in battle. It was given to honor a Greek athlete who was victorious in the games. This medal of honor often admitted the victor to certain feasts and entitled the victor to a triumphal entrance to his hometown. The overcomers at Pergamum were victorious in their battle against Satan. They'll be given a white stone as a medal of honor with a new name written on it.

The overcomer is declared not guilty of compromise by Christ, he is admitted to an inner circle of fellowship with Christ, and he is given a new name signifying his intimate fellowship with Christ.

Remember when Jacob's name was changed to Israel? From that time on he was closely associated with God. Remember when Saul's name was changed to Paul? From that time on he was closely associated with Jesus Christ. A name stands for all that you are. A new name could refer to a new life, a higher purpose, and a greater intimacy.

Have you guarded your heart and mind from moral and doctrinal compromise? Are you intentionally pursuing an intimate friendship with Christ? If so, you will receive a white stone with a new name.

5. AUTHORITY OVER NATIONS

The fourth church our Lord addresses is the church in Thyatira. This little band of believers was known for their love, their faith, their service, their perseverance, and their growth in good works. Yet they had one fatal flaw. They tolerated Jezebel. This false prophetess had led some of those believers into idolatry and immorality.

Christ warns of judgment on Jezebel and on those who follow her. Christ promises to give two rewards to those who overcome: *"authority over the nations"* (Rev. 2:26-27) and "*the morning star*" (Rev. 2:28).

Let's consider that first promise.

Jesus Christ was promised authority over the nations. In Psalm chapter two, verses eight and nine we read this declaration:

> Ask of Me and I will give You the nations for Your inheritance, and the ends of the earth for Your possession. You shall break them with a rod of iron; You shall dash them to pieces like a potter's vessel."

Here in this passage our Lord offers authority over the nations to the overcomers. Incredible as it seems, our Lord is going to share His authority in the kingdom age with those believers who share His humility in this age.

Jesus Christ humbled Himself, took on the form of a servant, and was obedient to the point of death. Because of His commitment and obedience, God the Father highly exalted him, and one day every knee will bow before Him. Even so, believers who overcome by their faithfulness to Christ, by their sacrifices for Christ, and in their suffering for Christ have the glorious promise of reigning with Christ. Consider these promises:

- The servants who are faithful to Christ will rule over cities (Lk. 19).
- The disciples who sacrificed for Christ will sit on thrones (Mt. 19).
- The believers who suffer with Christ will reign with Christ (Rom. 8).
- Those who endure with Christ will reign with Christ (2 Tim. 2:12).

Jesus Christ is going to rule as King of Kings and Lord of Lords. Those who are close to Him now will be close to Him then. Those who suffer for Christ now will reign with him then. These overcomers will rule and reign with Christ. They'll be like Him in their position.

Are you conforming to this world or are you being transformed by Christ? Do you understand that the wisdom that is from above is first of all pure and then peaceable? Never sacrifice purity on the altar of peace. Truth is far more important than toleration. That is a foreign concept in this world of political correctness. Stand for truth and suffer for Christ, and you will be given authority over nations!

6. THE MORNING STAR

The overcomers at Thyatira are given an additional goal to go after . . . *"the morning star"* (Rev. 2:28).

Jesus Christ testified saying, *"I am the Root and the Offspring of David, the Bright and Morning Star . . ."* (Rev. 22:16).

The reward of the morning star is not the gift of Christ, for every believer possesses Christ:

- Freely, as a gift (Rom. 6:23);
- Undeservedly, apart from works (Eph. 2:8-9);
- Eternally, from the point of redemption (1 Jn. 5:10-13).

The reward of the morning star is the privilege of being like Christ in royal splendor! Peter describes this glorious transformation in 2 Peter 1:19:

> And so we have the prophetic word confirmed, which you do well to heed as a light that shines in a dark

> place, until the day dawns and the morning star rises in your hearts.

Daniel predicts this glorious transformation with these prophetic words:

> Those who are wise shall shine like the brightness of the firmament, and those who turn many to righteousness like the stars forever and ever. (Dan. 12:3)

These two rewards are complementary:

- The reward of authority over nations is to be like Christ in His position.
- The reward of the morning star is to be like Christ in His person.

The overcomer will be granted dominion and authority like the Lord, and the overcomer will be granted glory and splendor like the Lord.

Now I don't know how this affects you, but I can tell you that this is a motivation big enough to move me. Can you even imagine radiating the glory and splendor of our Lord? What a joy it would be to be like Jesus Christ in my position and in my person! What a thrill it would be to be like Jesus Christ in my character and conduct! What a delight it would be to shine like The Bright Morning Star forever and ever. What an honor it would be to have my life bring glory and honor to God! What a fantastic opportunity lays before us . . . the hope of having our life reflect and magnify what Jesus Christ's life is really like.

It is my desire to live my life in such a way that I can say to others what Paul said to the Corinthian believers . . . "Imitate me, just as I also imitate Christ!" (1 Cor. 11:1). Paul is saying, "Just look at my life. Follow my example. Do as I do. I am seeking to become like Christ."

7. WHITE RAIMENT

The fifth church our Lord addresses is the Church in Sardis. The church of Sardis was dying. Oh, everyone around thought the church was alive, but God knew they were dead. God rebuked them for their immaturity and their impurity. On the other hand, He acknowledged that there were some believers in Sardis who had not defiled their garments. Concerning these believers, Jesus says, *"He who overcomes shall be clothed in white garments"* (Rev. 3:5).

It is obvious throughout Scripture that our garment says something about us.

- A priest wore a special kind of garment as a sign of his office.
- A garment laid on the ground for another to walk on was an indication of submission.
- A garment being ripped was a sign of great tragedy or wrongdoing being recognized.
- A garment of sackcloth and ashes was a sign of mourning and guilt.
- A garment of white was often a sign of celebration, a sign of purity, or a sign of triumph.

Jesus promises the overcomer the reward of being clothed in white. Revelation 19:7-8 gives us some very specific help in understanding this promise:

> Let us be glad and rejoice and give Him glory, for the marriage of the Lamb has come, and His bride has made herself ready. And to her it was granted to be arrayed in fine linen, clean and bright, for the fine linen is the righteous acts of the saints.

First, it should be noted that the bride clothed herself. Second, it should be noted that she clothed herself in her righteous acts.

Like Daniel, we must purpose in our heart not to defile ourselves (Dan. 1:8). A garment hanging in a store had this sign over it: "Slightly soiled, greatly reduced." God forbid that that sign could hang appropriately over our life.

At the transfiguration of Christ, that which was visible only to God was made visible to all. In a similar way, these overcomers will be honored with an outward manifestation of their righteous character and conduct.

Edward Mote put it this way,

> When He shall come with trumpet sound, O may I then in Him be found;
> Dressed in His righteousness alone, faultless to stand before the throne!

This concept has captured the heart of other songwriters as well . . .

> To him that overcomes the foe, white raiment shall be given.
> Oh to be worthy to walk with Him in white.

Has it captured your heart? It has captured mine. I am captured by His amazing love and His holy calling. Will you walk with Him in white? You will if there is a very personal, practical purity in your daily walk.

8. NAME CONFESSED BY CHRIST

The believers at Sardis also received this warning and challenge:

> He who overcomes . . . I will not blot out his name from the Book of Life; but I will confess his name before My Father and before His angels. (Rev. 3:5)

This promise, like the promise to the church of Smyrna, is a form of litotes . . . a figure of speech in which one statement is strongly negated in order to bring attention to a contrasting statement which is soundly affirmed. The negated statement is *"I will not blot out his name from the Book of Life."* The affirmed statement is *"I will confess his name before My Father and before His angels."*

First of all, the overcomer is assured that his name will not be erased from the book of life. That is the weaker statement, and is true of all believers. No believer's name will be erased from the book of life. Bennetch speaks clearly to this issue:

> The blotting out of names from the book of life calls for consideration. So far from intimating the possibility of losing personal salvation, the expression stresses the marvelous security enjoyed by the saint. Grace has gained the Christian his security—pure grace. Were salvation dependent upon works, most of the Sardian believers would surely have suffered loss. What indicates the note of grace in the present reference to the book of life is the obvious fact that Christ is addressing the overcomer. No one would question the security of the faithful overcomer, although some might doubt about the rest in Sardis. If the promise not to blot out the name is spoken to the conqueror, it must signify that even he merits everlasting condemnation. Only through divine grace can even a faithful saint reach the glory. The same grace that avails for the successful Christian then will certainly also bring the weakest saint home to God.[14]

So the overcomer's name is far above being blotted out. In fact, his name will be confessed by Christ before the Father and His angels. That is the expression that is being emphasized by Christ!

You see, the overcomer will not simply be present in heaven; he will be praised in heaven. The overcomer has far more awaiting him than personal admission into God's eternal abode; he will receive public recognition in God's eternal abode. Jesus will gladly acknowledge the overcomer before His Father in heaven.

This same truth is taught by the Lord Jesus Christ in Matthew 10:32-33, where He says:

> Therefore whoever confesses Me before men, him I will also confess before My Father who is in heaven. But whoever denies Me before men, him I will also deny before My Father who is in heaven.

Actually, the Scriptures are very clear. If we are ashamed of Christ, He'll be ashamed of us. If we refuse to honor Christ on earth, He'll refuse to honor us in heaven. If we publicly identify with Christ on earth, He'll publicly identify with us in heaven.[15]

> What will it be for you?
> A name simply written or a name graciously spoken?
> A person who is ashamed or a person who is acknowledged?
> A name sadly admitted, or a name gladly announced?

What a tremendous reward it will be to know that you have been an honor to Christ! What a fantastic reward it will be to have Christ honor you! What a marvelous joy it will be to know that Christ is pleased with you.

9. A PILLAR IN THE TEMPLE OF GOD

The sixth church our Lord addresses is the church in Philadelphia. The believers in Philadelphia have a little power and a lot of perseverance.

Satanic opposition to the church in Philadelphia was very powerful. The believers in Philadelphia were severely tempted to disobey God's Word and to deny God's name.

The battle was raging. Some would succumb to the pressure and persecution. Others would draw on Christ's power and overcome. To the overcomer in the church in Philadelphia, the Lord says:

> He who overcomes, I will make him a pillar in the temple of My God, and he shall go out no more. I will write on him the name of My God, and the name of the city of My God, the New Jerusalem, which comes down out of heaven from My God. And I will write on him My new name. (Rev. 3:12)

This overcomer will be a pillar in the temple of God. What does that mean? According to Merrill Tenney, this is one of a large number of symbols in the book of Revelation that are either novel in character or else unexplained by their context.[16]

In order to understand this phrase, we must look back at its use in other places in the New Testament. The Greek term for "pillar" is used four times in the New Testament, and every single reference is metaphorical.[17] Therefore it is most natural to take it metaphorically in this passage as well. Since the term for pillar is metaphorical, it follows that the term for temple would also be metaphorical. This interpretation is supported by the prophetic word in Revelation 21:11, which tells us that John saw no temple in the New Jerusalem because the Lord and the Lamb were the temple. Throughout the New Testament there are references to Christians as parts of a spiritual temple of which Jesus Christ is the Chief

Cornerstone.[18] In Galatians 2:9, Paul refers to Peter, James, and John as "pillars." Why would they be considered pillars? Peter, James, and John were chosen by Christ, taught by Christ, and followers of Christ. They were with Christ more than anyone else was. They were His closest associates. They could be depended on as representatives of Christ.

In First Timothy 3:15, Paul refers to the church as the pillar and support of the truth. A pillar is a symbol of stability and support. Apparently the believers in Philadelphia who stood for God's name instead of denying it were being pillars of truth!

Commenting on this promise, Theodore Epp very simply and forthrightly says:

> The overcomer is the one who surmounts difficulties, conquers foes, subdues enemies—in short is victorious here in this life over the enemies of God and the Bible.
>
> The promise to the overcomer of being made a pillar in the temple of God is without doubt figurative language. As someone pointed out, in the New Jerusalem, the Lord will be the temple. And so the suggestion is made that in Christ the overcomers will be pillars of strength in Him. So one day we shall be found in the New Jerusalem, standing as pillars in the radiant glory of His presence which shall not only rest upon us but also shine forth from us.[19]

To be called a pillar is to be recognized as one who is stable and supportive and trustworthy. It is a picture of one who has fought the good fight, finished the course, and kept the faith.

It is a picture of one who, in today's words, "kept on keeping on!"

The overcomer will be recognized as a pillar in the temple of God. The overcomer will have a prominent place in the kingdom, and he will never be removed from that place of prominence.

To have a name written upon you is a mark of identification. The overcomer will be identified as a close associate of God the Father, the Holy City, and God the Son.

Are you a pillar? Are you someone upon whom God can depend? Are you upholding the truth? Are you supporting the church? Are you closely identified with Christ? Are you a close associate of His? If you are, it is not an accident. You have made a commitment. You have drawn on His power. You have drawn close to Christ. You have become like Christ.

William Longstaff challenges us with these words:

Take time to be holy; speak oft with thy Lord;
Abide in Him always, and feed on His Word.
Make friends of God's children; help those who are weak
Forgetting in nothing His blessing to seek.

Take time to be holy, the world rushes on;
Spend much time in secret with Jesus alone
By looking to Jesus, like Him thou shalt be;
Thy friends in thy conduct His likeness shall see.

Take time to be holy, let Him be thy guide,
And run not before Him whatever betides;
In joy or in sorrow still follow thy Lord,
And looking to Jesus, still trust in his Word.

> Take time to be holy, be calm in thy soul;
> Each thought and each motive beneath His control;
> Thus led by His Spirit to fountains of love,
> Thou soon shalt be fitted for service above.

10. SEATED WITH CHRIST

The seventh (and last) church the Lord addresses is the church in Laodicea. This church was so sick it made Christ sick. This was the Church of the Upper Crust. They said, *"I am rich, have become wealthy, and have need of nothing"* (Rev. 3:17). Christ tells them, *". . . you do not know that you are wretched and miserable and poor and blind and naked"* (Rev. 3:17).

This church desperately needed to repent and renew their walk with Christ. To those who would be faithful, to those who would overcome, Christ promised:

> I will grant him to sit down with Me on My throne as I also overcame and sat down with My Father on His throne. (Rev. 3:21)

Wow! What a privilege . . . to be seated with Christ on His throne! How could this happen? What do we have to do? We are to overcome as He overcame. How did Christ overcome?

First, there was an unswerving commitment to do the will of God (Heb. 10:7; Jn. 4:24).

Second, there was an unwavering trust in the care of God (1 Pet. 2:21-25).

Walter Scott asks this same question, and his answer is worth quoting:

> How did Jesus reach His Father's throne and sit down with Him in that exalted seat? Not by inherent right only! But by His life of patience and death for His Father's glory. The conqueror's path lies open to us. His example is our cheer. His footprints our guide-marks.[20]

Just for a moment let's consider the temptation of Jesus in Matthew 4:8-10:

> Again the devil took him up on an exceedingly high mountain, and showed Him all the kingdoms of the world and their glory, and he said to Him, "All these things I will give You if You will fall down and worship me."
> Then Jesus said to him, "Away with you, Satan! For it is written, 'You shall worship the Lord your God, and Him only shall you serve.'"

Satan was saying, "Spare yourself. Sure you want to rule and reign. Sure you want the love and loyalty of all these people. But do it the easy way. Do it without the cross. Do it without the suffering. Do it without the rejection. Do it without the persecution. Just let me give it to you. Spare yourself."

Jesus did not take Satan's offer. Jesus was committed to God's will. He would only worship Him. Jesus was entrusting Himself to God's care. He would lay down His life.

Now Satan is offering you the same thing. "Spare yourself! Take what you want! Live life for yourself!"

Many believers do that. They place ego on the throne of their life. Jesus is shoved over into a convenient corner. Like the Laodicean believers, they live a life that is wretched and miserable and poor and blind and naked. But they don't know it! They are bogged down in the mire of mediocrity. They have settled for status quo. President Ronald Reagan once said, "*Status Quo* is Latin for 'the mess we're in.'"

Jesus was not only pushed off the throne, but He was shoved out of the throne room of these believers' lives. Their lives were lukewarm and nauseating to the Lord.

In this letter we see Jesus Christ standing at the door knocking. He wants to come in. He wants to dine with these believers. He longs for their fellowship. But it will not happen! Not until they repent!

If they repent and renew their love and fellowship with Christ, they will overcome the ignorance, the apathy, and the lukewarmness that have been destroying them. If they overcome, they will be given the privilege of reigning with Christ!

I want to ask you a personal question. Has apathy crept into your spiritual life? Have you shoved Christ aside and put self on the throne of your life?

If so, I want to challenge you to repent. I want to challenge you to re-admit Christ to the throne room of your life. Give Him the place that He alone deserves . . . the place of lordship and leadership. If you give Him the throne of your life now, He'll share His throne with you in eternity! And what a difference He will make in your life right now:

Replacing lukewarmness with fire.
    Replacing selfishness with sacrifice.

Replacing apathy with conviction.
Replacing ignorance with intimacy.

Don't live for yourself, live for your Savior! Don't take the easy way out—make a commitment. This promise has to do with throne rights. According to Romans 8:16-17, believers are joint heirs with Christ if they suffer with Him.

When David went to the cave of Adullam, he was being persecuted, rejected, and excluded by King Saul and his army. But there was a band of men who gathered around him who accepted him and befriended him: a band of men who were discontented, discouraged, and indebted. They became David's comrades. They became his companions. As for raw material, they were sorry; but with regard to their final outcome, they were super!

Those miserable men became mighty men. And when the day came that David was crowned King, they were with him. Because they were his companions in his rejection, they were also his companions in his reign. They ruled and reigned with David as his mighty men.

In a similar fashion, when Christ comes back, there are going to be those who have accepted being His companions in this world, His companions in suffering and in rejection and in persecution. Those very people will be His companions when He comes back to rule and reign and rejoice! Roles and ranks in heaven will be distinct but just. They will be distinct but appropriate.

I attended a wedding recently, and I noticed at the wedding that there were certain people that were closer to the bride and groom than others. There was the best man, the maid of honor, the bridesmaids, and the groomsmen.

When we sat down at the marriage supper, again those same people were closer to the bride and groom than others. But no one complained, because it was their rightful place.

In the same way, when Jesus Christ comes back as King of Kings and Lord of Lords, and we sit down for the marriage supper of the Lamb, there will be those who will be closer to Him than others. But that's going to be okay. It will please everyone, because it will be their rightful place. They will be where they belong, I will be where I belong, and you will be where you belong.

Pause for a moment and give this some thought. You and I need to ask ourselves some probing questions. *Where will I belong? What am I settling for? Am I a close associate of Christ's?*

Comrades in days of rejection will be co-regents in the days of reign.[21]

There will be tribulation now, but the King is coming.

There will be rejection now, but the King is coming.

There will be persecution now, but the King is coming.

Take heart! Look up! Exercise faith! Stay close! Perhaps these words from John Yates will be of encouragement to you:

Encamped along the hills of life,
        Ye Christian soldiers rise.
And press the battle ere the night
        Shall veil the glowing skies.
Against the foe unveiled below,
        Let all our strength be hurled.
Faith is the victory, we know,
        That overcomes the world.
To him that overcomes the foe,
        White raiment shall be given.

Before the angels he shall know
    His name confessed in heaven.
Then onward from the hill of light,
    Our hearts with love aflame,
We'll vanquish all the hosts of night
    In Jesus' conquering name.

Faith is the victory! Faith is the victory!
Faith is the victory that overcomes the world!

Study Guide – Chapter 9

"Satan tries to steal our faith, kill our hope, and destroy our love."
—Harlan D. Betz: *Setting the Stage for Eternity*

1. The tree of life. Rev. 2:7.

"The tree of life is a result of a life that is lived skillfully in the fear of the Lord and in fellowship with the Lord."
—Harlan D. Betz: Setting the Stage for Eternity

How is wisdom a tree of life?
How is the fruit of righteousness a tree of life?
How is a desire fulfilled a tree of life?
How is a healing tongue a tree of life?

2. The crown of life. Rev. 2:10-11.

"The crown of life is a richer, deeper, fuller capacity to enjoy life now and throughout eternity that is given to those believers who give their lives to God."
—Harlan D. Betz: *Setting the Stage for Eternity*

Describe an experience where you gave up something for the sake of the Lord, and found yourself receiving far more than you gave up.

3. The hidden manna. Rev. 2:17.

"Hidden manna pictures the life-sustaining nourishment of intimacy and fellowship with Christ that comes from spending time in the Word and standing firm in the truth."
—Harlan D. Betz: *Setting the Stage for Eternity*

Read Matthew 4:4 . . . What are you feeding on?
Read John 4:32-34 . . . What was Jesus' food?

4. The white stone with a new name. Rev. 2:17.

"The overcomer is declared not guilty of compromise by the Lord, he is admitted to an inner circle of fellowship with the Lord, and he is given a new name signifying his intimate fellowship with the Lord."

—Harlan D. Betz: *Setting the Stage for Eternity*

What areas of moral and doctrinal compromise are creeping into today's church?

What can we do in order to cultivate a closer friendship with the Lord?

5. Authority over nations. Rev. 2:26-27.

"Our Lord is going to share His authority in the kingdom age with those who share His humility in this age."

—Harlan D. Betz: *Setting the Stage for Eternity*

Discuss the promise of Christ in Matthew 19:27-30.

6. The morning star. Rev. 2:28.

"The reward of the morning star is the privilege of radiating the glory and splendor of our Lord!"

—Harlan D. Betz: *Setting the Stage for Eternity*

List some ways that you could lead someone to righteousness. Dan. 12:3.

7. White raiment. Rev. 3:5.

The overcomer will be clothed in his righteous acts.

"Like Daniel, we must purpose in our heart not to defile ourselves."

—Harlan D. Betz: *Setting the Stage for Eternity*

Our garment says something about us. Which of the following should be appropriate for a believer and why?

A sign of priesthood.
A sign of submission.
A sign of mourning over sin.
A sign of celebration.
A sign of purity.
A sign of triumph.

8. Name confessed in heaven. Rev. 3:5.

"The overcomer has far more awaiting him than personal admission into God's personal abode; he will receive public recognition in God's eternal abode. Jesus will gladly acknowledge the overcomer before His Father in heaven."

—Harlan D. Betz: *Setting the Stage for Eternity*

Read Matthew 10:32-33.

Consider carefully the possibilities. What will it be for you?

A name graciously spoken or a name simply written.
A time to be acknowledged or a time to be ashamed.
A name gladly announced or a name sadly admitted.

9. Pillar in the temple. Rev. 3:12.

"To be called a pillar is to be recognized as one who is stable, supportive, and trustworthy."

—Harlan D. Betz: *Setting the Stage for Eternity*

Think of some people who have been pillars in your life.

Think of some people who have been pillars in your church.

Are there some steps you could take to become a pillar in your church?

10. Seated with Christ. Rev. 3:21.

"If you'll give Christ the throne of your life now, He'll share His throne with you in eternity!"

—Harlan D. Betz: *Setting the Stage for Eternity*

How has ignorance, apathy, and lukewarmness infiltrated our churches today?

What would it mean to re-admit Jesus to the throne room of our life?

What can you do to stoke the fire of love for Christ in your heart?

---

[1] Harlan D. Betz, "The Nature of Rewards at the Judgment Seat of Christ." (unpublished Th.M. thesis, Dallas Theological Seminary, Dallas, Texas, 1974), 37-38. It seems best to understand the term *o nikon*_(the overcomer) as a technical term for the believer who in walking by faith is victorious over the world, the flesh, and the devil.

[2] William Hendriksen, *More than Conquerors* (Grand Rapids, Michigan: Baker Book House, 1940), p. 63.

[3] Leon Morris, *The Revelation of St. John* (Grand Rapids, Michigan: William B. Eerdmans Publishing Company, 1969), p. 62.

[4] The reading "those who do His commandments" is favored by a concurrence of all The Majority Text subgroups and the *1825 Oxford Textus Receptus*, and is accepted as the original reading as opposed to the reading "those who wash their robes," which is supported by Codex Sinaiticus, Codex Alexandrinus, and Codex Ephraemi Rescriptus. Zane Hodges and Arthur Farstad, *The Greek New Testament According to the Majority Text* (Nashville: Thomas Nelson Publishers, 1982), p. 799. H. C. Hoskier, *Concerning the Text of the Apocalypse* (London: Bernard Quartich, Ltd., 1929), II, 635-636, notes that the reading adopted above is supported by close to two hundred manuscripts; by Syrian, Armenian, Arabic versions, and the Old Latin manuscript Gigas; and by patristic evidence of Tertullian and Cyprian, both of whom antedate Codex Sinaiticus and Codex Alexandrinus. Thus the evidence for this reading is both widespread and ancient.

[5] Arndt and Gingrich, *Greek-English Lexicon*, p. 506-507. *Meros* should be translated here as "share." It refers to one's share, one's place, one's fellowship. This same term is used in John 13:8, Revelation 3:20. 21:8; 22:14.

[6] James Orr, gen. ed., *The International Standard Bible Encyclopedia* (Grand Rapids, Michigan: Wm. B. Eerdmans Publishing Co., 1960), V, 3010.

[7] John uses *didwmi* with the infinitive in 2:2, 17, 28, 3:21, and this phrase is appropriately translated "to grant." According to John Peter Lange, *Revelation*, as noted by Benedict, "The Use of NIKAW," p. 41. *Didwmi* with the infinitive means "to grant or authorize," not simply "to give." This reward is not bestowed without merit. It is a privilege that is granted because it has been earned.

[8] *Webster's New World Dictionary of the American Language* (New York: The World Publishing Company, 1966), p. 856. *Litotes: "a figure of speech in which something is expressed by a negation of the contrary. Examples: not a few (meaning "many"), no rare occurrence (meaning "a frequent occurrence")."*

[9] E. W. Bullinger, *Figures of Speech Used in the Bible* (Grand Rapids, Michigan: Baker Book House, 1968), p.155. Litotes is *A belittling of one thing to magnify another*. The affirmation of a fact by denying its opposite.

---

[10] Reagan Benedict, "The Use of Nikao," (unpublished Th.M. thesis, Dallas Theological Seminary, Dallas, Texas, 1966), pp. 9-10.
[11] Leon Morris, *The Revelation of St. John* (Grand Rapids, Michigan: William B. Eerdmans Publishing Company, 1969), p. 62. Morris suggests that there are at least seven plausible explanations.
[12] Moses Stuart, "The White Stone of the Apocalypse," *Bibliotheca Sacra*, (1843), 476-477.
[13] G. Campbell Morgan, *A First Century Message to Twentieth Century Christians* (Grand Rapids, Michigan: Baker Book House, 1980), pp. 104-106. The meaning of the white stone and the new name are also discussed by William Ramsay in *The Letters to the Seven Churches* (Grand Rapids, Michigan: Baker Book House, 1979), pp. 302-308.
[14] John H. Bennetch, "The Grace of the Lord Jesus Christ for the Seven Churches of the Apocalypse," *Bibliotheca Sacra*, XCVI (July-September, 1939), 358.
[15] This same interpretation is brought out in C. H. Lang, *The Revelation of Jesus Christ* (London: Oliphants, 1945), pp. 104-105. It is based upon the fact that Matthew 10:24-29, Luke 12:8-9, and 2 Timothy 2:11-13, like Revelation 3:5 are not promises of regeneration, but are promises of reward. They deal not with coming to Christ for the gift of justification, but with following after Him for growth in sanctification. It is essential to distinguish these two concepts!
[16] Merrill C. Tenney, *Interpreting Revelation* (Grand Rapids, Michigan: Wm. B. Eerdmans Publishing Company, 1957), p.189-190.
[17] Galatians 2:9; 1 Timothy 3:15; Revelation 3:12; 10:1.
[18] 1 Corinthians 3:16-17; 2 Corinthians 6:16; Ephesians 2:19-22; 1 Peter 2:4-5.
[19] Epp, *Revelation*, I, 201-211.
[20] Walter Scott, *Exposition of the Revelation of Jesus Christ* (London: Pickering & Inglis Ltd., n.d.), p.115. I would encourage a careful study of Philippians 2:1-11 and Matthew 20:20-29 when considering throne rights. Interestingly, in this passage the promise is not to sit on other thrones, but to sit with Christ on His throne!
[21] I highly recommend Jody Dillow's book, *The Reign of the Servant Kings.*

CHAPTER 10

THE FRUIT OF FAITHFULNESS

A miser sold all his valuable possessions and made an ingot of the gold that he got for them. He buried the gold in a special hiding place. Every day he would sneak out to the burial place and gloat over his treasure.

A laborer watched him sneaking around and guessed his secret. One night the laborer dug up the gold and took it for himself. When the miser came back, he found the hole was empty and the gold was gone. He tore his clothes in lament, he cried out in grief, and he fell on the ground in despair.

A passerby saw him and asked the reason for his grief. After the miser explained his sorrow, the passerby said, "Do not be downcast sir. Even when you had the gold, you might as well not have had it. Take a stone instead; put it in the earth, and imagine you have the gold there. It will serve the same purpose, for as far as I can see, even when you had it, you did not use it!"

He who has ears to hear, let him hear what the passerby said to the miser. For Christ teaches that same truth in a parable. **He alone possesses who uses and enjoys his possessions![1]**

Tremendous resources, marvelous opportunities, and fantastic privileges are made available to all who believe in Jesus Christ! The promises of God, the privilege of prayer, and the power of the Spirit are all entrusted to believers. But he alone possesses who uses and enjoys his possessions.

Time, talents, and treasures are entrusted to all believers. But he alone possesses who uses and enjoys his possessions. Good gifts and good news are entrusted to all believers. But he alone possesses who uses and enjoys his possessions. Unfortunately, too many Christians are not good stewards. Someone has said that if Jesus were to speak to the typical church in America today, he would be speaking to the multitude that loafs and fishes. Unfortunately, that is true in far too many churches.

The choice is up to each individual believer . . .

Will you appropriate or vegetate?
    Will you develop or atrophy?

Will you invest or ignore?
Will you be faithful or idle?

Jesus Christ speaks clearly on this issue in Luke 19. This parable reveals the fruit of faithfulness.[2]

First, we must reconstruct the setting.

Jesus was passing through Jericho. This city was famous because of its capture, which was totally by the grace of God through faith. While in Jericho Jesus went to the house of Zaccheus. Zaccheus was converted just as Jericho was conquered . . . by grace through faith. Jesus then speaks, probably from Zaccheus' courtyard, and the audience is divided. On the one hand there are antagonistic grumblers:

> But when they saw it, they all complained, saying, "He has gone to be the guest with a man who is a sinner." (Lk. 19:7)

On the other hand, there are enthusiastic followers:

> Now as they heard these things, He spoke another parable, because He was near Jerusalem and because they thought the kingdom of God would appear immediately. (Lk. 19:11)

Next, we should consider the significance.

What is a parable? A parable is a story drawn from the physical realm that teaches a truth in the spiritual realm. A parable is a simple story concerning everyday life that contains a profound truth concerning eternal life. A parable is an earthly story with a surface meaning containing a spiritual truth with a deeper meaning. Why did Jesus use this parable?

First, it was an act of mercy. He used the parable to avoid greater judgment for the unbelievers. They had already rejected Christ. They were already condemned. At this point, greater knowledge for them just meant greater judgment (Mt. 13:10-17).

Secondly, it was a word of challenge. He used this parable to give greater understanding among the believers. He wanted to let his followers know that the kingdom would not be set up immediately. Those who follow Him should be faithful until He comes, and they should live in the light of His coming.

Thirdly, it was a word of warning. He used this parable to teach the people that only those who are rightly related to Him will get into His kingdom. The institution of the kingdom will bring a spiritual judgment and a test of faithfulness.

Now the parable begins, and it has three basic parts: 1) the supreme responsibility, 2) the sovereign reckoning, and 3) the sobering results. Let's examine these as Christ presents them.

THE SUPREME RESPONSIBILITY

> Therefore He said, "A certain nobleman went into a far country to receive for himself a kingdom and to return. So he called ten of his servants, delivered to them ten minas, and said to them, 'Do business till I come.'
>
> But his citizens hated him, and sent a delegation after him saying, 'We will not have this man to reign over us.'" (Lk. 19:12-14)

Three figures are presented in these three paragraphs. They are fairly easy to identify.

1. The nobleman represents Jesus Christ.

The journey to a far country is His ascension to Heaven. The receiving of a kingdom is His reinstatement to the position of glory and honor which He willingly laid aside at the incarnation and the reward of exaltation and rulership over the entire universe for His suffering and death and victory over sin. The return is a reference to Christ's Second Coming to earth to rule and reign as Lord of lords and King of kings.

2. The servants represent believers in Christ.

They have a personal relationship with the nobleman. They accept him as heir to the throne. They willingly receive responsibilities from him. They are each given equal responsibilities—one *mina.* "A mina was a Greek coin worth 100 drachmas, the drachma being a laborer's daily wage."[3] This could picture any stewardship that believers have in common. All believers have a life to live, opportunities to use, and relationships to develop. All believers have the good news of the gospel and the opportunity of service. The master says to his servants, *"Do business till I come."* He is instructing them to trade and make business investments with the mina.[4] Jesus Christ is challenging His servants to make the most of the entrustment He has given to them. Believers are to faithfully and actively do business until Christ returns.

3. The citizens represent unbelievers.

While the servants have a personal relationship to the nobleman, the citizens only have a physical relationship. While the servants willingly accept him, the citizens actively reject him. The citizens represent unbelievers. Unbelievers reject Christ. They refuse to have Him as their Savior.

This parable was probably very vivid in the minds of Christ's listeners because they could relate it to events they knew about. Archelaus had a palace in Jericho. It could have been visible from Zaccheus' courtyard. Archelaus was the son of Herod the Great. After his father's death, he went to Rome to have Augustus Caesar confirm his right to rule over his father's kingdom. A delegation of Jews who didn't want him to rule followed him to Rome to dispute his claim to kingship. Caesar appointed Archelaus ruler over half of his father's kingdom.[5]

How do you suppose Archelaus treated those who supported him? How do you suppose he treated those who were seditious?[6]

There was definitely a day of reckoning. And there will be for us. The servants will give account of their stewardship. The citizens will be dealt with for their rejection. Jesus spells this out in the next part of the parable.

THE SOVEREIGN RECKONING

> And so it was that when he returned, having received the kingdom, he then commanded these servants, to whom he had given the money, to be called to him, that he might know how much every man had gained by trading. (Lk. 19:15)

In verses 16 and 17, we see **the most faithful servant:**

> Then came the first, saying, "Master, your mina has earned ten minas."
>
> And he said to him, "Well done, good servant, because you were faithful in a very little, have authority over ten cities."

He increased his entrustment by ten times. He was given authority over ten cities. The cities were not given to him as a possession, for they belong to the king, but he was given the right to rule over the cities and the right to participate in the king's authority.

In verses 18 and 19 we see **a less faithful servant:**

> And the second came, saying, "Master, your mina has earned five minas."
>
> Likewise he said to him, "You also be over five cities."

He increased his entrustment by five times. He was given authority over five cities. He was faithful to a smaller degree, so he was rewarded in a smaller measure; but he was faithful! Our Lord is pointing out that there are degrees of faithfulness.

In verses 20 to 25 we see **the unfaithful servant:**

> Then another came, saying, "Master, here is your mina, which I kept put away in a handkerchief; for I feared

> you, because you are an austere man. You collect what you did not deposit, and reap what you did not sow."
>
> And he said to him, "Out of your own mouth I will judge you, you wicked servant. You knew that I was an austere man, collecting what I did not deposit and reaping what I did not sow. Why then did you not put my money in the bank, that at my coming I might have collected it with interest?"
>
> And he said to those who stood by, "Take the mina from him, and give it to him who has ten minas."
>
> But they said to him, "Master, he has ten minas."

Several things should be noted about this third servant.

First of all, he was a lazy sluggard and not a faithful steward. His entrustment was put away instead of put to work, idle instead of increasing, and neglected instead of invested.

Secondly, he was a negative steward and not a positive steward. He saw his master as rigorous, not righteous, and as exacting, not enabling. The Greek term for "exacting" *is austeros*, and means severe, austere, exacting, or strict.[7] It refers to "a man who expects to get blood out of a stone."[8]

Thirdly, he was a condemned steward and not a commended steward. His master called him a worthless servant.

Was this third servant a believer? Some commentators would say the third servant was an unbeliever because he is called worthless. But this reason must be rejected because the Bible says all believers will give an account of what they have done in the body whether those things are "good or bad."[9] The Bible also indicates that a believer's life could go up in smoke. It could be characterized by wood, hay, and stubble, and in that case he would certainly be considered a worthless servant.[10]

Some commentators would also say the third servant is an unbeliever because his entrustment was taken away. But this reason must also be rejected because the Bible indicates that a believer could lose what he has and that he could fail to receive a full reward.[11]

I believe all the servants in this parable are believers. Let me highlight three reasons why the third servant should be considered a believer:

- The third servant, like the first two servants, is called a "servant" by Christ. The citizens were called "enemies" by Christ.
- The punishment for the faithless servant was "loss of reward." The punishment for the unbelieving citizen was "loss of life!"
- The third servant enters the kingdom. The citizens don't!

For believers, there are two very distinct possibilities . . . faithfulness and rewards or unfaithfulness and disgrace. The principle for judging believers is found in verse 26:

> For I say to you, that to everyone who has (more) will be given, and from him who does not have, even what he has will be taken away from him.

The principle is clear. He alone possesses who uses and enjoys his possessions. One of life's most valuable possessions is time. God has granted believers the opportunity to serve as stewards of the time we have here on earth. This truth is captured by a poem that my Gram Betz shared with me:

> I have only just a minute,
> Only sixty seconds in it,
> Forced upon me, can't refuse it,
> Didn't seek it, didn't choose it,
> But it's up to me to use it,
> I must suffer if I lose it,
> Give account if I abuse it,
> It is only just a minute,
> But eternity is in it!

The Apostle Paul challenged the saints in Ephesus to be good stewards of their time:

> See then that you walk carefully, not as fools but as wise, redeeming the time, because the days are evil.[12]

The Apostle Paul challenged the believers in Colossae to be good stewards of their time, writing, "*Walk in wisdom toward those who are outside, redeeming the time.*"[13]

Whoever makes full use of opportunities to serve Christ will receive further opportunities to serve Christ, and will have a greater capacity to serve Him in eternity.

Now while the servants will be rewarded by the king, the citizens will be rejected by the king. Notice verse 27:

> But bring here those enemies of mine, who did not want me to reign over them, and slay them before me.

The term "but" occurs only two times in this parable.[14] In both cases, it is the last verse in the section. In both cases, it separates the servants from the citizens. In both cases, it serves to contrast the believers from the unbelievers. Verse 14 shows that while servants accept the heir to the throne, the citizens reject the heir to the throne. Verse 27 shows that while servants are rewarded and admitted to the kingdom the citizens are punished and restricted from the kingdom.

The servants' entrance is permitted because they are personally related to the master. The citizens' entrance is prohibited because they are not personally related to the master. The servants accepted the king and will be rewarded by the king.

Granted, the third servant was punished, but there is a huge difference between the stripping of a servant and the execution of a citizen. A fatal end awaits all who refuse to acknowledge Jesus Christ and accept His free gift of eternal life. The servants gained authority; the citizens got the axe.

Actually, the citizens got what they asked for. They did not want to be with the king. They do not have to be with the king. In fact, they do not get to be with the King. They had a choice to make. They made it. We have a choice to make. We will live or die with the consequences.

THE SOBERING CONCLUSION

There are three categories of people:

- Those whose entrance is blessed.
- Those whose entrance is barren.[15]
- Those whose entrance is barred.

Entrance into the kingdom is a gift by grace through faith. Inheritance in the kingdom is a reward by grace through faithfulness.

Have you trusted in Christ for eternal life? If so, you have a personal relationship with Him and your entrance is secure. You have been entrusted as a servant.

How will you answer the Master?

"Master, your mina has made ten more."

"Master, your mina made five more."

"Master, I have buried your mina."

The faithful believer's entrance will be blessed with rewards. The unfaithful believer's entrance will be barren. While a barren entrance would be sad, a barred entrance would be a tragedy. Let me remind you that entrance into the kingdom is a gift of God. If your entrance is barred, it is barred because you have not yet accepted God's offer of eternal life through Jesus Christ as payment for your sin.

In Vienna, Austria, there is a famous chapel where royal members of the Hapsburg family have been buried over the past 500 years. When a member of the family dies, he is taken to the chapel where an impressive ceremony takes place. The chaplain performs the funeral service in the palace. Then he leads the procession to the chapel for the burial. Upon arriving at the chapel, the prior of the chapel comes to the door but does not open it. Instead he cries out, "Who is there?"

When the Emperor Franz Josef was being buried, the chaplain answered, "I ask admittance for the body of Franz Josef, Emperor of Austria, King of Hungary, King of the Romans, King of Illyria." The prior spoke back through the wicket, "I know no Franz Josef, Emperor of Austria, King of Hungary, King of the Romans, King of Illyria."

Once more the chaplain knocked. Again the prior asked, "Who is there?" Again the chaplain answered, "I ask admittance for the body of Franz Josef, Emperor of Austria, King of Hungary, King of the Romans, King of Illyria." Once again the prior responded, "I know no Franz Josef, Emperor of Austria, King of Hungary, King of the Romans, King of Illyria."

The chaplain hesitated a minute, knocked a third time, and said; "I ask admittance for Franz Josef, a poor sinner." The prior immediately swung the door open and said, "Enter, Franz Josef, poor sinner."

Do you want the eternal gates to open for you? Then you must recognize your need for Christ. You must trust in Him and Him alone for forgiveness of sin and entrance to the Kingdom of God.

All believers will enter the kingdom. This is the question. *What kind of entrance will you have?* It is required of a servant that he be found faithful. We may know the most famous servants, but we don't know the most faithful servants. Only God knows, and He will reward them!

For God is not unjust (so as) to forget your work and the labor of love you have shown toward His name.

What opportunities for ministry do you possess? What treasures do you possess? What talents do you possess? He alone possesses who uses and enjoys his possessions.

One of my family's favorite summertime meals on the farm was bacon, lettuce, and tomato sandwiches. We had plenty of tomatoes and lettuce because we grew them in our own garden. But bacon was scarce because most of our hogs were sold for cash to make ends meet, and very few were ever butchered for us to eat ourselves. Consequently, we were often limited to four slices of bacon . . . about enough for two sandwiches.

On one occasion I decided to secretly hide one of my BLT sandwiches so I could pull it out and eat it in front of my brother and sister later. The thought of teasing them was delightful enough to enable me to resist eating it right away.

About a week later I heard mom shriek as she pulled back the curtain in our family room. There on the window sill was an old and cold, moldy and musty BLT sandwich. I had hidden the sandwich away, and I had forgotten to get it back out.

Not only did I miss the opportunity to tease my brother and sister, I missed the opportunity to enjoy the sandwich at all. I had just as well never had it in the first place. He alone possesses who uses and enjoys his possessions.

Do you have abilities? Invest them.
Do you have opportunities? Seize them.
Do you have gifts? Exercise them.

Let's be faithful, not slothful;
active, not passive;
and blessed, not barren!

Study Guide – Chapter 10 – Faithfulness

"He alone possesses who uses and enjoys his possessions!"
—Harlan D. Betz: *Setting the Stage for Eternity*

1. What terms come to your mind when you think of faithfulness?
   Synonyms?
   Antonyms?

"It is high time that the ideal of success should be replaced by the ideal of service." —Albert Einstein

2. What people come to your mind when you think of faithfulness?

Polycarp, at his martyrdom, was pressed by the Pro-consul to take an oath reviling Christ in order that he might be set free. Polycarp boldly replied, "Eighty and six years I have served Him, and He hath done me no wrong; how then can I blaspheme my King who saved me?"

3. Consider this quote:
   "It is, however, only by fidelity in little things that a true and constant love to God can be distinguished from a passing fervor of spirit." —Francois Fenelon: *Letters and Reflections*

4. What are some of the entrustments that God has placed under your care?
   What about your time? Psa. 90:12; Jn. 9:4; Jas. 4:13-17
   What are your spiritual gifts? Rom. 12; 1 Cor. 12, Eph. 4; 1 Pet. 4
   What are your skills and talents?

5. What are some of the opportunities God is placing before you?
   Do you have family you can minister to?
   Do you have a church family you can minister to?
   Do you have co-workers or classmates you can reach?
   Do you have acquaintances and friends who do not yet know Christ personally?

6. Discuss the meaning and merits of the following quotes:
   "Service can never become slavery to one who loves."
   —J. L. Masse
   "Each day comes bearing its gifts. Untie the ribbons."
   —Ann Shabacker
   "Opportunity is often missed because we are broadcasting when we should be tuning in." —National Safety News
   "About the only golden opportunity some men can recognize are blondes." —Maynerd Bradford
   "The reason so many people never get anywhere in life is because, when opportunity knocks, they are out in the back yard looking for four-leaf clovers."
   —Walter P. Chrysler
   The reason some people don't recognize opportunity is because it often comes disguised as hard work or as a difficult problem.

7. Discuss the options that lie before mankind:
   If a person's entrance to heaven is barred, why will it be barred?
   If a person's entrance to heaven is barren, why will it be barren?
   If a person's entrance to heaven is blessed, why will it be blessed?

8. Will your entrance be barred, barren, or blessed?
   Are there some steps you need to take?
   Is there someone you need to talk to?

---

[1] This will be demonstrated in an exposition of the parable in Luke 19:27. NB especially Luke 19:26.

[2] The parable of the laborers in the vineyard in Matthew 20:1-16 warns us not to be among the first who become last. It focuses our attention on having the right attitude. The right attitude in service . . . have you done what you've done to simply secure the reward or have you done what you've done to whole-heartedly serve the Lord? Guard against selfishness. Do you have the right attitude towards others? Do you feel a need to be the greatest, or are you happy for others who serve the Lord faithfully and are rewarded generously? Guard against envy. Do you have the right attitude toward your Master? Are you willing to trust the Lord to be faithful, just, and generous? God has the right to do what He wishes, and He will do what is right! Genuine, wholehearted service for the Lord is not simply a sacrifice, it is an investment; and God can be trusted to grant a bountiful and gracious reward (Matthew 19:27-29; cf. also Hebrews 6:10). Guard against demandingness and doubt.

[3] William Hendricksen, *New Testament Commentary: Exposition of the Gospel According to Luke* (Grand Rapids, Michigan: Baker Book House, 1978), p.859-860

[4] Moulton and Milligan, *Vocabulary of the Greek New Testament*, p. 532

[5]Josephus, *Josephus: Complete Works*, translated by William Whitson (Grand Rapids, Michigan: Kregel Publications, 1960), *The Antiquities of the Jews*, Book XVII, 366-375.

[6] Josephus, *Antiquities*, p. 375. "When Archelaus was entered on his ethnarchy, and was come into Judea, he accused Joazar the son of Boethus, of assisting the seditious, and took away the high priesthood from him, and put Eleazar his brother in his place. He also magnificently rebuilt the royal palace that had been at Jericho."

[7] Arndt and Gingrich, *Greek-English Lexicon*, p. 121.

[8] Moulton and Milligan, *Vocabulary*, p. 93.

[9] 2 Corinthians 5:9-10.

[10] 1 Corinthians 3:11-15.

[11] 2 John 8.

[12] Ephesians 5:15-16.

[13] The phrase, "Making the most of the opportunity," could be translated, "Redeeming the time!"

[14] Luke 19:14; Luke 19:27. The distinctions are clarified and charted in Appendix 9.

[15] Unfaithful believers will not hear Christ's voice saying, "Well done!" Unfaithful believers will not be honored with the privilege of ruling and reigning with Christ. Unfaithful believers will not be intimately associated with Christ. For the unfaithful believer this will be a time of disappointment, loss, and shame. This experience is variously described as being in "the darkness outside the lighted banquet hall" and as a time of profound regret described as "weeping and gnashing of teeth."

Granted, these terms are sometimes used to refer to the unregenerate in hell, but they are also used to refer to the unfaithful regenerate in the kingdom. The terms must be understood in their context! Joseph Dillow, in his book, *The Reign of the Servant Kings*, discusses this on pages 344-353. He concludes by making this comment: *"Those Christians who fail to persevere to the end, who are carnal, will experience three negatives at the future judgment: (1) a stinging rebuke (Mt. 24:45-51); (2) exclusion from the wedding banquet (Mt. 22:1-14; Mt. 25:1-13); and Millennial disinheritance (Mt. 25:14-30)."* This same concept is presented by G. H. Lang in his book *Pictures and Parables*, pp. 306-308. This same concept is also presented by Arlen Chitwood in his book, *Judgment Seat of Christ*, pp. 167-176.

CHAPTER 11

THE NATURE OF THE REWARDS

It is almost impossible to understand the future if you don't understand the past. A clear understanding of history can provide the foundation for a clear understanding of prophecy. Even so, the Apostle Paul, under the guidance of the Holy Spirit, takes his readers from history (the Olympic Games) to prophecy (the judgment seat of Christ). In so doing he is taking them from the known (in their experience) to the unknown (in his explanation).

A clear understanding of the historic nature of rewards at the Olympic Games will give us insight into the prophetic nature of rewards at the judgment seat of Christ.

HISTORY

The Isthmian games were held in Corinth, Greece, every other year. The Olympic Games were held in Olympia, Greece, every four years. In his challenge to the Corinthians, Paul refers to the games in 1 Corinthians 9:24-27:

> Do you not know that those who run in a race all run, but (only) one receives the prize? Run in such a way that you may obtain it. And everyone who competes for the prize exercises self-control in all things. Now they do it to obtain a perishable crown, but we for an imperishable crown. Therefore I run thus: not with uncertainty. Thus I fight: not as one who beats the air. But I discipline my body and bring it into subjection, lest, when I have preached to others, I myself should become disqualified.

This passage tells us three things about the victor at the games:

First, the victor must win at the cost of great personal sacrifice. *"And everyone who competes for the prize exercises self-control in all things . . . I discipline my body and bring it into subjection . . . ."*[1] The rewards must be won, and they are won at the cost of great personal sacrifice. Those athletes committed themselves to at least ten months of training. During that time they had to restrict themselves from many pleasures that other people might normally enjoy . . .

No lazy days,
No late nights,
No fatty foods,
No strong drinks.

In order to be victorious in the games, the contestant had to pay the price in terms of personal sacrifice.

Second, the victor is rewarded for his work. *"They do it to receive a perishable crown."*[2] The victor was crowned with a wreath of laurel, olive, or ivy. That wreath was like the gold medal awarded to victorious athletes in the modern Olympic Games because receiving that reward was a tremendous honor, and it brought glory and fame to the victor. The crowning was followed by celebrations, parades, media attention, and financial benefits. The victor was richly rewarded for his work.

Third, the victor is closely associated with the god that he is honoring.[3] The athletes not only prepared for the games with physical disciplines (exercise and training), but also with spiritual disciplines (prayers and sacrifices). The games were held in honor of the gods. The Olympic Games were held in honor of Zeus, the supreme god of Greek mythology. The Isthmian Games were held in honor of Poseidon, the sea-god. The Pythian Games were held in honor of Apollo, the sun-god. The victor was crowned with a wreath made from a sacred tree. The wild olive tree was sacred to Zeus, so the victors at the

Olympic Games received a wild olive wreath. The laurel tree was sacred to Poseidon, so the winners at the Isthmian games were crowned with a laurel wreath. The spruce tree was sacred to Apollo, so the winners at the Pythian Games received a spruce wreath. When the victor was crowned, the blessing of his god came upon him. When the victor was crowned, his god was honored. "To the average citizen, a victory in the Olympic games symbolized man's closest approach to the qualities of the gods."[4]

PROPHECY

I see three specific characteristics of the rewards given to athletes at the games that give us insight into the nature of the rewards that will be given to believers at the judgment seat.

Number one—the rewards must be won at the cost of great personal sacrifice. Anyone who competes in the game exercises self-control in all things. *"I run thus: not with uncertainty. Thus I fight: not as one who beats the air. But I discipline (buffet) my body and bring it into subjection."* The Apostle Paul likens the Christian life to the major events of the Games—running, boxing, and wrestling.

The running word-picture looks forward to the heavenly goal of becoming like Christ (Phil. 3:12-14). The boxing word picture looks inward to the battle with our sinful flesh (1 Cor. 9:24-27). The wrestling word picture looks outward to the enemy around us and our battle against Satan ((Eph. 6:10-13).

As a runner, are you running with endurance the race that is set before you? Are you laying aside every sin and weight?

Are you keeping your eyes fixed on Jesus? Are you becoming like Him?

As a boxer, do you buffet (read "buffet") your body or do you buffet (read "buffay") your body? Is your body honed and toned? Is your body firm and fit? Is your body disciplined and devoted? Are your physical desires characterized by holiness? Are your physical desires controlled by the Holy Spirit?

As a wrestler, are you standing firm against the schemes of the devil? Do you know his target? Do you know his strategy for your defeat? Are you finding your strength in the Lord and in the power of His might? Have you put on the full armor of God?

Rewards are won at the cost of great personal sacrifice. As many of today's athletes like to remind us—if there is no pain, there is no gain! Is your body your slave or your master? Does your body say, "Hey, I'm hungry! Feed me!"? Do you say, "Yes sir! Your wish is my command."? Do you tell your body when it can eat, or does your body tell you when it can eat? Is your body your slave or your master? If it longs for some pleasure, does it get it? If it longs for some possession, does it get it? Paul said, *"I buffet my body and bring it into subjection, lest, when I have preached to others, I myself should become disqualified."*

Jesus teaches this same truth in Matthew 16:24-27:

> Then Jesus said to His disciples, "If anyone desires to come after Me, let him deny himself, and take up his cross, and follow Me. For whoever desires to save his life will lose it, but whoever loses his life for My sake will find it. For what profit is it to a man if he gains the whole world, but loses his own soul? Or what will a

man give in exchange for his soul? For the Son of Man will come in the glory of His Father with His angels, and then He will reward each according to his works."

If you try to save your life for yourself, Jesus Christ says you will lose it. But if you lose your life for the sake of Jesus Christ, you will find it. Rewards must be won at the cost of great personal sacrifice. *"If anyone desires to come after Me,"* Jesus Christ said, *"let Him deny himself, and take up his cross, and follow Me."* We must deny the pleasures, possessions, prestige, and power that bring us closer to the world and draw us further away from Christ. We must say "no" *to selfishness* and say "yes" *to service* . . . the service of Christ. We must take up our cross and follow Him!

Many people come to Christ for regeneration. Few people follow after Him in discipleship. The challenge is to deny yourself worldly pleasures and give yourself to heavenly pursuits. The promise is that those who do this will experience life in its fullest sense—a life that is genuinely satisfying, truly abundant, and greatly rewarded. Those who humble themselves before God now will be exalted with Christ through eternity.

I like what Paul says in 2 Corinthians 4:16-17. He's talking about what happens when you take up your cross and follow Christ. He says, *"Therefore, we do not lose heart. Even though our outward man is perishing, yet the inward man is being renewed day by day! For our light affliction, which is but for a moment, is working for us a far more exceeding and eternal weight of glory."*

The trials and troubles that we face in giving up our life to God are a momentary light affliction that is not worthy to be compared to the eternal weight of glory that awaits us. The rewards are indescribable!

Yes, the rewards must be won at the cost of great personal sacrifice, but if you begin to catch a glimpse of the glory that is awaiting you, then I think the word "sacrifice" will probably take on new meaning. Because, as Jim Elliot once said, "He is no fool who gives up what he cannot keep to gain what he cannot lose."[5]

We can't keep these things that we see—these material possessions, positions, and the pleasures that we might temporarily enjoy. We can't keep those. And he is no fool who gives up what he cannot keep in order to gain what he cannot lose. We cannot lose those things that are eternal—becoming like Christ in your character, becoming like Christ in your conduct, leading others to a personal faith in Christ, building Jesus Christ into the lives of others, maturing spiritually. We can't lose those things.

Where is your time being invested—in things that are temporary or eternal? Where are your skills being invested—in things that are temporary or eternal? Where is your money being invested—in things that are temporary or eternal? Where is your life being invested—in things that are temporary or eternal? It may mean sacrifice, but the rewards are worth it. The rewards must be won at the cost of great personal sacrifice!

Number two—the rewards will be according to our work. In 2 Corinthians 5:9-10 Paul says,

> Therefore, we make it our aim, whether present or absent, to be well pleasing to Him. For we must all appear before the Judgment Seat of Christ, that each one may receive the things done in the body, according to what he has done, whether good or bad.

God's Word makes it very clear that while we are not given eternal life because of our good works, we are given eternal life so we can do good works[6] (Eph. 2:8-10). God's Word also makes it very clear that God will remember our works and reward us accordingly. Take a look at these declarations:

"For God is not unjust." (Heb. 6:10)
"For we must all appear." (2 Cor. 5:10)
"Do not be deceived." (Gal. 6:7)

Notice the declaration in 1 Corinthians 3:13-15. The work remains! The reward of a lasting work is that it is lasting!

- Those who become righteous because of the love of Christ's return will receive the crown of righteousness (2 Tim. 4:8).
- Those who share in Christ's suffering here will share in Christ's glory hereafter (Rom. 8:16-18).
- Those who have the joy of building Christ into others' lives in time will have the joy of that impact in eternity (1 Thess. 2:19-20).

- Those who are willing to die to self and live for Christ now, will have the crowning experience of life forever (Jas. 1:12).
- Those who bring the light of the gospel to men in this life will shine like stars for ever and ever (Dan. 2:3).

Yes, the rewards Christ will unveil at the judgment seat of Christ will be according to our work. And those works, to be of any value, must be done for the glory of God the Father, out of a love for God the Son, and in the power of God the Spirit!

Number three—the rewards will be related to our likeness to Christ. The Bible says, *"A disciple, when he is fully trained, will be like his teacher."*[7] Jesus Christ is our teacher. We don't want to simply come to Him for regeneration; we want to follow after Him in discipleship. And a disciple, when he is fully trained, will be like his teacher. Isn't that an exciting concept? This hope was evident in Paul's life and ministry. Look carefully at his words:

> According to my earnest expectation and hope that in nothing I shall be ashamed, but with all boldness, as always, so now also Christ will be magnified in my body, whether by life or by death."[8]

What is God's desire for you? The first part of Romans 8:28 is quoted over and over. *"We know that all things work together for good."* But that great comfort is qualified in the same verse: "*We know that all things work together for good to those who love God, to those who are the called according to His purpose.*" What is His purpose? The very next verse tells us. It is that we might be . . . "*conformed to the image of His Son.*"

His Son learned obedience through suffering.

His Son set an example for us.

His Son gave His life for others.

His Son accomplished the work God had for Him to do.

Consider Ephesians 1:18 for a moment. Here is Paul's prayer, and it's a prayer that I've been praying for years. I pray that the eyes of your heart may be enlightened, "*that you may know what is the hope of His calling.*"

What is the hope of His calling? It is Christ in you, the hope of glory.[9] The hope of His calling is believers being changed from glory unto glory, even unto the image of Christ![10] The hope of His calling is to have the character of Christ revealed in and through our lives.

Now, notice the second phrase: I pray that you may know "*what are the riches of the glory of His inheritance in the saints.*" Whose inheritance? His inheritance. The term "His" refers to Christ! Think about it—*His inheritance in the saints.* Do you know the riches of the glory of Christ's inheritance? You! You are His inheritance. The rich inheritance of Christ is believers who have become like Him. His inheritance is believers who have become trophies of His grace. His inheritance is believers who have become reflections of His image. You are the riches of the glory of His inheritance!

You, as a believer, are the bride of Christ. The more you love Him, the more you will live for Him. The more you live for Him, the more you will look like Him. The more you look like Him, the richer His inheritance will be! That's the motivation for Christ-like living. That's what the judgment seat of Christ is all about!

The judgment seat of Christ is designed to reveal how much we've become like Him, and to reveal just how rich His inheritance has really become.

It is our privilege to give Jesus Christ a rich inheritance!

It is our privilege to be a rich inheritance!

Yes, the rewards will be related to our likeness to Christ.

Now notice the third phrase: I pray that you may know *"what is the exceeding greatness of His power toward us who believe!"* God's power is the key. How can we fulfill His calling and press toward the prize of becoming like Jesus Christ? By God's grace and power. How can we be victorious over sin and Satan? By God's grace and power. How can we become a rich inheritance for Christ? By God's grace and power. It is not by our own strength or might or intellect. It is by the grace and power of God. We must tap into His grace and power!

THE NATURE OF THE REWARDS

Now I'd like to call your attention to three things the Bible indicates about the nature of rewards at the judgment seat of Christ.

First, the rewards are directly related to our capacity to enjoy eternal life. The Psalmist in Psalm 16:11 says, *"In Your presence is fullness of joy; at Your right hand are pleasures forevermore."* One aspect of a believer's reward at the judgment seat of Christ is an increased capacity to enjoy and experience the blessings of God. For example, the person who takes the time in this life to feed on God's Word will be given the privilege of feasting on heavenly manna. He will have the capacity to feed on heavenly food that others who are in heaven won't have the privilege of eating. Some will have the privilege of reigning with Jesus Christ, and some will not. Some will be close associates with Christ, and others will not.

Your reward is directly related to your capacity to enjoy and experience the riches and privileges of eternal life.

- The riches of divine commendation—*"Well done, good and faithful servant"* (Mt. 25:21).
- The riches of divine joy—*"enter into the joy of your Lord"* (Mt. 25:21).
- The riches of public acknowledgment by Christ—*"before My Father who is in heaven"* (Mt. 10:32).
- The riches of treasure in Heaven—*"where neither moth nor rust destroys and where thieves do not break in or steal"* (Mt. 6:20).

The privilege of ruling with Christ (2 Tim. 2:11-12), being glorified with Christ (Rom. 8:16-17), and serving Christ (Rev. 22:3).

These are phenomenal riches and fantastic privileges. The capacity to experience these riches and privileges is a reward for faithfulness in this life! Faithfulness in this life will be rewarded in the next life. Increased faithfulness increases our capacity to experience the joys and the blessings of eternal life. There will be degrees of reward. A believer could settle for entrance or earn the reward of abundant entrance (2 Pet. 1:11).

A believer could settle for joy or earn the reward of exceeding joy (1 Pet. 4:13).

F. J. Horsefield speaks about increased capabilities as a reward:

> It would rather seem to indicate that some of the redeemed will be capable of greater joy, and blessing, and service, than others . . . it is simply a question of capacity—a capacity that will have been, to a larger or smaller extent, developed by the employment of our talents here; by the opportunities of service of which we have availed ourselves; by the cultivation of the Christ-like spirit. The man who, in this life, has yielded himself unreservedly to the control of the Holy Spirit, living in the very atmosphere of fellowship with Christ, and seeking in every possible way the extension of the Kingdom of God, will thus have enlarged his capacity for the employment of the yet more perfect communion of the life to come, and will doubtless be given some form of service in the Church triumphant that none other could undertake.[11]

Second, rewards are directly related to the work that is rewarded. If you become righteous, you'll have the honor of manifesting His righteousness. If you through faithfulness in suffering bring glory to God, you'll have the wonderful privilege of reflecting Christ's glory throughout eternity. If you're involved in building Christ into the lives of others in this life, they will be a cause for rejoicing throughout eternity. If you feed on the Word of God now, you'll feast on heavenly manna then. If you suffer with Christ here, you will reign with Christ hereafter, for suffering leads to glory. If you die to self and live for Christ now, you will have an increased capacity to enjoy the divine life throughout eternity. If you publicly acknowledge Christ before men, He'll publicly acknowledge you before the angels and the Father.

C. S. Lewis, in *The Weight of Glory*, makes this statement:

> We must not be troubled . . . when they say that this promise of reward makes the Christian life a mercenary affair. There are different kinds of reward. There is the reward which has no natural connection with the things you do to earn it, and is quite foreign to the desires that ought to accompany those things. Money is not the natural reward of love; that is why we call a man a mercenary if he married a woman for the sake of her money. But marriage is the proper reward for a real lover, and he is not mercenary for desiring it...the proper rewards are not simply tacked onto the activity for which they are given, but are the activity itself in consummation.[12]

Third, the rewards will be directly related to our intimacy to Christ. The church is the bride of Christ. The intimate loving relationship between a husband and wife is a picture of the relationship between Christ and the church (Eph. 5:22-33). Jesus laid down His life for His bride. Jesus has gone to His Father's house to prepare a place for His bride. He is coming back to receive His bride unto Himself, that where He is, there we may be also (John 14:1-3). Jesus loves

His bride. His love is a realistic love. His love is a sacrificial love. His love is a purposeful love. His love is a captivating love. His love is a life-changing love. Isaac Watts once wrote: "Love so amazing, so divine, demands my life, my soul, my all!" Jesus wants to present His bride to His Father without spot or wrinkle. Satan does not want that to happen. Satan's method is deceit and his target is the mind. Just as Satan led Eve astray, even so he is seeking to lead believers' minds astray from the simplicity and purity of devotion to Christ! (2 Cor. 11:1-3).

What is the greatest command? Jesus said, "You shall love the Lord your God with all your heart, all your soul, and with all your mind!" (Mt. 22:37). We love Him because He first loved us! (1 Jn. 4:19). The love of Christ serves as a powerful motivation in our lives. As Paul said, "The love of Christ constrains me!" As Jesus said, if we love Him, we will obey Him (John 14:21). We can be obedient without loving God, but we cannot love God without being obedient! If we love Him, we will live for Him. If we love Him, we will intentionally and consciously spend time with Him. If we love Him, we will find joy in His presence. I can identify with the heart of David as he says to his Lord, *"You will show me the path of life; in Your presence is fullness of joy; at Your right hand are pleasures forevermore"* (Psa. 16:11). That verse expresses the joy of intimacy with the Almighty!

Jesus said, "A disciple, when he is fully trained, will be like his teacher" (Luke 6:40). A believer, when he is fully matured, will be like Jesus Christ! Jesus was committed to bringing glory to God the Father (J. 17:1-3). We need to be committed to bringing glory to God the Father. Jesus was committed to doing the will of God the Father (Heb. 10:5-10). We need to be committed to doing the will of God. Jesus finished the work God gave Him to do (Jn. 17:1-3). We need to finish the work God has given us to do!

We are created in Christ for good works (Eph. 2:10). God will recognize our work, remember our work, and reward us according to our work. In order for a work to be imperishable and rewardable, it must be done for the glory of God the Father, out of a love for God the Son, and in the power of God the Spirit.

"Service is the outflow of a grateful heart to the One who has redeemed us."[13] By God's grace we can become like Christ in our character and in our conduct. God rewards Christ-likeness in character with the privilege of being like Christ in our person, radiating His glory. God rewards Christ-likeness in our conduct with the privilege of being like Christ in our position, sharing His reign. Rewards will come to those who have abided in Christ—those who have been intimately associated with Christ.[14] Rewards will come to those who have tapped into the riches of His grace. We are redeemed by grace, we are matured by grace, we are used by grace, and we are rewarded by grace! The reward will be an increased opportunity to abide with Him and to share in His fellowship.

When good King Richard the Lionhearted was away, evil King John took over. Robin Hood was an intelligent man and a great warrior. He could have sided with the powerful and evil King John. He could have served King John and experienced the accompanying privileges, pleasures, and joys. He could have been banqueting, reveling, and enjoying the riches of evil King John's rule. Instead, he chose to say "No" to selfish pleasures and possessions and to fight for what was right. Therefore he was considered an outlaw during evil King John's reign. Fortunately, good King Richard came back and reclaimed the throne. Evil King John got his just recompense. King Richard the Lionhearted heard of Robin Hood's bravery and support. He not only recognized Robin Hood; he also rewarded him. Do you remember the scene? Robin Hood walks down the center aisle and walks up towards King Richard. When Robin Hood gets in front of the King he kneels down, and King Richard honors him and exalts him with knighthood. The crowd cheers because they know that it is Robin Hood's rightful reward. From that time on, Robin Hood is a close confidante and faithful friend of Richard the Lionhearted.

Some day soon Jesus Christ is going to return, and there will be a day of reckoning at the judgment seat of Christ. You will come before Him for judgment. What will it be like for you? Will His judgment reveal that you fought the good fight, kept the faith, and finished the course? Will His judgment reveal that you manifested His character and magnified His name? Will His judgment reveal that you had a passionate love for Christ and a commitment to live for Christ? Will your life be a rich inheritance for Christ? Will you be honored and exalted? Will you be forever identified as a close confidante and faithful friend of Jesus Christ?

It is possible for you to come before Him, to kneel before Him, and to hear Him say, *"Well done, good and faithful servant. Enter into my joy."*[15] What an exciting possibility! What a fantastic privilege! What a marvelous hope!

Do you have that hope? You can, if you genuinely love the Lord Jesus Christ. You can, if you personally live for the Lord Jesus Christ. You can, if you tap into His power and His grace. You can, if you're waiting patiently and working faithfully. You can count on it. God will bless you, and you will be a blessing to God!

Study Guide – Chapter 11 – The Nature of the Rewards

"He is no fool who gives what he cannot keep to gain what he cannot lose."

—Jim Elliott, missionary and martyr to the Auca Indians

1. Rewards will be directly related to our capacity to enjoy eternal life.

List some situations where present capacity sets the stage for future capacity?

"Faithfulness in this life will be rewarded in the next. Increased faithfulness increases our capacity to experience the joys and the blessings of eternal life. A believer could settle for entrance or earn the reward of an abundant entrance." (2 Pet. 1:11)

—Harlan D. Betz: *Setting the Stage for Eternity*

2. Rewards will be directly related to the work that is rewarded.

Discuss the meaning of Hebrews 6:10.

"God will recognize our work, remember our work, and reward us according to our work."

—Harlan D. Betz: *Setting the Stage for Eternity*

"In order for a work to be imperishable and rewardable it must be done for the glory of God the Father, out of a love for God the Son, and in the power of God the Spirit."

—Harlan D. Betz: *Setting the Stage for Eternity*

3. Rewards will be directly related to our likeness to Christ.

"A disciple, when he is fully trained, will be like his teacher."

—Jesus Christ

Why did Jesus come to the earth? (Heb. 10:9. MK. 10:45. Lk. 19:10.

4. Rewards will be directly related to our intimacy with Christ.

What is the basis for a great love for God? 1 John 4:19

What is the nature of a great love for God? Matthew 22:37; John 14:21; Psalm 1:1-3; 31:23; 34:18; 63:3-8; 84:10; 104:33-34; 119:97-98.

Discuss the mystery of this picture of love and intimacy. Ephesians 5:22-33.

Discuss the meaning and merits of these quotes about love:

"A believer, in order to be fully trained, must love his Lord."

—Harlan D. Betz: *Setting the Stage for Eternity*

"Our Lord told his disciples that love and obedience were organically united. The final test of love is obedience!"

—A. W. Tozer

"Let everyone understand that real love of God does not consist in . . . that sweetness and tenderness for which we usually long, just because they console us, but in serving God in justice, fortitude of soul, and humility."

—Theresa of Avila

"You called, you cried, you shattered my deafness, you sparkled, you blazed, you drove away my blindness, you shed your fragrance, and I drew in my breath, and I pant for you."

—Saint Augustine

"I never knew up until that time that God loved us so much. This heart of mine began to thaw out . . . I just drank it in . . . I tell you that there is one thing in this world that draws above everything else in the world and that is love.

—D. L. Moody

"Love is the oldest, the newest, the greatest, and the most encompassing of all the commandments!"

—Harlan D. Betz

---

[1] 1 Corinthians 9:24-27
[2] 1 Corinthians 9:24-25.
[3] For more information on the games and the rewards, see Grundmann's article on "stephanos" in *Theological Dictionary of the New Testament*, translated by Geoffrey Bromiley, edited by Gerhard Kittel and Gerhard Friedrich, vol. 7, pp. 615-636.
[4] Umberto Albini, *The World*, vol. 28, p. 51-52.
[5] Elisabeth Elliot, *Shadow of the Almighty* (New York: Harper & Brothers, Publishers, 1958), p. 19
[6] Ephesians 2:8-10.
[7] Luke 6:40.
[8] Philippians 1:20.
[9] Colossians 3:27-28; Romans 8:28-29.
[10] 2 Corinthians 3:18; Ephesians 4:13.
[11] F. J. Horsefield, *The Church and The Coming King*, p. 72
[12] C. S. Lewis, *The Weight of Glory* (New York, New York: Macmillan Publishing Company, Inc., 1980), pp. 3-4.
[13] H. A. Ironside, *Miscellaneous Papers,* "Salvation and Reward," p. 1.
[14] 1 John 4:19; John 15:1-11; Psalm 42:1; 73:25-26; 91:1-2.
[15] Matthew 25:21.

CHAPTER 12

THE HOPE OF GLORY

When I was a kid, I actually believed that if I had the right tennis shoes, I could run faster. Back then there were no Adidas, Nike, or Reebok tennis shoes. It was just Converse, P.F. Flyers, and Red Dot. I believed, as the advertisers told me, that P.F. Flyers would make me run really fast. I finally came to realize that the key was not the shoe; the key was who was in the shoe!

The Bible challenges us as believers to run with endurance the race that is set before us, keeping our eyes fixed upon Jesus! Dear fellow believer, never forget this. The key is not you, but Who is in you! As the Bible says, *"Christ lives in me"* (Gal. 2:20) and *"I can do all things through Christ"* (Phil. 4:13). *"Christ in you, the hope of glory"* (Col. 1:27-28). Christ in you is the key! *"We have this treasure in earthen vessels that the excellence of the power may be of God and not of us"* (2 Cor. 4:7).

> For you see your calling, brethren, that not many wise according to the flesh, not many mighty, not many noble are called. But God has chosen the foolish things of the world to put to shame the wise, and God has chosen the weak things of the world to put to shame the things which are mighty; and the base things of the world and the despised God has chosen, and the things which are not, to bring to nothing the things that are, that no flesh should glory in His presence. But of Him you are in Christ Jesus, who became for us wisdom from God—and righteousness and sanctification, and redemption—that, as it is written, "He who glories, let him glory in the Lord." (1 Cor. 1:26-31).

The key is not **who** you are; it is **whose** you are. It is not a matter of scholarship; it is a matter of relationship. It is not a matter of human strength; it is a matter of divine power. It is not a matter of noble ancestry; it is a matter of divine adoption! You have been bought by the blood of the Son, you have been adopted by the grace of the Father, and you have been indwelt by the power of the Spirit. The power and presence of God in you—that is the key!

The Calling

God has called us to a very high calling—to glorify Him by becoming like His Son! What a glorious calling! What a fabulous hope! That hope can become a reality because of the indwelling Christ. It is God who enables us to desire and to do His good pleasure. (Phil. 2:13).

Are you doing His good pleasure? Are you living your life in the light of Christ's return? Are you becoming like Jesus Christ?

The Apostle Paul was motivated to press toward the prize of the high calling of God—to be conformed to the image of His Son (Phil. 3:13-14; Rom. 8:28-29). It was Paul's deep desire that Jesus Christ would be magnified by his life and by his death (Phil. 1:20-21). In everything Paul did, he wanted to do all to the glory of God (1 Cor. 10:31).

Are you seeking to be conformed to the image of Christ? Is it your desire to magnify Christ by your life and your death? Do you intentionally purpose to do all to the glory of God? Remember, God is not asking for perfection, He is asking for progression. Are you moving in the right direction? Even the Apostle Paul was willing to acknowledge that he hadn't arrived. But that did not cause him to give up his quest. Listen to his testimony:

> Brethren, I do not count myself to have laid hold of it yet; but one thing I do, forgetting those things which are behind and reaching forward to those

> things which are ahead, I press toward the goal for the prize of the upward call of God in Christ Jesus. (Phil. 3:13-14)

The apostle assumes that all believers will have this same passion and purpose!

> Therefore **we make it our aim** . . . to be well pleasing to Him. For we must all appear before the judgment seat of Christ, that each one may receive the things done in the body, whether good or bad (2 Cor. 5:9-10).

We have discovered that the bottom line is not our success; it is our faithfulness! The key to faithfulness is our motives. God will evaluate what we have done and become by our motives. We will be considered faithful if we do what we do for the glory God the Father, out of a love for God the Son, and in the power of God the Spirit.

The Challenge

How can we match Paul's passion to bring honor and glory to God? How can we cultivate Paul's commitment to manifest the purity of Christ and to magnify the person of Christ? Paul gives us some insight in his letter to Titus:

> For the grace of God that brings salvation has appeared to all men, teaching us that, denying ungodliness and worldly lusts, we should live soberly, righteously, and godly in the present age,

> looking for the blessed hope and glorious appearing of our great God and Savior Jesus Christ, who gave Himself for us, that He might redeem us from every lawless deed and purify for Himself His own special people, zealous for good works. (Ti. 2:11-14).

This is a call to purity and passion. Jesus is the key to purity and passion.

Jesus gave Himself that He might redeem us from sin and remake us like Him. His grace *teaches us that, denying ungodliness and worldly lusts, we should live soberly, righteously and godly in this present age.* That is purity.

His grace teaches us to be looking for *the blessed hope and glorious appearing of our God and Savior* and to be *zealous for good works.* That is passion.

Through obedience to His Word, we can be purified from ungodliness (Jn. 17:17). Through the power of His life, we can be passionate about doing good works (Rom. 5:10).

We come to Christ by grace and through faith; we are to follow after Christ by grace and through faith.

Remember, the key is not you; it is Who is in you! As we run the race of the Christian life, we must fix our eyes on Jesus, and we can find our hope in Jesus!

John's heart echoes Paul's heart in his passion for purity. John gently and lovingly addresses believers as little children and gives us this plea:

> And now little children, abide in Him, that when He appears, we may have confidence and not be ashamed before Him at His coming. If you know

> that He is righteous, you know that everyone who practices righteousness is born of Him.
>
> Beloved, now we are children of God, and it has not yet been revealed what we shall be, but we know that when He is revealed, we shall be like Him, for we shall see Him as He is. And every one who has this hope in Him purifies himself, just as He is pure. (1 Jn. 2:28-29; 3:2-3)

This is a very tender and passionate plea from the heart of the beloved Apostle John. He is calling believers to righteousness and purity in the light of the return of Christ.

John is challenging believers to abide in Christ. The concept of abiding in Christ was clearly spelled out by our Lord Jesus Christ in the upper room and is recorded by John in the fifteenth chapter of his gospel.[1] Jesus Christ is the vine, and believers are the branches. As branches in Christ, believers can bear no fruit, some fruit, more fruit, or much fruit.

Abiding in Christ is the condition for fruit-bearing, and obedience is the condition for abiding. God the Father is glorified by the branch that bears much fruit. Christ is magnified by the branch that bears much fruit. John makes it very clear that if we abide in Christ, we will prove to be His disciples. A disciple, when he is fully trained, is like His master. A fully trained, fruitful disciple will reflect the character of Christ!

John is challenging believers to purify themselves. The believer who abides in Christ will be setting himself apart from sin and devoting himself to righteousness. This process of sanctification will enable us to reflect ever more clearly the beauty and purity of Jesus Christ.

John is explaining how Christ's appearing should affect us. When Christ returns, every believer will be like Him. We will all be children of God. We will all have eternal life. We will all be free from sin. In this sense we will bear a likeness to Christ—a family likeness. But some believers, John tells us, will bear far more than a family likeness. Those who abide in Christ will bear a special likeness of Jesus Christ—they will reflect the very righteousness and purity of Christ.

If you abide in Christ, your character and conduct will gradually, but surely, conform more and more into a reflection of the righteousness of Christ. Consequently, you will be eager for His return. If, on the other hand, you fail to abide in Christ, you will fail to become like Him, and you will be ashamed of yourself at Christ's return.

If there is going to be a transformation, there must be a transformer. We can experience transformation of our minds through the power of the Written Word—The Bible (Rom.12:1-2). We can experience transformation of our lives through the power of the Living Word—Jesus Christ (Gal. 2:20).

John goes on to describe the reward for this practical righteousness . . . the crown of righteousness:

> Let us be glad and rejoice and give Him glory, for the marriage of the Lamb has come and His bride has made herself ready. And to her it was granted to be arrayed in fine linen, clean and bright, for the fine linen is the righteous act of the saints." (Rev. 19:7-8)

Several significant truths were expressed in that passage:

- The white linen is the **righteous acts** of the saints!
- The bride **made herself** ready!
- The glory goes to **Jesus Christ!**

It is obvious that the crown of righteousness does not come from gritting your teeth, squaring your shoulders, clenching your fists, and saying, "I am going to be righteous." One does not become righteous by gutting it out in the flesh.

Remember, the key is not you; it is Who is in you! As Jesus reminded the disciples, "Without Me, you can do nothing!" (John 15:5). Transformation comes as a result of Christ abiding in you, your abiding in Christ, and God's Word abiding in you. Transformation is the result of Christ's power in an abiding earthen vessel. You must run this Christian race with endurance, keeping your eyes fixed upon Jesus!

The Collaboration

One of the real life experiences that burned itself into the minds of most Americans during the 1992 Olympics is a beautiful picture of this truth. Derek Redmon, a British runner, tore a ligament midway through his race. The sudden tear caused him to collapse on the track while the rest of the runners finished the race. However, something happened that drew the attention of those in the stands and those watching on television. Derek struggled to get back on his feet and began hobbling around the track, determined to cross the finish line.

It was evident that he was in a lot of pain. He was struggling to push himself on, but it didn't look as if he would be able to reach the finish line. Suddenly a man came out of the stands and started toward Derek. The security guards tried to stop him, but he was not about to be stopped. He put his arm around Derek's waist, and Derek put his arm around this man's shoulder. Together they began walking toward the finish line. The television sportscasters confirmed what most of us suspected. It was Derek's father. The crowd began to cheer Derek on. Eventually the father and his son crossed the finish line. There was a thunderous applause. With his father's help and strength, Derek was able to finish his race.

In a similar way, each of us stumbles and falls. Each of us needs the help and the strength of our Father to enable us to run the race and finish the course. By His grace, we can walk with Him. By His power, we can become like His Son.

The Consummation

Almeda J. Pearce expresses my prayer:

When He shall come, resplendent in His glory,
to take His own from out of this vale of night,
O may I know the joy of His appearing,
only at morn to walk with Him in white!

When He shall call, from earth's remotest corners,
all who have stood triumphant in His might,
O to be worthy then to stand beside them,
and in that morn to walk with Him in white![2]

Guy King gives us a touching picture of this divine collaboration when he says:

> I so well remember, many years ago, being appointed to supervise the "Little Its" at a Children's Special Service Mission Birthday Sports. I gave the wee people their handicap—all, of course, sheer guesswork; and one Delectable Dumpling I placed well in front of the rest, for she could only toddle—or waddle. I then explained the rules, and gave the word "Go!" I greatly hope that the governing Body of the Athletic Association will not, at this distance of time, declare the decision of the race void when I confess that, besides being the starter, I also myself ran with the competitors—running backwards in front of my little friend, luring her on to catch me! The result was that she won the race, although she was really too young to realize what was happening. Surprised by all the clapping and cheering, she looked up at me and said, "What has me done?" Ah, my friend, if, at the end of the race, you receive the plaudits of the Master, and a prize at His hand, I know that you will say, "But, Lord, what have I done?" [3]

You will simply have loved Him because He loved you. Your love for Him caused you to long for His return. Your longing for His return caused you to live in the light of His return. Living in the light of His return resulted in character and conduct empowered by Christ and reflecting the righteousness and purity of Christ. That reflection is a reward to you and an honor to Christ!

It is important that we realize that every reward given to a believer is ultimately an honor to the Christ who indwells and empowers him.

Consequently, the focus encouraged by the old hymn is appropriate:

> The bride eyes not her garment, But her dear Bridegroom's face.
> I will not gaze at glory, But on my King of grace.
> Not at the crown He giveth, But on His pierced hand;
> The Lamb is all the glory Of Immanuel's land.

The songwriter's heart is right! After all, even the rewards are ultimately tokens of His grace and testimonies to His goodness! So our last focus in this book is not on the reward and its presentation, but on the Lord and His appearing. A proper understanding of rewards plays a significant role in motivating a believer to Christ-likeness. These rewards provide a powerful motivation in the present and a fabulous hope for the future! One can hardly imagine the thrill of honoring and being honored by our Lord Jesus Christ as a close associate, a Christ-like friend, and a victorious believer. What an incredible joy it would be to look in our dear Savior's eyes and hear him say, "Well done, good and faithful servant, come and share my joy." I agree with the person who said, "I don't want 'Well done!' on my tombstone to simply mean that I was cremated!" I love the Lord, and I want Him to be pleased with my love and my life. I want my life to be an honor to Him. I want my life to bring joy to His heart. I want to run this race with endurance. I want to finish the course!

Surely Satan will try to lead our minds astray from the simplicity and purity of such devotion to Christ!

The Commitment

Greek mythology brings forth a very fitting truth in the tale of Atlanta. It seems that a number of men had fallen in love with this very capable and athletic woman. In order to handle this problem, she merely challenged them to a foot race, knowing full well that she could outrun any man alive. Man after man had challenged her, and man after man had been defeated.

But at last there came one who used his head as well as his heels, and that man was Hippomenes. He had secured three beautiful golden apples through the graciousness of Aphrodite. There was not a person in the world that could look at these golden apples and not want them.

Atlanta took off, as swift as an arrow, and was beginning to leave him behind when he rolled one of the apples in front of her. She stopped briefly, picked it up, and soon was outstripping him again. Once again, he threw out a golden apple, and once again she stopped to pick it up. Finally, as they were nearing the goal, and she was rapidly passing him, he threw the last apple over to the side of the track. She saw the gleam of the beautiful apple, and could not resist it. As she turned to pick it up, Hippomenes, panting and almost winded, crossed the goal. She was his.[4]

In a similar manner, three golden apples are sidetracking many Christians from their prizes. They are sidetracked by the lust of the flesh, the lust of the eyes, and the pride of life. At the judgment seat of Christ, every man's work shall be tried, and the Christian who was sidetracked will suffer loss, while the victorious Christian will be rewarded. The quality of one's life on earth sets the bounds for the quality of one's life in eternity.

Right now you are setting the stage for eternity! Faithfulness here will be rewarded hereafter, for God will be debtor to no man.[5] As Christ declares in the last chapter of the Revelation, *"Behold I am coming quickly, and My reward is with Me, to give to every one according to his work"* (Rev. 22:12).

If the awe and inspiration of this truth grips your heart, you will make it your aim to please Christ and by God's grace to become like Christ.

This longing and commitment is expressed well in the Angel Stadium Declaration, April 17, 2005, by John Fischer.[6] Perhaps you could make this commitment right now!

> Today I am stepping across the line. I'm tired of waffling and I'm finished with wavering; I've made my choice, the verdict is in and my decision is irrevocable. I'm going God's way. There is no turning back now! I will live the rest of my life serving God's purposes with God's people on God's planet for God's glory. I will use my life to celebrate His presence, cultivate His character, participate in His family, demonstrate His love, and communicate His word.

Since my past has been forgiven and I have a purpose for living and a home waiting in heaven, I refuse to waste any more time or energy in shallow living, petty thinking, trivial talking, thoughtless doing, useless regretting, hurtful resenting, or faithless worrying. Instead, I will magnify God, grow to maturity, serve in ministry, and fulfill my mission in the membership of His family.

Because this life is preparation for the next, I will value worship over wealth, "we" over "me," character over comfort, service over status, and people over possessions, position, and pleasures. I know what matters most and I'll give it all I've got. I'll do the best I can with what I have for Jesus Christ today.

I won't be captivated by culture, manipulated by critics, motivated by praise, frustrated by problems, debilitated by temptation, or intimidated by the devil. I'll keep running my race with my eyes on the goal, not the sidelines or those running beside me. When times get tough, and I get tired, I won't back up, back off, back down, back out or backslide. I'll just keep moving forward by God's grace. I'm Spirit-led, purpose-driven, and mission-focused so I cannot be bought, I will not be compromised, and I shall not quit until I finish the race.

I'm a trophy of God's amazing grace so I will be gracious to everyone, grateful for every day, and generous with everything that God entrusts to me.

To my Lord and Savior Jesus Christ, I say: However, Whenever, Wherever, and Whatever you

> ask me to do, my answer is yes! Wherever you lead and whatever the cost, I'm ready. Anytime, Anywhere. Anyway. Whatever it takes Lord; Whatever it takes. I want to be used by you in such a way that on that final day I'll hear you say, "Well done, thou good and faithful one. Come on in, and let the eternal party begin."

The judgment seat of Christ will be an intensely personal and emotionally powerful event. For some, a time of exquisite sorrow and anguish. For others, a time of exceptional joy and delight. May God so work in your heart and life that the **bema** will be a time of joy for you and a time of delight for your Lord. May you hear the Lord Jesus Christ say to you, "Well done, my loving and faithful servant. Come and share my joy, my glory, and my reign."

In closing this book, I open my heart . . .

Christ is coming back for me,
And I'd find it a great delight
If I could watch for Him eagerly,
And not shrink back in shame or fright.

When I stand before the Judgment Seat,
And Christ's discerning eyes fall on me,
I long to hear Him say, "Well done,
You have served Me faithfully."

Oh what pain, and oh what anguish
There will be in store for me,
If I fail to live for God
And forfeit much that I could be.

I want to be like You, Lord Jesus,
In all I am and all I do.
Help me deny self and take up my cross,
So Your image comes shining through.

Now I call upon You, Lord Jesus,
How I need Your grace and power.
Help me stay on fire for You
Every day and every hour.

Even so, come Lord Jesus,
Make me ready day or night.
As my love for You increases,
May I bring You much delight!

Oh what joy and great delight
To see You face to face.
And more than that, to magnify You
As a trophy of Your grace.

— Harlan D. Betz

Study Guide – Chapter 12 – The Hope of Glory

"Those who are living in the light of Christ's return will be rewarded by the warmth of Christ's embrace, the thrill of Christ's praise, and the blessing of Christ's joy!"

—Harlan D. Betz: *Setting the Stage for Eternity*

1. **Read & Discuss Titus 2:11-14.**

   "Jesus gave Himself that He might redeem us and remake us. Jesus is the key to purity and passion. Through His Word we can be purified, and through His work we can be passionate!"

   —Harlan D. Betz: *Setting the Stage for Eternity*

2. **Read & Discuss Galatians 6:6-10.**

   "God does not expect perfection, but He does expect progression. Failure is not fatal. Giving up is fatal! Do not grow weary in becoming what God is calling you to be nor in doing what God is calling you to do, for in His time you will be rewarded if you do not give up!" —Harlan D. Betz: *Setting the Stage for Eternity*

3. **Read Romans 12:1-2.**

   Discuss the meaning of transformation.

   "If there is going to be a transformation, there must be a transformer. We can experience transformation of our minds through the power of the Word, and we can experience transformation of our lives through the power of the Lord."

   —Harlan D. Betz: *Setting the Stage for Eternity*

4. Take a few moments to do some personal inventory?

   Have you responded to the invitation of the gospel? John 3:16.

   Have you trusted in Christ as your own personal Savior?

Have you fallen in love with the Lord? Matthew 22:37.
Are you basking in the warmth of His love?
Is He basking in the warmth of your love?
Are you living your life for Him?
Have you tapped into His grace and power?
Are you abiding in Him? John 15:5.
Are you seeking His grace? Hebrews 4:16.
Are you living in the light of eternity? 1 John 2:28-3:3.

"Rewards will provide a powerful motivation in the present and a fabulous hope for the future." —Harlan D. Betz

Have you honored this One who longs to honor you? Lk. 19:17.

5. Discuss the meaning of 2 Corinthians 4:7 and Philippians 4:13.
   How do those verses relate to John 15:5 and Philippians 2:13?

   Take some time to discuss this quote:
   "Rewards are ultimately tokens of His grace and testimonies of His goodness." —Harlan D. Betz: *Setting the Stage for Eternity*

6. Commit yourself to the following:
   Keep on coming to Him and calling upon Him. Heb. 4:14-16.
   Keep on loving Him and longing for His return! 2 Tim. 4:6-8.
   Keep on looking to Him and living for Him. Heb. 12:1-2.

7. Picture yourself standing before Christ at the judgment seat.
   Imagine the joy of reflecting and honoring Him!
   Imagine the thrill of hearing Him saying "Well done!"
   Imagine the blessing of intimate fellowship with Him!

---

[1] The concept of abiding in Christ is critical to victorious Christian living. It is very clearly explained in Bruce Wilkinson's little book, *The Secret of the Vine.* I highly recommend a careful reading of his book. First of all, because I completely agree with his interpretation of John 15. Secondly, because he says everything I would want to say about abiding in Christ far better than I ever could.

[2] Almeda J. Pearce, "When He Shall Come."

[3] Guy King, *To My Son* (Fort Washington, Pennsylvania: Christian Literature Crusade, 1944), p. 123.

[4] Edith Hamilton, *Mythology* (New York: The American Library, 1940), pp. 173-177.

[5] "God is not unjust so as to forget your work and the love which you have shown toward His name, in having ministered, and in still ministering to the saints" (Hebrews 6:10). "For whoever gives you a cup of water to drink because you are followers of Christ, truly I say to you, he shall not lose his reward" (Mark 9:41).

[6] This declaration is similar to The Expendables Creed and The Creed of a Bold Follower of Jesus Christ. It was written by John Fischer who is the Senior Writer for Purpose Driven Life Daily Devotionals. It was read together by all those who attended the 25th anniversary of ministry at Saddleback Church, which was held at Angel Stadium in Anaheim, California.

APPENDICES

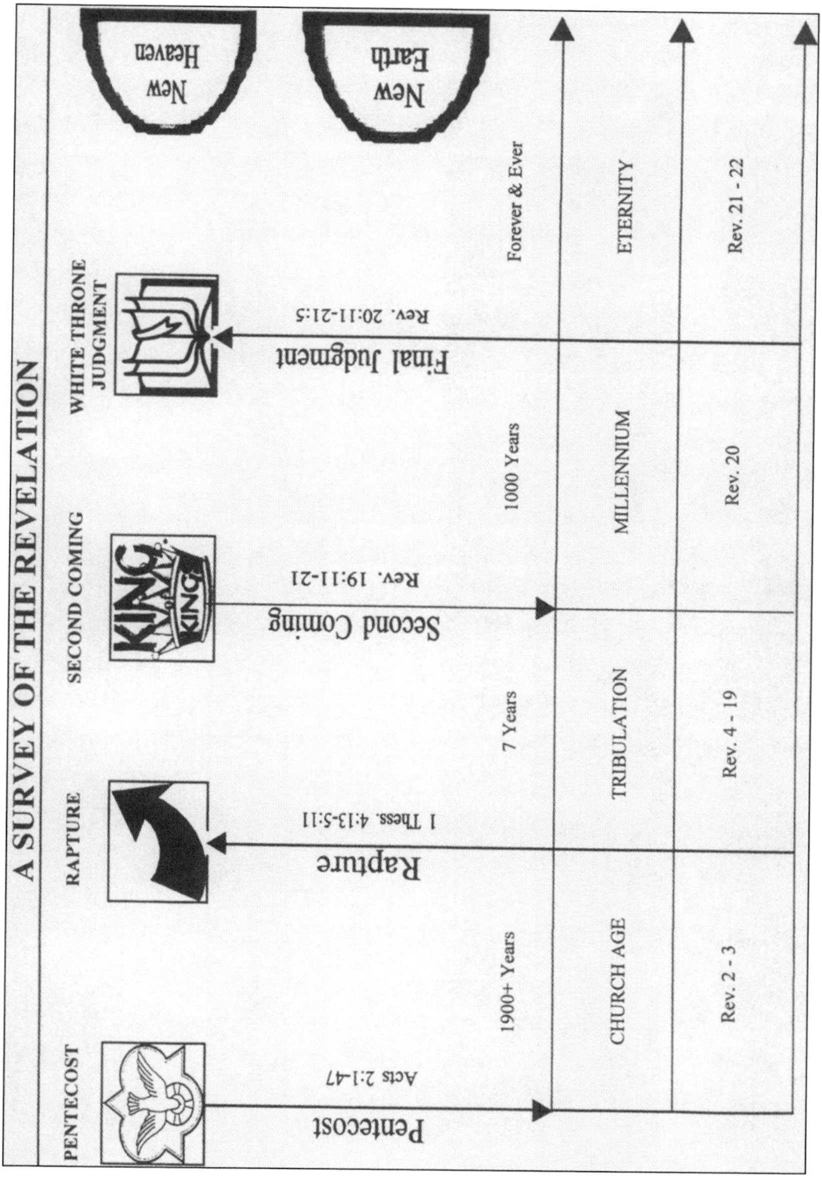
A SURVEY OF THE REVELATION
PENTECOST
RAPTURE
SECOND COMING
WHITE THRONE JUDGMENT
Pentecost
Acts 2:1-47
Rapture
I Thess. 4:13-5:11
Second Coming
Rev. 19:11-21
KING of KINGS
Final Judgment
Rev. 20:11-21:5
New Heaven
New Earth
1900+ Years
7 Years
1000 Years
Forever & Ever
CHURCH AGE
TRIBULATION
MILLENNIUM
ETERNITY
Rev. 2 - 3
Rev. 4 - 19
Rev. 20
Rev. 21 - 22

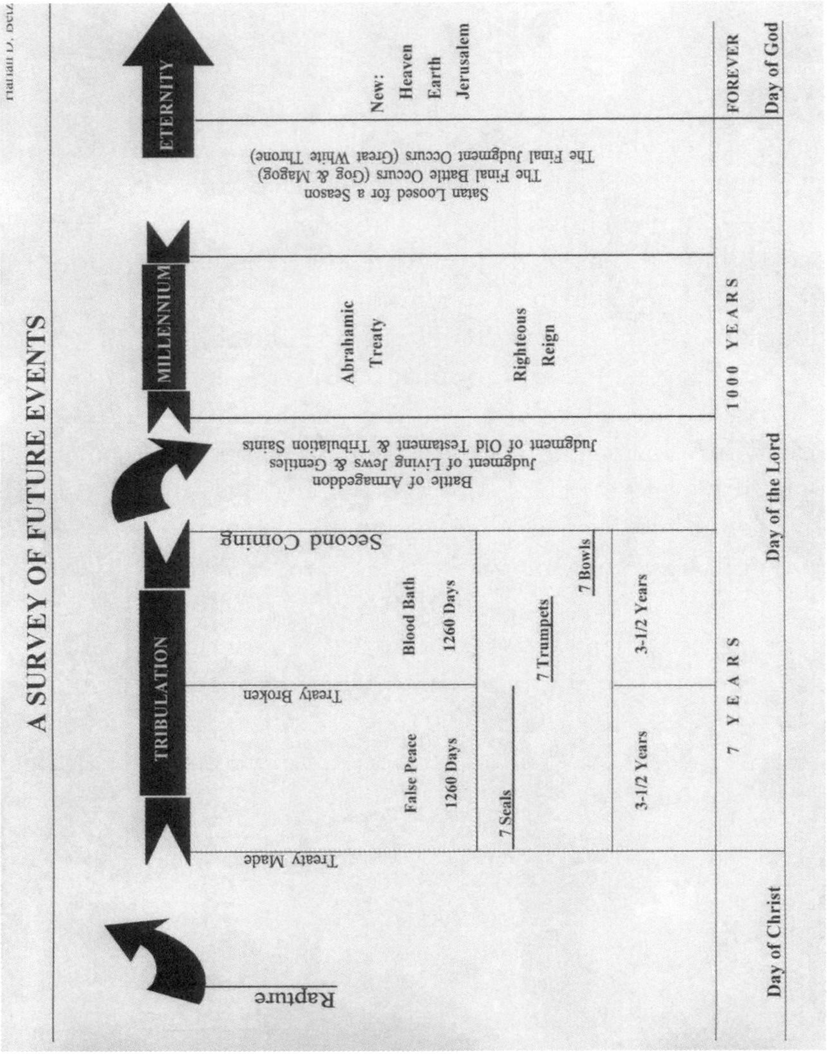
A SURVEY OF FUTURE EVENTS
Rapture
Treaty Made
TRIBULATION
False Peace
1260 Days
Treaty Broken
Blood Bath
1260 Days
Second Coming
7 Seals
7 Trumpets
7 Bowls
3-1/2 Years
3-1/2 Years
Battle of Armageddon
Judgment of Living Jews & Gentiles
Judgment of Old Testament & Tribulation Saints
MILLENNIUM
Abrahamic
Treaty
Righteous
Reign
Satan Loosed for a Season
The Final Battle Occurs (Gog & Magog)
The Final Judgment Occurs (Great White Throne)
ETERNITY
New:
Heaven
Earth
Jerusalem
7 YEARS
1000 YEARS
FOREVER
Day of Christ
Day of the Lord
Day of God

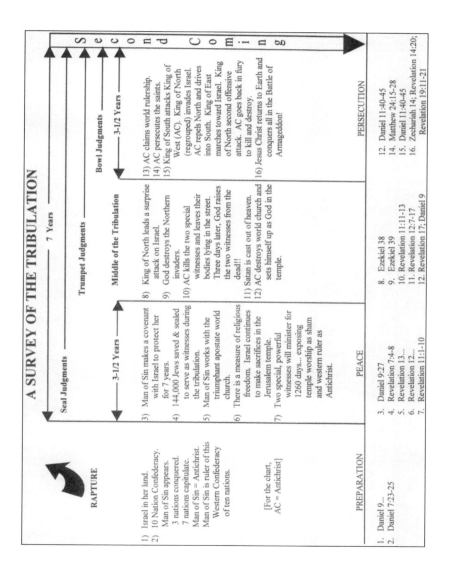

A SURVEY OF THE TRIBULATION

RAPTURE

7 Years

Seal Judgments

Trumpet Judgments

Bowl Judgments

Second Coming

PREPARATION

1) Israel in her land.
2) 10 Nation Confederacy.
   Man of Sin appears.
   3 nations conquered.
   7 nations capitulate.
   Man of Sin = Antichrist.
   Man of Sin is ruler of this Western Confederacy of ten nations.

[For the chart, AC = Antichrist]

1. Daniel 9...
2. Daniel 7:23-25

PEACE

3-1/2 Years

3) Man of Sin makes a covenant with Israel to protect her for 7 years.
4) 144,000 Jews saved & sealed to serve as witnesses during the tribulation.
5) Man of Sin works with the triumphant apostate world church.
6) There is a measure of religious freedom. Israel continues to make sacrifices in the Jerusalem temple.
7) Two special, powerful witnesses will minister for 1260 days... exposing temple worship as sham and western ruler as Antichrist.

3. Daniel 9:27
4. Revelation 7:4-8
5. Revelation 13...
6. Revelation 12...
7. Revelation 11:1-10

Middle of the Tribulation

8) King of North leads a surprise attack on Israel.
9) God destroys the Northern invaders.
10) AC kills the two special witnesses and leaves their bodies lying in the street. Three days later, God raises the two witnesses from the dead!!
11) Satan is cast out of heaven.
12) AC destroys world church and sets himself up as God in the temple.

8. Ezekiel 38
9. Ezekiel 39
10. Revelation 11:11-13
11. Revelation 12:7-17
12. Revelation 17; Daniel 9

PERSECUTION

3-1/2 Years

13) AC claims world rulership.
14) AC persecutes the saints.
15) King of South attacks King of West (AC). King of North (regrouped) invades Israel. AC repels North and drives into South. King of East marches toward Israel. King of North second offensive attack. AC goes back in fury to kill and destroy.
16) Jesus Christ returns to Earth and conquers all in the Battle of Armageddon!

12. Daniel 11:40-45
14. Matthew 24:15-28
15. Daniel 11:40-45
16. Zechariah 14; Revelation 14:20; Revelation 19:11-21

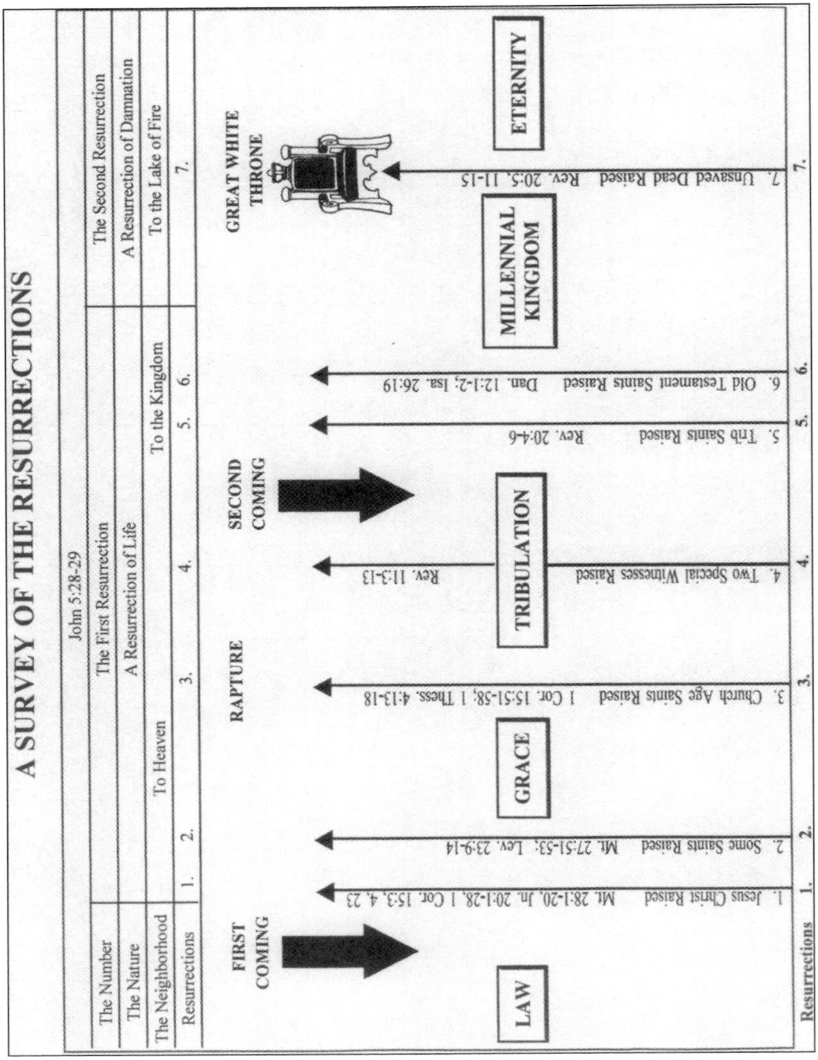
A SURVEY OF THE RESURRECTIONS
John 5:28-29
The Number
The First Resurrection
The Second Resurrection
The Nature
A Resurrection of Life
A Resurrection of Damnation
The Neighborhood
To Heaven
To the Kingdom
To the Lake of Fire
Resurrections
1. 2. 3. 4. 5. 6. 7.
LAW
FIRST COMING
GRACE
RAPTURE
TRIBULATION
SECOND COMING
MILLENNIAL KINGDOM
GREAT WHITE THRONE
ETERNITY
1. Jesus Christ Raised Mt. 28:1-20, Jn. 20:1-28, I Cor. 15:3, 4, 23
2. Some Saints Raised Mt. 27:51-53; Lev. 23:9-14
3. Church Age Saints Raised I Cor. 15:51-58; I Thess. 4:13-18
4. Two Special Witnesses Raised Rev. 11:3-13
5. Trib Saints Raised Rev. 20:4-6
6. Old Testament Saints Raised Dan. 12:1-2; Isa. 26:19
7. Unsaved Dead Raised Rev. 20:5, 11-15
Resurrections
1. 2. 3. 4. 5. 6. 7.

A SURVEY OF THE JUDGMENTS

NAME	SUBJECTS	TIME	PLACE	BASIS	RESULTS
1. Judgment Seat of Christ	All Church Age Believers - Rom. 14:10-12; 1 Cor. 3:11-15; 2 Cor. 5:10	After the rapture.	Heaven	Works performed during earthly life.	Either rewards or the loss of rewards. Revelation of personal character and eternal rewards.
2. Judgment of the Beast & False Prophet	Beast (Antichrist) & False Prophet - Rev. 19:11-20	After the tribulation. At the 2nd Advent.	Earth	Rejection of Christ. Deceit of others.	Eternal condemnation in the Lake of Fire.
3. Judgment of Israel	Living Jews - Mal. 3:2-5; Ezek. 20:33-38; Mt. 25:31-46	After the 2nd Advent & the regathering of Israel.	Earth	Israel's response to God - Mt. 18:3.	Unbelievers = Lake of Fire. Degrees of punishment. Believers = Into Kingdom. Degrees of reward.
4. Judgment of the Nations	Living Gentiles - Joel 3:1-2; Mt. 25:31-46, Ezek. 20:32-38	After the 2nd Advent & the judging of Israel.	Earth	Gentile's response to God (Mt. 24:14) as revealed in treatment of believing Israel.	Unbelievers = Lake of Fire. Degrees of punishment. Believers = Into Kingdom. Degrees of reward.
5. Judgment of O.T. & Tribulation Saints	All O.T. & Trib. Saints (resurrected after the Great Tribulation) - Dan. 12:1-3; Mt. 25:1-13, Rev. 20:4-6	After the 2nd Advent	Earth	Works performed during earthly life	Either rewards or the loss of rewards... Positions in the Kingdom.
6. Judgment of Satan & Fallen Angels	Satan & Fallen Angels - 2 Pet. 2:4; Jude 6; Mt. 25:41; Rev. 20:10	After the Millennium	Possibly Angelic Sphere	Rebellion against God and sins against people.	Eternal torment. Lake of Fire.
7. Great White Throne Judgment	All Unjudged Unbelievers; physically and spiritually dead - Rev. 20:11-15	After the Millennium	Between Heaven and Earth	Rejection of Christ. Works performed during earthly life.	Eternal separation from God; Lake of Fire; The "second death." Degrees of punishment.

The Rapture and The Second Coming

The Rapture	The Second Coming
The amazing conclusion of the church age	The awesome climax of the tribulation period
Imminent - can happen at any moment	Predicted - can't happen until signs are fulfilled
Not revealed in the Old Testament	Revealed in the Old Testament
Promised to the Church	Promised to Israel
Christ comes as Groom	Christ comes as King
He comes for His Bride	He comes with His Bride
Jesus stops in the air	Jesus comes to the Earth
He gathers up His Church	He sets up His Kingdom
Jesus goes back to Heaven	Jesus stays here on Earth
Followed by God's wrath on Earth	Followed by God's blessing on Earth
Followed by the Tribulation	Followed by the Millennial Kingdom
Followed by the Antichrist's reign	Followed by the True Christ's reign
Precedes outpouring of God's wrath	Follows outpouring of God's wrath
Takes place silently	Takes place violently
A private event	A public event
People saying "peace and safety"	People saying "kill and destroy"
Time of hope for the believer	Time of horror for the unbeliever
Time of eating, drinking, marrying	Time of war, panic, holocaust
Removing of the Restrainer	Binding of the Destroyer
Followed by judgment seat of Christ	Followed by judgment of the sheep and goats

The following books can serve as a resource for the above chart:

Dr. John F. Walvoord, *Prophecy: 14 Essential Keys to Understanding the Final Drama* (Nashville: Thomas Nelson Publishers, 1993).

Dr. John F. Walvoord, *The Return of the Lord* (Grand Rapids, Michigan: Zondervan Publishing House, 1955).

Leon J. Wood, *The Bible and Future Events* (Grand Rapids, Michigan: Zondervan Publishing House, 1973).

Regeneration vs. Rewards

Regeneration	Rewards
1. A gift based on the work of Christ	1. A reward based on the work of the believer
2. Giving entrance into the kingdom	2. Granting inheritance in the kingdom
3. Unmerited favor	3. A merited honor
4. Not by works of righteousness	4. Based on works of righteousness
5. Given at moment of faith in Christ	5. Granted at time of judgment seat of Christ
6. A present possession	6. A future attainment
7. Adopted as a child	7. Honored as a son
8. Freely given by grace appreciated	8. Fully deserved by grace appropriated

* Isaiah 64:6; Matthew 10:42; Luke 19:17; John 3:16, 36; 4:10; 5:24; Romans 6:23; 1 Corinthians 9:24-25; Ephesians 2:8-9; 2 Timothy 4:7-8; Titus 3:5-6; Revelation 19:7-8; 22:12.

The Barren Believer vs. The Faithful Follower

Barren Believer	Faithful Follower
1. Entrance into Heaven	1. Inheritance in Heaven
2. Have the gift of eternal life	2. Experience the fullness of eternal life
3. Ashamed at Jesus' coming	3. Confident at Jesus' coming
4. Kept life for self	4. Gave up life for God
5. Lived a carnal life	5. Lived a spiritual life
6. Conformed to cosmos	6. Conformed to Christ
7. Failed to overcome world, flesh, and devil	7. Faithful to overcome world, flesh, and devil
8. No commendation from Christ	8. Public commendation from Christ
9. Foolish servant	9. Faithful servant
10. A shame to Christ	10. An honor to Christ
11. Focused on temporal	11. Focused on eternal
12. Conformed to world	12. Transformed by Word
13. Lived for glory of self	13. Lived for glory of God
14. Loves the world	14. Loves the Lord
15. Excluded from honors - regretting	15. Included in honors - reigning

* Matthew 10:32-39; 25:14-30; Mark 8:34-38; Luke 9:23-27; 19:11-27; Romans 8:16-17; 12:1-2; 14:10-17; 1 Corinthians 3:10-15; 4:1-5; 10:31; 2 Corinthians 5:9-11; 1 John 2:15-17; 2:28-3:3; Revelation 2:26; 3:5, 12, 21. There will be varying degrees all the way from the barren unfaithful believer to the blessed faithful follower!

Parable of the Minas
Luke 19:11-27

Servants (Saved)	**Citizens** (Unsaved)
Relationship to the King (11-13)	**Relationship to the King (14)**
Personal relationship	Physical relationship
Belonged to Him ... servants	Did not belong to Him... citizens
Received Him ... believers	Rejected Him... unbelievers
Relationship to the Kingdom (15-26)	**Relationship to the Kingdom (27)**
Servant's entrance permitted	Citizen's entrance prohibited
Servants received	Citizens rejected
(16-19) Entrance blessed; Inheritance: A reward, Merited (20-25) Entrance barren; Entrance: A gift, Received	(27) Entrance barred; Entrance: A gift, Rejected
Character of the Person	**Character of the Person**
(16-19) Faithful: (16-17) More Faithful, (18-19) Less Faithful (20-25) Unfaithful: (20-25) Unfaithful	(27) Faithless

Calvinism vs. Biblicism vs. Arminianism
By Dr. Harlan D. Betz

Five Points of Calvinism

1. Total Inability

Man is not able to respond to the grace of God. Man has no ability to come to Christ. Man cannot choose to come to Christ. God must overpower man and cause him to turn to Christ. The man who does not place his faith in Christ does not do so because he cannot do so! Man does not have the ability to respond to Christ or to come to Christ. Man cannot choose to trust in Christ. God must force man to trust in Him. Man cannot decide to come to Christ. God must make man come to Him.

2. Unconditional Election

God has elected some to go to Heaven and others to go to Hell and that election is unconditional. The decision is wholly God's. The individual has absolutely nothing to do with it. God has chosen some to be saved, and those who are saved are saved without their choosing to believe. God has determined that certain people will perish. These people were created for eternal damnation and predestined to Hell. God does not desire for them to be saved and God does not

Five Truths of the Bible

1. Total Depravity

Man is totally depraved. Every facet of man's nature and faculties is corrupted by the sin nature. There is nothing in man that can enable him to earn or deserve eternal life. God, in grace, draws all men (John 12:32; Titus 2:11). Man is able to receive and respond to the grace of God (Mt 23:37; John 5:24-25; Eph. 2:8-9). Man is a free moral agent with responsibility to respond to God's grace (John 1:1-9; 3:16-17). Man can respond to God's grace and come to Christ and he is called to do so (Rev. 22:17)!

2. Unmerited Election

God elects a man without regard to that man's merit! In fact, man cannot merit God's saving grace! Election is an act of God's grace (Eph. 1:4-6). Believing is a response to God's grace. The Bible teaches both God's sovereignty in choosing and man's responsibility in believing. The Bible places foreknowledge before predestination (Rom. 8:28-30). God desires for all men to be saved (1 Tim. 2:4). God is not desirous that any should perish (2 Pet 3:9). Whosoever

Five Points of Arminianism

1. Partial Depravity

Man is partially depraved. He inherited pollution from Adam, but guilt was not imputed to any of Adam's descendants. Some facets of man's nature and faculties are not corrupted by the sin nature.

2. Conditional Election

God's election of a man is conditioned upon the foreseen merit of that man. God's decrees are based on foreknowledge, and election is based on foreseen faith, and reprobation is based on foreseen resistance to grace. God elects on the basis of foreseen faith. Election is based on man's will to believe. In effect, man's foreseen faith precedes God's election and is the basis for God's election. This makes election a response to man's faith rather than an act of God's grace.

3. Governmental Atonement

Christ died for all men and for every man, although only believers are saved. The atonement makes salvation possible for all men, although it becomes effectual only when accepted by the repentant believer. The atonement was not only offer salvation to them.

3. Limited Atonement

Christ died only for the elect. He did not die for those He planned and ordained to go to Hell. Those who were not elected by God cannot believe and be saved. Christ did not die for those who were not elect. God did not desire for them to be saved and Christ did not die for them and salvation is not available to them.

4. Irresistible Grace

God's grace overpowers people and forces them to believe. God's grace cannot be resisted by man. Men cannot believe in Christ until after they are born again. Man is made spiritually alive by God apart from faith and before faith!

5. Perseverance of the Saints

"Once saved, always saintly." That is…if a person is a believer, he will live like a godly saint; if a person does not live like a godly saint, then he is not a believer. Assurance of eternal life is not possible in this life, for the believer must endure to the end. Temporary assurance comes from the evidence of works of righteousness. If he perseveres, he is saved. If he fails to persevere, he was not truly saved in the first place.

believes in Jesus has eternal life (John 3:16)! Men who go to Hell, go there because they are sinners who rejected God's grace.

3. Limitless Atonement

Christ died for all mankind (Isa. 53:6; John 4:14, 42; 1 Tim. 2:3-6; Heb. 2:9; 1 John 2:2). His death is sufficient for all, but efficient only for those who believe (John 3:15-17; Rom. 4-5).

4. Instrumental Grace

God's common grace reaches all people and enables them to respond to Him (Mt 5:45; Tit 2:11; Psa. 19; Rom. 1). God, in His grace, offers salvation to all. Some resist God's grace and remain condemned (John 5:40); others respond to His grace and at the very moment they place their faith in Christ, they are made alive and have eternal life. They are saved by grace. (Eph. 2:8-9). Faith and regeneration in Christ are simultaneous (Jn. 1:11-13; 3:1-17).

5. Preservation of the Saints

"Once saved, always saved." A believer is secure because of God's preservation. If a person has placed his faith in Christ alone for salvation, he is guaranteed eternal life, regardless of what he thinks, says, or does. If a person is a believer, he should live like it, but if he doesn't, God will discipline him. He may sin, but he is still saved (Rom. 8:31-39; Heb. 12:1-11).

unlimited, but also unnecessary. It was a way in which God chose to manifest His love. The atonement was not strictly penal or substitutionary, but was rather designed to safeguard the interests of the moral government of God.

4. Resistible Grace

There is no common grace to be distinguished from special grace. The external call of the gospel is accompanied by a universal sufficient grace, which can be resisted. The human will is viewed as one of the causes of regeneration (synergism). Repentance and faith are seen as preceding regeneration. Faith is a good work and a ground of acceptance with God. There is no imputation of righteousness to the believer.

5. Perseverance of the Saints

While saintly, still saved. That is…a believer who perseveres in his faith and works is saved only as long as he perseveres. Assurance of eternal life is not possible in this life. As long as a man lives, he may fall from grace and lose his salvation altogether. If he perseveres, he is saved. If he fails to persevere, he is no longer saved.

Biographical Sketch

Dr. Harlan D. Betz

Harlan Betz is the Senior Pastor at Kingwood Bible Church in Kingwood, Texas. Harlan grew up on a farm northwest of Ladora, Iowa. It was there, through the influence of his parents and his older brother that he came to realize his need for Jesus Christ and at the age of seven, he placed his faith in Christ for forgiveness of sins and for eternal life.

Harlan has earned a B.A. in Classical Greek from the University of Iowa (1970), a Th.M. in New Testament Literature and Exegesis from Dallas Theological Seminary (1974), and a Ph.D. in Biblical Studies from Cambridge Graduate School (1998).

Harlan served as Youth Pastor at Irving Bible Church, Irving, Texas, from 1972-1976, as Church Planting Pastor at LeMars Bible Church, LeMars, Iowa, from 1976-1982, as first full-time Pastor at Lake Ray Hubbard Bible Church, Rockwall, Texas, from 1982-1992, as Senior Pastor at First Baptist Church, Spencer, Iowa, from 1992-1998, and as Senior Pastor of Kingwood Bible Church, Kingwood, Texas, from 1998 to the present.

Sharon is Harlan's partner in life and in ministry. Sharon serves on the Women's Ministries Leadership Team and she sings in Choir. She enjoys playing tennis with Harlan. Sharon and Harlan have two children: Joshua, a graduate of Midwestern State University, is married to Jill Thompson, lives in Houston, Texas, and has three children—Madison and Noah and Micah; and Sarah, a graduate of Wheaton College, is married to Mark Loeffler, lives in Temecula,

California, and has two children—Luke and Benjamin. Harlan and Sharon enjoy being "Papa" and "Mema" (both names pronounced with a strong Texas accent) to these five grandkids!

Harlan enjoys being outdoors, he enjoys hunting, and he enjoys playing tennis and golf. Harlan has a great love for the Lord and a genuine love for people. Harlan's passion is to see lives transformed into conformity with Christ through the teaching of the Scriptures. He finds great delight in studying the Word, putting it into practice, and sharing its truths with others. He is well known for his expository preaching and his Bible teaching. His teaching is personal, practical, motivational, enthusiastic, and life-changing!

Notes

Notes

Notes

Notes

Notes

Notes

Notes